Refactoring at Scale
Regaining Control of Your Codebase

Maude Lemaire

Beijing · Boston · Farnham · Sebastopol · Tokyo

Refactoring at Scale

by Maude Lemaire

Published by O'Reilly Media, Inc., 1005 Gravenstein Highway North, Sebastopol, CA 95472.

O'Reilly books may be purchased for educational, business, or sales promotional use. Online editions are also available for most titles (*http://oreilly.com*). For more information, contact our corporate/institutional sales department: 800-998-9938 or *corporate@oreilly.com*.

Acquisitions Editor: Melissa Duffield
Development Editor: Jeff Bleiel
Production Editor: Christopher Faucher
Copyeditor: nSight, Inc.
Proofreader: Christina Edwards

Indexer: Potomac Indexing, LLC
Interior Designer: David Futato
Cover Designer: Karen Montgomery
Illustrator: Kate Dullea

October 2020: First Edition

Revision History for the First Edition
2020-10-13: First Release

See *http://oreilly.com/catalog/errata.csp?isbn=9781492075530* for release details.

978-1-492-07553-0

[LSI]

Table of Contents

Part I. Introduction

Part II.   Planning

Part III. Execution

Preface

While there are a number of books about refactoring, most of them deal with the nitty-gritty of improving small bits of code one line at a time. I believe that the most difficult part of a refactor is usually not finding the precise way to improve the code at hand, but rather everything else that needs to happen around it. In fact, I might also go so far as to say that for any large software project, the little things rarely matter; coordinating complex changes is the biggest challenge of all.

Refactoring at Scale is my attempt at helping you figure out those difficult pieces. It's the culmination of many years of experience carrying out all sorts of refactoring projects of various scales. During my time at Slack, many of the projects I've led have allowed the company to scale dramatically; our product has gone from being able to support customers with 25,000 employees to those with a whopping 500,000. The strategies we developed to refactor effectively needed to tolerate explosive organizational growth, with our engineering team growing nearly sixfold during the same period. Successfully planning and executing on a project that affects both a significant portion of your codebase and an increasing number of engineers is no small feat. I hope this book gives you the tools and resources you need to do just that.

Who Should Read This Book

If you work in a large, complex codebase alongside dozens (or more) of other engineers, this book is for you!

If you're a junior engineer seeking ways to start building more senior skills by making a difference at your company, a large refactoring effort can be a great way to achieve that. These kinds of projects have broad, meaningful impact extending well beyond your individual team. (They're also not so glamorous that a senior engineer might snap it up right away.) They're a great opportunity for you to acquire new professional skills (and strengthen the ones you already have). This book will teach you how to navigate this kind of project smoothly from start to finish.

This book is also a valuable resource for highly technical senior engineers who can code themselves out of any problem, but are feeling frustrated that others aren't understanding the value of their work. If you're feeling isolated and are looking for ways to level-up others around you, this book can teach you the strategies you need to help others see important technical problems through your eyes.

For the technical managers seeking to help guide their team through a large-scale refactor, this book can help you understand how to better support your team every step of the way. There isn't a substantial amount of technical content contained within these pages, so if you are involved with a large-scale refactor in just about any capacity (engineering manager, product manager, project manager), you can benefit from the ideas herein.

Why I Wrote This Book

When I set out on my first large-scale refactor, I understood *why* the code needed to change and *how* it needed to change, but what puzzled me most was how to introduce those changes safely, gradually, and without stepping on everyone else's toes. I was eager to have cross-functional impact and didn't pause to acknowledge the ramifications the refactor might have on others' work, nor how I might motivate them to help me complete it. I simply plowed through. (You can read about this refactor in Chapter 10!)

In the years that followed, I refactored many, many more lines of code and ended up on the receiving end of a few ill-executed refactors. The lessons I'd learned from these experiences felt important, so I began speaking about them at a number of conferences. My talks resonated with hundreds of engineers, all of whom, like me, had experienced problems effectively refactoring large surface areas of code within their own companies. It seemed clear that there was some sort of gap in our software education, specifically around this core aspect of what it means to write software professionally.

In many ways, this book attempts to teach the important things that aren't covered in a typical computer science curriculum, simply because they are too difficult to teach in a classroom. Perhaps they cannot be taught in a book either, but why not give it a try?

Navigating This Book

This book is split into four parts and organized in rough chronological order of the work required to plan and execute a large-scale refactor, outlined as follows.

- Part I introduces important concepts behind refactoring.
  - Chapter 1 discusses the basics of refactoring and how refactoring at scale differs from smaller refactors.
  - Chapter 2 describes the many ways code can degrade and how this plays into effective refactoring.
- Part II covers everything you need to know about planning a successful refactor.
  - Chapter 3 provides an overview of the many metrics you can use to measure the problems your refactor seeks to solve before any improvements are made.
  - Chapter 4 explains the important components of a comprehensive execution plan and how to go about drafting one.
  - Chapter 5 discusses different approaches to get engineering leadership to support your refactor.
  - Chapter 6 describes how to identify which engineers are best suited to work on the refactor and tips for recruiting them.
- Part III focuses on what you can do to make sure that your refactor goes well while it is underway.
  - Chapter 7 explores how best to promote good communication within your team and with any external stakeholders.
  - Chapter 8 looks at a number of ways to maintain momentum throughout the refactor.
  - Chapter 9 provides a few suggestions for how to ensure that the changes introduced by your refactor stick around.
- Part IV contains two case studies, both pulled from projects I was involved with while working at Slack. These refactors affected a significant portion of our core application, truly at scale. I hope these will help illustrate the concepts discussed in Parts I–III of the book.

This ordering is not prescriptive; just because we've reached a new phase doesn't mean we shouldn't revisit our previous assumptions if necessary. For example, you might be kicking off your refactor with a strong sense of the team you'll be working with, only to discover halfway through drafting your execution plan that you'll need to bring in more engineers than you had initially anticipated. That's ok; it happens all the time!

Conventions Used in This Book

The following typographical conventions are used in this book:

Italic
> Indicates new terms, URLs, email addresses, filenames, and file extensions.

`Constant width`
> Used for program listings, as well as within paragraphs to refer to program elements such as variable or function names, databases, data types, environment variables, statements, and keywords.

> This element signifies a tip or suggestion.

> This element signifies a general note.

Using Code Examples

Supplemental material (code examples, exercises, etc.) is available for download at *https://github.com/qcmaude/refactoring-at-scale*.

This book is here to help you get your job done. In general, if example code is offered with this book, you may use it in your programs and documentation. You do not need to contact us for permission unless you're reproducing a significant portion of the code. For example, writing a program that uses several chunks of code from this book does not require permission. Selling or distributing examples from O'Reilly books does require permission. Answering a question by citing this book and quoting example code does not require permission. Incorporating a significant amount of example code from this book into your product's documentation does require permission.

We appreciate, but do not require, attribution. An attribution usually includes the title, author, publisher, and ISBN. For example: "*Refactoring at Scale* by Maude Lemaire (O'Reilly). Copyright 2021 Maude Lemaire, 978-1-492-07553-0."

If you feel your use of code examples falls outside fair use or the permission given above, feel free to contact us at *permissions@oreilly.com*.

O'Reilly Online Learning

O'REILLY® For more than 40 years, *O'Reilly Media* has provided technology and business training, knowledge, and insight to help companies succeed.

Our unique network of experts and innovators share their knowledge and expertise through books, articles, and our online learning platform. O'Reilly's online learning platform gives you on-demand access to live training courses, in-depth learning paths, interactive coding environments, and a vast collection of text and video from O'Reilly and 200+ other publishers. For more information, visit *http://oreilly.com*.

How to Contact Us

Please address comments and questions concerning this book to the publisher:

O'Reilly Media, Inc.
1005 Gravenstein Highway North
Sebastopol, CA 95472
800-998-9938 (in the United States or Canada)
707-829-0515 (international or local)
707-829-0104 (fax)

We have a web page for this book, where we list errata, examples, and any additional information. You can access this page at *https://oreil.ly/refactoring-at-scale*.

Email *bookquestions@oreilly.com* to comment or ask technical questions about this book.

For news and information about our books and courses, visit *http://oreilly.com*.

Find us on Facebook: *http://facebook.com/oreilly*

Follow us on Twitter: *http://twitter.com/oreillymedia*

Watch us on YouTube: *http://youtube.com/oreillymedia*

Acknowledgments

Writing a book is not an easy task, and this one was no exception. *Refactoring at Scale* would not have been possible without the contributions of many people.

First, I'd like to thank my editor at O'Reilly, Jeff Bleiel. Jeff turned an inexperienced writer (me) into a published author. His feedback was always spot-on, helping me organize my thoughts more cohesively, and encouraging me to cut whenever I was being too wordy (which is something that happened quite frequently). I simply can't imagine working with a better editor.

Second, I want to thank the handful of friends and colleagues who read early versions of a few chapters: Morgan Jones, Ryan Greenberg, and Jason Liszka. Their feedback assured me that my ideas were sound and would be valuable to a wide range of read-ers. For the words of encouragement and thought-provoking conversations, thanks go to Joann, Kevin, Chase, and Ben.

I'd like to thank Maggie Zhou for all her help cowriting the second case study chapter (Chapter 11). She is one of the most thoughtful, intelligent, energetic coworkers I've ever had the pleasure to work with and I'm thrilled for the world to read about our adventures together!

A huge thank you to my technical reviewers, David Cottrell and Henry Robinson. David has been a close friend since university and has led a number of large-scale refactors in his many years at Google. He's since founded his own company. Henry is a colleague at Slack who's made countless open-source contributions and seen explo-sive growth at Silicon Valley companies firsthand. They are both incredibly conscien-tious engineers, and the book greatly benefited from their guidance and wisdom. I am endlessly grateful for the many hours they spent verifying its contents. Any inaccura-cies in the final manuscript are mistakes of my own.

Thank you to everyone who's ever refactored something with me. There are too many of you to name, but you know who you are. You all have had a hand in shaping the ideas in this book.

Thank you to my family (Simon, Marie-Josée, François-Rémi, Sophie, Sylvia, Gerry, Stephanie, and Celia) for cheering me on from the sidelines.

Finally, thank you to my husband, Avery. Thank you for your patience, for giving me the time, space, and encouragement to write. Thank you for letting me hijack count-less afternoons to talk through an idea or two (or three or four). Thank you for believing in me. This book is just as much yours as it is mine. I love you.

PART I

Introduction

CHAPTER 1

Refactoring

Someone once asked me what it was that I liked so much about refactoring. What kept me coming back to these types of projects at work so often? I told her that there was something addicting about it. Maybe it's the simple act of tidying, like neatly cataloging and ordering your spices; or maybe it's the joy of decluttering and finally deprecating something, like bringing a bag of forgotten clothes to Goodwill; or maybe yet it's the little voice in my head reminding me that these tiny, incremental changes will amount to a significant improvement in my colleagues' daily lives. I think it's the combination of it all.

There's something in the act of refactoring that can appeal to us all, whether we're building new product features or working on scaling an infrastructure. We all must strike a balance in our work between writing more or writing less code. We must strive to understand the downstream effects of our changes, whether intentional or not. Code is a living, breathing thing. When I think about the code that I've written living on for another five, ten years, I can't help but wince a little bit. I certainly hope that by that time, someone will have come along and either removed it entirely or replaced it with something cleaner and, most importantly, more suited to the needs of the application at that time. This is what refactoring is all about.

In this chapter, we'll start by defining a few concepts. We'll propose a basic definition for refactoring in the general case and build on top of it to develop a separate definition for refactoring at scale. To frame some of the motivations of this book, we'll discuss why we should care about refactoring and what advantages we can bring to our teams if we've honed this skill. Next, we'll dive into some of the benefits to expect from refactoring and some of the risks we should keep in mind when considering whether to do it. With our knowledge of the trade-offs, we'll consider some scenarios when the time is right and when the time is wrong. Finally, we'll walk through a short example to bring these concepts to life.

What Is Refactoring?

Very simply put, *refactoring* is the process by which we restructure existing code (the *factoring*) without changing its external behavior. Now if you think that this definition is incredibly generic, don't worry; it purposefully is! Refactoring can take many equally effective forms, depending on the code it's applied to. To illustrate this, we'll define a "system" as any defined set of code that produces a set of outputs from a set of inputs.

Say we have a concrete implementation of such a system called S, pictured in Figure 1-1. The system was built under a tight deadline, encouraging the authors to cut some corners. Over time, it's become a large pile of tangled code. Thankfully, consumers of the system aren't exposed to the internal mess of the system directly; they interact with S, using a defined interface and rely on it to provide consistent results.

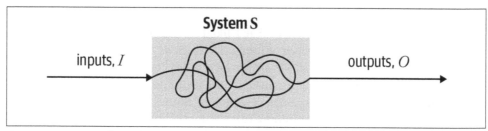

Figure 1-1. A simple system with inputs and outputs

A few brave developers cleaned up the internals of the system, which we'll now call S', picture in Figure 1-2. While it might be a tidier system, to the consumers of S', absolutely nothing has changed.

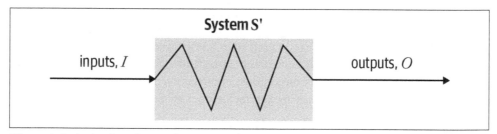

Figure 1-2. A simple refactored system with inputs and outputs

System S could be anything; it could be a single `if` statement, a ten-line function, a popular open source library, a multimillion-line application, or anything in between. (Inputs and outputs could be equally diverse.) The system could operate on database entries, collections of files, or data streams. Outputs aren't limited to returned values, but could also include a number of side effects such as printing to the console or issuing a network request. You can see how a RESTful (*https://oreil.ly/jrk1p*) service responsible for operating on user entities might map to our definition of a system in Figure 1-3.

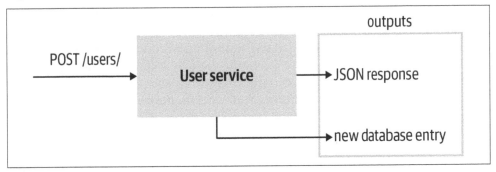

Figure 1-3. A simple application as a system

As we continue to build on our definition of refactoring and begin exploring different aspects of the process, the best way to ensure we're all on the same page is to connect each idea to a single, concrete example.

Using real-world programming examples is difficult for a few reasons. Given the breadth of experiences in our industry, choosing just one example over another immediately gives one group of readers a leg up. On the flip side, those deeply familiar with the example might be frustrated when some concepts are simplified for brevity or when certain nuances are ignored to apply a concept more cleanly. In hopes of establishing a level playing field, whenever we seek to illustrate a generic problem at a high level, we'll use as our example a business familiar to (hopefully) most of us: a dry cleaning establishment.

Simon's Dry Cleaners is a local dry cleaning business with a single location on a busy street in Springfield. It's open Monday through Saturday during regular business hours. Customers drop off both regular laundry and dry-clean-only items. Depending on the quantity, urgency, and difficulty of each item, the items are cleaned and returned to the customers any time between two and six business days later.

How does this map to our definition of a system? The dry cleaning operation housed within the business is the system itself. It processes customers' dirty clothing as inputs and returns them cleaned to their owners as outputs. All of the intricacies of the dry cleaning operation are hidden from the consumer; all we need to do is drop off our clothes and hope the cleaners are able to do their job. The system itself is quite complex; depending on the type of input (leather jacket, pile of socks, silk skirt), it may respond by performing one or more operations to ensure the proper output (a clean garment). There is ample opportunity for something to go wrong between drop-off and pickup: a belt might get lost, a stain overlooked, a shirt accidentally returned to the wrong customer. However, if the employees proactively communicate with one another, the machines are in good condition, and the receipts are kept in order, the system will continue to operate smoothly and it'll be easy to fulfill orders.

Let's say Simon's still ran its operations using paper carbon-copy receipts. All customers coming in to drop off their clothes would write their name and phone number on the provided slip, and the clerk would take note of their order. If customers misplaced their receipts, Simon's could easily locate the copy by leafing through their recent orders alphabetized by last name. Unfortunately, when customers are late to pick up their dry cleaning and they've misplaced their receipts, the clerk has to fetch archived slips from boxes in the back office. Although almost all orders are successfully retrieved, it takes much more time for the customer to pick up their apparel and be on their way again. Paper receipts are also inconvenient when the owners calculate their earnings at the end of each month; they have to match up all transactions (both credit card and cash) manually with completed orders. Eager to modernize and refactor their process, the team decided to upgrade their systems to use a point-of-sale system and erase the pain points of paper. Ta da, refactoring complete! Customers continue to drop off their dry cleaning and retrieve it a few days later with minimal perceived change, but now everything behind the front desk runs much more smoothly.

What Is Refactoring at Scale?

In late 2013, amidst a tumultuous launch, all major American news outlets declared Healthcare.gov a complete fiasco; the website was plagued with security concerns, hours-long outages, and a slew of serious bugs. Before launch, not only had the cost ballooned to nearly two billion dollars, the codebase had blown up to over five million lines of code. While much of the failure of Healthcare.gov was due to failed development practices caught up in bureaucratic federal government policies, when the Obama administration later announced that it was planning to invest heavily in improving the service, the undeniable difficulty involved with rearchitecting and refactoring overgrown software systems became mainstream news. In the subsequent months, the teams tasked with rewriting Healthcare.gov dove headfirst into a near-complete overhaul of the codebase, a refactor at scale.

A refactor at scale is one that affects a substantial surface area of your systems. It typically (but not exclusively) involves a large codebase (a million or more lines of code) powering applications with many users. As long as legacy systems exist, there will be a need for these kinds of refactors, ones where developers need to think critically about code structure at breadth and how it can be measurably improved effectively. What makes refactoring multimillion-line codebases different from refactoring smaller, more well-defined applications? While it might be easy for us to see concrete, iterative ways to improve small, well-defined systems (think individual functions or classes), it becomes nearly impossible to determine the effect a change might have when applied uniformly across a sprawling, complex system. Many tools exist to identify code smells or automatically detect improvements within subsections of code, but we are largely unable to automate human reasoning about how to restructure large applications in codebases that are growing at an increasingly rapid pace, particularly at high-growth companies.

Some may argue that you can make a measured improvement to this kind of system by continuously applying small, additive transformations. This method might begin to tilt the scales in a positive direction, but progress is likely to drop off significantly when most of the low-hanging fruit is gone and it becomes trickier to introduce these changes carefully (and gradually).

Refactoring at scale is about identifying a systemic problem in your codebase, conceiving of a better solution, and executing on that solution in a strategic, disciplined way. To identify systemic problems and their corresponding solutions, you'll need a solid understanding of one or more broad sections of an application. You'll also need high stamina to propagate the solution properly to the entire affected area.

Refactoring at scale also goes hand in hand with refactoring live systems. Many of us work on applications with frequent deployment cycles. At Slack, we ship new code to our users about a dozen times per day. We need to be mindful of how our refactoring efforts fit into these cycles, to minimize risk and disruption to our users. Understanding how to deploy strategically at various points during a refactoring effort can oftentimes make the difference between a quiet rollout and a complete service outage.

What might Simon's Dry Cleaners look like when considering scale? Say deploying a point-of-sale system dramatically optimized the business—so much so, in fact, that it managed to open five new locations in neighboring towns in just two years! Now that it's operating multiple locations, growing the scale of their business, they have a different set of problems. To keep costs low, only two of their six locations have dry cleaning equipment on-site. When customers drop off dry cleaning at one of the four locations that do not have dry cleaning equipment on-site, the apparel must be sent to the closest facility via the company van. The van stops at all four storefronts to pick up clothes, dropping them off in large bins on the loading docks of the two dry cleaning locations. Simon's employees work hard to sort through the heaps of clothes, clean them, and return them to the correct storefront. Most days, however, it's a harrowing process. Both dry cleaning locations process apparel from both their own location and the four smaller ones. It's not uncommon for clothes to get separated or tangled when dropped into the processing bins by the van drivers. More urgent orders often get lost in the heap and cleaners have to dig through the entire shipment to identify them first.

How can Simon's improve its operations most efficiently? Should it dedicate a specific dry cleaning center for each location so that each facility is handling orders from a maximum of three storefronts? If so, should it consider rerouting the vans in a specific way? What if it did both? Would it be cost-efficient to open yet another dry cleaning facility if it enables the business to decrease turn-around time? How should it set up its loading docks so that fewer clothes get tangled? Could the drivers be taught to hang and categorize orders properly by urgency before driving off to make another round? Should the company limit pickups to right after lunchtime and shortly after closing to give the dry cleaning locations more time to organize the drop-offs? There are quite a few options to consider, many of which could be combined and executed on numerous orders or simultaneously. Imagine being faced with all of these possibilities and having to decide which lever to pull first. It's positively paralyzing! Turns out, refactoring large applications feels the same way.

Why Should You Care About Refactoring?

Refactoring might sound compelling in theory, but how do you know that reading the rest of this book won't be a waste of time? I certainly hope that all readers can walk away from this book with a few new tools in their tool belt, but if there's a single reason I can provide to keep you reading it's this:

Confidence in your ability to refactor allows you to lean toward action and start building a system sooner, well before you've developed a strong understanding of all the moving pieces, pitfalls, and edge cases. If you know you'll be able to identify opportunities to improve components effectively throughout the development process, and will continue to be able to do so as the system grows more complex, you won't need to spend as much time architecting a program upfront. Once you've honed the skills required to manipulate code effortlessly, you'll spend less time worrying about boxing yourself in with any single design decision. While programming, you'll find yourself opting to write something simple that works given the current circumstances rather than stepping back and planning your next half-dozen moves. You'll recognize that there is always a (sometimes tricky) path to a better solution.

Programming isn't a game of chess. When given a board configuration and assuming optimal opponents, the best competitive players deftly play out dozens of complete matches within minutes. Unfortunately, in our line of work, we aren't provided a fully enumerated set of possible moves and there is no predetermined end state. I don't mean to imply that there is no value in sitting down and brainstorming a robust solution to a problem, given a reasonable set of requirements; however, I do want to caution you against spending any significant time ironing out the final 10 percent to 20 percent. If you've honed your ability to refactor, you'll be able to evolve your solution to handle the final specifications just fine.

Benefits of Refactoring

Refactoring can have some tangible benefits beyond the ability to start confidently problem-solving sooner. Though it might not be the correct tool for every problem, it can certainly have a lasting, positive impact on your application, engineering team, and broader organization. We discuss two major benefits: increased developer productivity and greater ease identifying bugs. While some might contend that there are many more benefits to refactoring than those discussed here, I argue that they all boil down to the two themes presented here.

Developer Productivity

One of the primary goals of refactoring is yielding code that is easier to understand. Simplifying a dense solution as you reason through it not only helps you gain a better grasp of what the code is doing, it also helps everyone who comes after you do the same. Code you can easily comprehend elevates absolutely everyone on your team, no matter their tenure or experience level.

If you are a tenured engineer on the team, you tend to be very familiar with some parts of the codebase but, as the codebase grows, more and more parts are unfamiliar to you, and your code is increasingly likely to develop dependencies on those parts. Imagine that you're implementing a new feature and in weaving your solution through the system, you venture from code you know rather well to unfamiliar territory. If the area unknown to you is well maintained and regularly refactored to take into account evolving product requirements and bug fixes, you'll be able to narrow down the ideal location for your change *and* intuit an effortless solution much more quickly. If the code has instead deteriorated over time by accruing patchy bug fixes and ballooning in length, you'll spend exponentially more time wading through each line, trying first to understand what the code is doing and how it's doing it before you're able to spend any time reasoning through an acceptable solution. (It's not uncommon to drag someone else into the tortured-code rabbit-hole, whether it's another engineer working alongside you or one who's intimately familiar with the code to answer your questions.)

> ## Evolution of Codebase Familiarity
>
> For smaller codebases with just a handful of engineers, it's not uncommon for most engineers to be highly comfortable with all parts of the codebase. The familiarity will gradually decrease over time as more modules are added and modified, and the engineers begin to specialize; eventually, the codebase reaches a critical mass where it's impossible for any single engineer (even the first hire!) to be familiar with everything.

Let's flip the scenario. What if a colleague on another team who isn't familiar with your team's code had to take a stab at reading through it. Would they have an easy time understanding how it works? Are you more likely to expect questions and confused looks, or a request for code review?

What if you were a new engineer on the team. Perhaps this was you just recently or maybe you recently onboarded someone to your team, whose experiences you can pull from. They have absolutely no mental model of the codebase. Their ability to gain confidence with any area of the code is directly proportional to the code's legibility. Not only will they be able to organically build up an accurate mental representation of the relationships between different units in your codebase, they'll be able to reason out what the code is doing without needing to tag teammates for questions. (It's worth noting that knowing when and how to ask questions of your colleagues is an incredibly important skill to hone. Learning to evaluate how much time is appropriate for you to build your own understanding before seeking help is difficult but critical to growing as a developer. Asking questions isn't a bad thing, but if you're the tenured engineer on the team and you're feeling bombarded with them, maybe it's time to write some documentation and refactor some code.)

We're all prone to copying established patterns when developing something new. If the solutions we reference are clear and concise, we're more likely to propagate clear and concise code. The converse is also true: if the only solutions we have as reference are cluttered, we'll propagate cluttered code. Ensuring that the best patterns are the most prevalent ones is particularly crucial in establishing a positive feedback loop with developers who are just starting out. If the code that they interact with on a regular basis is easy to understand, they'll emulate a similar focus in their own solutions.

Identifying Bugs

Tracking down and solving bugs is a necessary (and fun!) part of our jobs. Refactoring can be an effective tool in accomplishing both of these tasks! By breaking up complex statements into smaller, bite-sized pieces, and extracting logic into new functions, you can both build up a better understanding of what the code is doing and, hopefully, isolate the bug. Refactoring as you are actively writing code can also make it easier to spot bugs early in the development process, allowing you to avoid them altogether.

Consider the scenario in which your team deployed some new code to production a few hours ago. A few of the changes were embedded in a handful of files that everyone fears modifying: the code is impossible to read and contains a minefield of bugs waiting to happen. Unfortunately, your tests didn't cover one of many edge cases and someone from customer service reaches out about a pesky bug users are starting to run into. You and your team immediately start digging in and quickly realize that the bug is, as expected, in the scariest part of the code. Thankfully, your teammate's able to reproduce the problem consistently and, together, you write a test to assert the correct behavior. Now you have to narrow down the bug. You take methodical steps to break down the hairy code: you convert lengthy one-liners into succinct, multiline statements and migrate the contents of a few conditional code blocks into individual functions. Eventually, you locate the bug. Now that the code's been simplified, you're able to fix it swiftly, run the test to verify that it works, and ship a fix to your customers. Victory!

To the customer, sometimes bugs are only a minor nuisance, but other times, bugs can prevent the customer from using your application altogether. While more disruptive bugs generally require urgent remediation, it's imperative that your team be able to solve bugs of all severity levels quickly to keep users happy. Working in a well-maintained codebase can dramatically decrease the time developers need to hone in on and fix a bug, delighting you when it's shipped to production in record time.

Risks of Refactoring

While the benefits of refactoring might be compelling, there are some serious risks and pitfalls to consider before setting out on a journey to improve every inch (or centimeter) of your codebase. I may be starting to sound like a broken record, but I will reiterate it nonetheless: refactoring requires us to be able to ensure that behavior remains identical at every iteration. We can increase our confidence that nothing has changed by writing a suite of tests (unit, integration, end to end), and we should not seriously consider moving forward with any refactoring effort until we've established sufficient test coverage. However, even with thorough testing, there is always a small chance that something slips through the cracks. We also must keep in mind our ultimate goal: bettering the code in a way that is clear to both you and future developers interacting with the code.

Serious Regressions

Refactoring untested code is very dangerous and highly discouraged. Development teams equipped with the most thorough, sophisticated testing suites still ship bugs to production. Why? With every change, large or small, we disrupt the equilibrium of the system in a measurable way. We strive to cause as little disruption as possible, but whenever we alter our systems, there is a risk that it might lead to unanticipated regression. As we refactor the exceptionally frightening, puzzling corners of our codebase, introducing a serious regression is of particular concern. These areas of the codebase are frequently in their current state because they've had plenty of time to deteriorate. At fast-growing companies, they are also frequently both integral to how your application works and the least tested. Attempting to detangle these files or functions can feel like trying to walk across a minefield unscathed—it's possible, but very dangerous.

Unearthing Dormant Bugs

Just as refactoring can help you identify bugs, it can unintentionally unearth dormant bugs. Here, I classify dormant bugs as regressions that are most commonly exposed by restructuring code. We'll revisit Simon's Dry Cleaners to illustrate. The business has started ordering cleaning products in bigger batches at the same delivery cadence to unlock a better deal from the supplier. Unfortunately, there's not much room to store the products in the back of the main storefront, so Simon's decides to start stacking boxes closer to the loading dock door. After a few weeks of rain, the team notices that some of the boxes closest to the door are wet and falling apart. The owner notices that the back door is poorly sealed and allows water to seep through on wet days. Simon's had never encountered a problem with storing supplies close to the loading dock door because they'd simply never done it before; exercising a new storage pattern exposed a critical flaw in their infrastructure, which they might have never discovered otherwise.

Scope Creep

Refactoring can be a little bit like eating brownies: the first few bites are delicious, making it easy to get carried away and accidentally eat an entire dozen. When you've taken your last bite, a bit of regret and perhaps a twinge of nausea kick in. Experiencing immediate, highly significant improvements when you're making focused, localized changes is incredibly rewarding! It's easy to get carried away and allow the surface area of your changes to exceed *reasonable bounds*. What do I mean by reasonable bounds? Depending on the codebase, this can refer to a single functional area or a small, interdependent set of libraries. Ideally, the refactored code is limited to a set of changes another developer can comfortably review within a single changeset.

When mapping out a larger refactoring effort, especially one that might take several months or more, it's absolutely imperative to keep a tight scope. We all run into unexpected quirks when refactoring small surface areas (a few lines of code, single functions); while we can sustainably chain a few enhancements to handle these new quirks effectively, this approach becomes dangerous when tackling a significant surface area. The larger the surface area of the planned refactor, the more problems you'll encounter that you likely haven't anticipated. That doesn't make you a bad programmer, it simply makes you human. By keeping to a well-defined plan, you decrease the chances of causing a serious regression or running into dormant bugs, and promote productivity. Sustained, methodical refactoring efforts are already difficult; having a moving goalpost simply makes them unachievable.

Unnecessary Complexity

Be wary of over designing at the start and be open to modifying your initial plan. The primary goal should be to produce human-friendly code, even at the cost of your original design. If the laser focus is on the solution rather than the process, there's a greater chance your application will end up more more contrived and complicated than it was in the first place. Refactoring at all levels should be iterative. By taking small, deliberate steps in one direction and maintaining existing behavior at each iteration, you're better able to maintain focus on your ultimate goal. This is much easier to do when tackling only enough code as fits on your screen rather than three dozen libraries at a time. When we plan a new project, most of us generally try our best to develop a detailed specification document and execution plan. Even with a large refactoring effort, it's important to have a good sense of what the resulting code should look like upon completion.

When to Refactor

It would be easy simply to say "when the benefits outweigh the risks," but that wouldn't be a helpful answer. Yes, in practice, refactoring is a worthwhile effort when the benefits outweigh the risks, but how do we properly assign weight to each piece of the puzzle? How do we know when we've reached the tipping point and should consider a refactor?

In my experience, the tipping point is more of a tipping *range*, and it is different for everyone and every application. Determining your upper and lower bounds for this range is what makes refactoring a bit more of a subjective science: there is no formula we can use to give us a decisive "yes" or "no" answer. Fortunately, we can rely on some empirical evidence from others' experiences to guide us in making our own decisions.

Small Scope

When looking to refactor a small, straightforward section of well-tested code, there should be very little holding you back. Unless you're uncertain that your refactored solution is an objective improvement to its predecessor, or you're fearful the change affects too large of a surface area, it's likely a worthwhile endeavor. Carefully craft a few commits and get your changes rolling! We'll see an example that clearly falls into this category later in this chapter.

Code Complexity Actively Hinders Development

There are times when we have to venture into parts of our codebase we fear. Every time we read over the code, our brows furrow, our hearts pound, our neurons start firing. Then comes the moment when we have to bite the bullet, dig in, and make the change we came to make. But developing under duress is a surefire way to inadvertently cause more problems. When you're so hyper-focused on doing precisely the correct thing, holding the many dimensions of the problem in your head, you risk losing sight of your *actual* goal. How can you execute adequately on that goal when your mind is elsewhere?

If this particular section of the code hasn't bitten us yet, we'll often take our chances and make it. If it's bitten us or a fellow teammate already (sometimes more than once), the risk involved in taking a scalpel to the code now to prevent future mistakes might outweigh the risk of letting it linger in its current state any longer. If you're unsure which way the scales tilt, talk it over with your teammates and collect some data on the number of bugs caught in the past six months that you can trace back to this part of the codebase.

Shift in Product Requirements

Drastic shifts in product requirements can frequently map to drastic shifts in code. As hard as we might try to write abstract, extendable solutions for each piece of functionality in our application, we can't predict the future; and while our code might be easy to adapt for small deviations, it is seldom perfectly adaptable to larger ones. These shifts give us the rare business-related opportunity to go back to the drawing board and reconsider our design.

You may be thinking that these sorts of shifts can't possibly preserve behavior. Given the same inputs, now we must provide different outputs! How is this an opportune time for refactoring? If your code in its current state doesn't lend itself well to the new requirements, you must come up with a solution that continues to support today's functionality and will seamlessly support tomorrow's. You can make a case for refactoring your code first, and then (and only then!) implement the new functionality atop it. This way, you continue to set a standard of high-quality code, cashing in all the benefits of refactoring, all the while supporting business objectives. Again, it's a win, win, win!

Performance

Improving performance can be a difficult task; you must first build a deep understanding of the existing behavior and then be able to identify which levers you might be able to use to tilt the scales in a positive direction. Beginning with a clean slate (or building one as a first step) will best enable you to do that. Properly isolating the levers you've identified so that they are easier to manipulate without risk of downstream effects is also key.

 Not all developers believe that performance improvements are a valid reason to refactor; some assert that a system's performance is innately part of its behavior and therefore altering it in some way alters the behavior. I disagree. If we continue to define refactoring by using our generic system to which we provide a set of inputs, and continue to produce an expected set of outputs, then improving the speed (or memory burden) required to generate these outputs is a valid form of refactoring.

Refactoring for this purpose is unique in one important way: it does not ensure more approachable code as an outcome. Sometimes we'll be reading through a codebase and come across a lengthy comment block warning about the code below it. In my experience, most of these comment blocks caution the reader about one (or more) complications: strange application behavior, temporary workarounds, and a peculiar performance patch. Most performance improvements prefaced by these short stories are written cleverly and leverage a deep understanding of the code base as a means of minimizing the surface area affected. These "improvements" are more susceptible to degradation over a shorter period and as such are not good examples of the sustainability that refactoring is meant to foster. The worthwhile performance improvements, the ones worthy of falling under the refactoring umbrella, are profound and far-reaching; they are examples of effective refactoring deployed at scale. We'll cover these changes in greater depth in Part II.

Using a New Technology

In the world of software development, we're regularly adopting new technologies. Whether it's to keep up with the newest trends in our industry, boost our ability to scale to more users, or mature our product in a new way, we're perpetually evaluating new open-source libraries, protocols, programming languages, service providers, and more. Making the decision to use something new is not something we do lightly; this is partly due to the cost of integration within our existing codebases. If we opt to *replace* an existing solution with a new one, we have to craft a deprecation plan by identifying all affected callsites and migrating them (sometimes one at a time). If we opt to *adopt* a new technology moving forward, we have to identify high-leverage candidates for early adoption, with a plan to expand usage to all relevant use cases.

I won't enumerate each of the ways using a new technology can affect your system (there are many), but it's clear from these two scenarios that each requires a careful audit of your current system. Fortunately, an audit can reveal prime opportunities for refactoring! I want to take the time to acknowledge that this is a somewhat controversial opinion. Because of the risks involved with adopting a new technology alone, other developers may discourage you from making any other changes. However, I strongly believe that the worst way to introduce something new into your system is to stick it right in alongside a huge, tangled mess. To give it the best chance to fulfill its purpose, I think it's best to take the time to clean up the areas it'll come in contact with first.

We can easily apply this concept to Simon's Dry Cleaners. Let's say it just recently put in an order for some new state-of-the-art, eco-friendly dry cleaning machinery. In figuring out an installation plan, the owners realize that their existing floor plan has some serious inefficiencies. Employees have to walk all the way along the line of machines to pick up presorted garments from the racks nearly thirty feet away. If they reorient the machinery so that employees can walk just a few feet to reach the racks, they might shave a few minutes off of every cycle. They make the decision to install the new machines in the revised configuration. Simon's may have decreased its impact on the environment and increased the productivity of their employees. Win, win!

When Not to Refactor

Refactoring can be an astonishingly useful tool to a developer. Many developers believe that time devoted to refactoring is always time well spent, but it isn't so simple. There is a time and a place for refactoring, and the most mature developers understand the importance of knowing when to refactor and when *not* to refactor.

For Fun or Out of Boredom

Close your eyes for a minute and imagine yourself sitting in front of your computer. You're looking at a particularly gnarly function. It's too long; it tries to do too many things. Its name has long since ceased to describe its responsibility meaningfully. You're itching to fix it. You'd love to split it up into well-defined, succinct units complete with better variables names. It'd be *fun*. But is it the most important thing you could be doing right now? Perhaps your teammate's been waiting for your code review for a few days or you've been putting off writing some tests? If you're digging into some crufty old code and shifting it around to keep yourself entertained, you might be doing yourself (and your teammates) a disservice.

Chances are, if you're refactoring for fun, you're not focusing on the impact that your change will have on the surrounding code, the overall system, and your coworkers. We have different motivations when we're refactoring for fun: we're more likely to use more far-fetched language features or try out a brand new pattern we've been wanting to give a whirl. There is a time and place for trying new things and stretching our programming muscles, but refactoring isn't that time. Refactoring should be a deliberate process where the focus is strictly on providing the (ideally) smallest change for the biggest positive impact.

Because You Happened to Be Passing By

Picture this: you write some code, ship it to production, and start working on a new feature. You come back to your code a few months later to expand on the feature. Unfortunately, it looks nothing like what you originally wrote. A million questions are racing through your mind. What happened here?

You may have fallen prey to the drive-by refactorer. This is a coworker who is experienced enough to have developed some well-informed opinions about how to write code. They are someone whom other engineers consult with about design decisions.

They also have an unfortunate tendency to rewrite others' code as they encounter it. They think they're doing everyone a favor by doing this.

You might be tempted to agree, but consider this: if this engineer modified code in an area of the codebase where they are not an active contributor, it's likely they've decreased the productivity of those that are responsible for it. We are most productive when we are familiar with the code for which we are responsible. When we're tasked with quickly resolving an issue, whether it is a serious incident in production or a small bug, we use our mental model of the code to narrow a set of files, classes, or functions where the problem might exist. If we open up our editor and find that nothing is where we left it, we're disoriented and unable to fix the issue as quickly. This is incredibly costly to our employers in engineering hours, customer service hours, and potentially lost business.

Not telling the original author about the refactor is a disservice in two distinct ways. First, they have actively eroded the author's trust. As much as we try to divorce ourselves from our code, we always leave a tiny piece of personal pride and ownership in the code that we've written. I'd much prefer if someone were honest with me about the shortcomings of my solution and shows me how to fix it rather than find out about the problems after they've already been addressed. This is particularly harmful when it comes to newer engineers. Imagine yourself just one year out of school; you come into work one day only to find that the code that you'd taken weeks to cobble together had been rewritten in a few hours by a much more senior engineer whom you've never talked to. It doesn't feel great.

Second, they may not be aware of the initial circumstances surrounding the code at the time it was written. This is particularly troublesome when dealing with code that the drive-by refactorer is not actively maintaining. Why is this important? Programming is all about trade-offs; we can write a faster solution by using a more memory-intensive data structure or reduce our memory footprint by approximating rather than making precise calculations. Likewise, every line of "bad" code attempted to solve a problem. By blindly refactoring it, you may fall prey to a bug or weakness the original authors were carefully trying to avoid.

About Original Code Authors

Unfortunately, not everyone stays at the same company for their entire working career. The original code author may no longer be in your ranks. Fortunately, folks tend to relay information to their team before heading off to greener pastures, so there's likely a team you can sync with to get more perspective on the code.

Don't be a drive-by refactorer, be a *well-intentioned* refactorer. Rarely refactor code that you are not actively maintaining, and when you do, make sure you're doing it with the input of those responsible for it.

To Making Code More Extendable

Many refactoring gurus advocate for refactoring as a means to render code more readily extendable. While this can be a clear outcome of a good refactor, rewriting code for the sake of future malleability is likely unwise. Time spent refactoring without a clear understanding of the immediate, tangible wins might be a wasted effort; your changes might not pay off within a reasonably short period, nor, in the absolute worst case, within the lifetime of the code.

If you can make adequate changes to a block of code to advance your project, you probably shouldn't be refactoring it. Most companies have new features to develop and bug fixes to ship. Generally speaking, these are almost always of higher priority. Unless you have a concrete set of goals, and a compelling argument that it will directly affect your company's bottom line, your management chain will be unconvinced. But don't dismay! We'll help you build a business case for refactoring in the coming chapters.

When You Don't Have Time

The only thing worse than code in dire need of refactoring is code half-refactored. Code in limbo is confusing to developers interacting with it. When there is no clear point in time when the code will be fully refactored, it takes on semi-permanent disorder. It's often difficult for the reader to discern the direction or implementation to follow when reading code mid-refactor, especially if the refactorer left no comments in their wake. You might even make an incorrect assumption about which code will be adopted long-term and implement a necessary change in a block that's headed for deprecation. These kinds of mistakes pile up quickly, leading to faster, more serious erosion of the code you hoped to improve in the first place.

When setting out to refactor something, make sure you have enough time to see your plans through to completion. If not, try to scope down your changes so that you can still make some improvements but comfortably reach the finish line. No temporary benefits reaped from an incomplete refactor outweigh the confusion and frustration of future developers interacting with it.

Our First Refactoring Example

Now that we've built a solid foundation with which to begin understanding the goals of refactoring and how, under the right circumstances, it can enable us to be better programmers, let's bring it all to life with a small example. This example is much smaller in scope than the kinds of refactoring efforts we'll be discussing in this book, but it helps illustrate some of the concepts on a smaller scale so that we can get familiar with them early.

Let's pretend we're working at a university where we develop and support a rudimentary program that teaching assistants (TAs) use to submit assignment grades. The TAs use the program to verify that assignment grades fall within a certain range specified by the professor. This range is configurable because professors structure assignments differently, so not all problem sets are graded on a 0 to 100 point scale. Take, for example, a problem set with 10 questions. Each question is worth a maximum of 6 points. If you answer all questions correctly, your final grade is 60 out of 60. If you don't submit the assignment at all, you'll get 0 points.

Professors use the same tool to ensure that the average score for a given assignment falls within an expected range. Given our previous example, say the professor would like the average for the problem set to be within 42 and 48 points (for a percentage score between 70% and 80%). They can provide this expected range to the program, which then processes the final grades and determines whether the average falls within those bounds.

The function responsible for this logic is called checkValid and is shown in Example 1-1.

Example 1-1. A small, confusing sample of code

```
function checkValid(
  minimum,
  maximum,
  values,
  useAverage = false)
{
  let result = false;
  let min = Math.min(...values);
  let max = Math.max(...values);
  if (useAverage) {
    min = max = values.reduce((acc, curr) => acc + curr, 0)/values.length;
  }

  if (minimum < 0 || maximum > 100) {
    result = false;
  } else if (!(minimum <= min) || !(maximum >= max)) {
    result = false;
  } else if (maximum >= max && minimum <= min) {
    result = true;
  }
  return result;
}
```

Right off the bat, we can spot some problems. First, the function name doesn't fully capture its responsibilities. We're not entirely certain what to expect from a function with a generic name like `checkValid` (especially if there isn't any documentation atop the function declaration). Second, it's unclear what the inlined values (`0, 100`) represent. Given what we know about the function's expected behavior, we can deduce that these numbers represent the absolute minimum- and maximum-allowed point values for any assignment. Within the context, the minimum value of `0` makes sense, but why assert an upper bound of `100`? Third, the logic is difficult to follow; not only are there quite a few conditions to reason through, the inlined logic can be complex, making it difficult for us to reason through each case quickly. At a quick glance, it's nearly impossible to know whether the function contains a bug. We could spend considerable time enumerating the many issues contained within these few short lines of code, but to keep things simple, we'll stop here.

How could so few lines of code be so tough to understand? Code in active development is regularly modified to handle small, low-impact changes (bug fixes, new features, performance tweaks, etc.). Unfortunately, these modifications pile up, oftentimes resulting in lengthier, more convoluted code. From the code structure, we can identify two changes that probably occurred after the function was initially written:

- The ability to perform range validation on the average of the provided set of values rather than the sum of those values. I can infer that this functionality was introduced later for two reasons; `useAverage` is an optional Boolean argument with a default value of `false`, implying that there are existing callsites that do not expect a fourth argument. Boolean arguments are a code smell; we'll address that shortly. Further, the code overwrites both `min` and `max` to reflect the single, new average value for convenience. This indicates that the author was looking for the easiest way to handle this requirement while modifying the least amount of code.

- Ensuring that no provided range fell below `0` nor exceeded `100`. It seems strange to disallow professors from creating assignments worth more than 100 points, but we can assume that this was intended behavior for now. Although it isn't a conclusive clue, we can guess this behavior was introduced as an afterthought because of the placement of the conditional to verify the range's absolute limits. Why would we not immediately verify that the provided minimum and maximum bounds are within the acceptable range? The author of the change likely quickly identified the series of conditionals and thought the easiest place to add a new condition would be at the very end. We could confirm our hypothesis by looking through the version history and hopefully finding the original commit with a helpful commit message.

Simplifying Conditionals

First, let's simplify some of the `if` statement logic. We can easily do that by returning a result from the function early rather than evaluating every branch and returning a final value. We'll also return early in the case that the provided minimum and maximum values fall outside the 0, 100 range, as shown in Example 1-2.

Example 1-2. A small sample with early returns

```
function checkValid(
  minimum,
  maximum,
  values,
  useAverage = false
) {

  if (minimum < 0 || maximum > 100) return false; ❶

  let min = Math.min(...values);
  let max = Math.max(...values);

  if (useAverage) {
    min = max = values.reduce((acc, curr) => acc + curr, 0)/values.length;
  }

  if (!(minimum <= min) || !(maximum >= max)) return false; ❷
  if (maximum >= max && minimum <= min) return true; ❷

  return false;
}
```

❶ Return early if the minimum or maximum is out of range.

❷ Simplify the logic by returning early when we can.

Now we're getting somewhere! Let's see whether we can further simplify the logic by reasoning through all of the cases for which the function would return false: there's the case where the calculated minimum is smaller than the provided minimum and the case where the calculated maximum is greater than the provided maximum. We can replace the current conditions by failing early and only returning a `true` result after verifying each of these simple failure cases instead. Example 1-3 illustrates each of these changes.

Example 1-3. A small sample with simplified logic

```
function checkValid(
  minimum,
  maximum,
```

```
  values,
  useAverage = false
) {

  if (minimum < 0 || maximum > 100) return false;

  let min = Math.min(...values);
  let max = Math.max(...values);

  if (useAverage) {
    min = max = values.reduce((acc, curr) => acc + curr, 0)/values.length;
  }

  if (min < minimum) return false; ❶
  if (max > maximum) return false; ❶
  return true; ❷
}
```

❶   Simplify logic by reasoning through the cases and only having one condition per
    `if` statement.

❷   Fail early and return `true` only if we're certain that the values are valid.

Extracting Magic Numbers

Our next step will be to extract the inlined numbers (or magic numbers) into variables with informative names. We'll also rename `values` to `grades` for clarity. (Alternatively, we could define these as constants within the same scope as the function
declaration, but we'll keep things simple for now.) Example 1-4 demonstrates these
clarifications.

Example 1-4. A small sample with clearer variables

```
function checkValid(
  minimumBound, ❶
  maximumBound, ❶
  grades, ❶
  useAverage = false
) {

  // Valid assignments should never allow fewer than 0 points
  var absoluteMinimum = 0; ❷

  // Valid assignments should never exceed more than 100 possible points
  var absoluteMaximum = 100; ❷

  if (minimumBound < absoluteMinimum) return false; ❸
  if (maximumBound > absoluteMaximum) return false; ❸
```

```
  let min = Math.min(...grades);
  let max = Math.max(...grades);

  if (useAverage) {
    min = max = grades.reduce((acc, curr) => acc + curr, 0)/grades.length;
  }

  if (min < minimumBound) return false;
  if (max > maximumBound) return false;
  return true;
}
```

❶ Renaming the parameter to describe its role.

❷ Magic numbers are appropriately named for added context.

❸ Further simplifying logic by splitting up the complex conditional into two simpler if statements.

Extracting Self-Contained Logic

Next, we can extract the average calculation into a separate function, as shown in Example 1-5.

Example 1-5. A small sample with more functions with clear responsibilities

```
function checkValid(
  minimum,
  maximum,
  grades,
  useAverage = false
){
  // Valid assignments should never allow fewer than 0 points
  var absoluteMinimum = 0;

  // Valid assignments should never exceed more than 100 possible points
  var absoluteMaximum = 100;

  if (minimumBound < absoluteMinimum) return false;
  if (maximumBound > absoluteMaximum) return false;

  let min = Math.min(...grades);
  let max = Math.max(...grades);

  if (useAverage) {
    min = max = calculateAverage(grades);
  }

  if (min < minimumBound) return false;
```

```
  if (max > maximumBound) return false;
  return true;
}

function calculateAverage(grades) { ❶
  return grades.reduce((acc, curr) => acc + curr, 0)/grades.length;
}
```

❶ Extracted average calculation into a new function.

As we iterate on our solution, it becomes more obvious that the logic to handle the average of the set of grades seems increasingly out of place. Next, we'll continue to improve our function by creating two functions: one that verifies that the average of a set of grades fits within a set of bounds and another that verifies that all grades within a set occur within a minimum and a maximum value. We could reorganize the code into more focused functions at this point in a number of ways. There is no right or wrong answer so long as we've found a way to divorce the logic for the two distinct cases effectively. Example 1-6 shows one such way of further simplifying our check Valid function.

Example 1-6. A small sample with better-defined functions

```
function checkValid(
  minimum,
  maximum,
  grades,
  useAverage = false
){

  // Valid assignments should never allow fewer than 0 points
  var absoluteMinimum = 0;

  // Valid assignments should never exceed more than 100 possible points
  var absoluteMaximum = 100;

  if (minimumBound < absoluteMinimum) return false;
  if (maximumBound > absoluteMaximum) return false;

  let min = Math.min(...grades);
  let max = Math.max(...grades);

  if (useAverage) {
    return checkAverageInBounds(minimumBound, maximumBound, grades); ❶
  }

  return checkAllGradesInBounds(minimumBound, maximumBound, grades); ❷
}

function calculateAverage(grades) {
```

```
    return grades.reduce((acc, curr) => acc + curr, 0)/grades.length;
}

function checkAverageInBounds(
  minimumBound,
  maximumBound,
  grades
){ ❶
  var avg = calculateAverage(grades);
  if (avg < minimumBound) return false;
  if (avg > maximumBound) return false;
  return true;
}

function checkAllGradesInBounds(
  minimumBound,
  maximumBound,
  grades
){ ❷
  var min = Math.min(...grades);
  var max = Math.max(...grades);

  if (min < minimumBound) return false;
  if (max > maximumBound) return false;
  return true;
}
```

❶   Extract logic to determine whether the average of the grades is within minimum and maximum bounds in its own function.

❷   Extract logic to determine whether all the grades are within minimum and maximum bounds in a separate function.

Ta da! We've successfully refactored checkValid in six simple steps.

A More Refined Solution

In this case, a truly complete revision of this function would involve a few additional changes. We'd write a new function to encapsulate the logic on lines 7 through 14. Next, we'd call this function as a first step in both checkAverageInBounds and check AllGradesInBounds. Finally, we'd identify all of the callsites in checkValid and replace them with either a direct call to checkAverageInBounds if useAverage was set to true or checkAllGradesInBounds if useAverage was either omitted or set to false. We would no longer have to look at the function definition for checkValid to understand what the optional Boolean parameter controls were, nor would we have to read through the code to understand what we mean by a "valid" set of grades. We could finally remove checkValid from the codebase entirely.

Our new version has some clear benefits. With just a glance, we can develop a solid sense of what the code aims to do. We've also made it the slightest bit more performant and simplified bug-prone logic by simplifying our conditions. All in all, the next developer is more likely to be able to extend on this solution without too much trouble. This is just a sneak peak into the potentially positive impact strategic refactoring at a microscopic level can have on your application; now imagine the impact that it can have when applied *at scale*.

But before we can sit down at our keyboards and start diligently refactoring, we need to orient ourselves properly. We need to understand the history of the code we want to improve, and for that, we need to understand how code degrades.

CHAPTER 2

How Code Degrades

Successfully running a marathon is an impressive feat. While I've personally never taken on the challenge, quite a few of my friends have. What may surprise you, however, is that the large majority of these friends were not avid runners before deciding to sign up for their first half or full marathon. By sticking to a regular, sustainable training schedule, they were able to build up the necessary endurance in just a few months.

Most of my friends were already in good physical shape, but if your goal is to run a marathon and most of your current physical activity involves getting up from the couch to grab a bag of chips from your pantry, you will have a much more difficult time. Not only will you first have to build up the cardiovascular and physical endurance of a regularly active person, you'll have to adopt new habits around habitual exercise and eating healthy food (even when all you want to do is settle into a comfy chair with a big, cheesy slice of pizza).

Small fluctuations in training can lead to serious setbacks. If you haven't gotten enough sleep or get caught off-guard by a scorching-hot day, you will tire more quickly, compromising your ability to run your target distance. Even in peak marathon form, you have to be prepared for the unknowns on the day of the race. It might rain; your laces might break; you might be stuck in a tight crowd of runners. You learn to master the variables you can control but must be willing and ready to think on your feet.

Being a programmer is a little bit like being a marathon runner. Both take sustained effort. Both build atop preceding progress, commit by commit, mile by mile. Making an earnest effort to maintain healthy habits can make the difference between being able to get back into marathon-running shape or peak development pace in a matter of weeks and having to take months to do so. Maintaining a high level of vigilance over both your internal and external environments and adjusting accordingly is key to completing the race successfully. The same can be applied to development: a high level of vigilance over the state of the codebase and any external influences is key to minimizing setbacks and ultimately ensuring a smooth path to the finish line.

In this chapter, we'll discuss why understanding how code degrades is key to a successful refactoring effort. We'll look at code that is either stagnant or in active development and describe ways in which each of these states can experience code degradation, with a few examples pulled from both recent and early computer science history. Finally, we'll discuss ways in which we can detect degradation early, and how we might prevent it altogether.

Why Understanding Code Degradation Matters

Code has degraded when its perceived utility has decreased. What this means is that the code, while once satisfactory, either no longer behaves as well as we would like or isn't as easy to read or use from a development perspective. It's for these precise reasons that degraded code is a great candidate for refactoring. That said, I firmly believe that you cannot set out to improve something until you have a solid grasp of its history.

Code isn't written in a vacuum. What we might deem to be bad code today was likely good code when it was originally written. By taking the time to understand the circumstances under which the code was originally written, and how, over time, it might have gone from good to bad, we can build a better awareness of the core problem, get a sense of the pitfalls to avoid, and, thus, have a better shot at taking it from bad back to good.

Broadly speaking, there are two ways in which code can degrade. Either the requirements for what the code needs to do or how it needs to behave have changed, or your organization has been cutting corners in an attempt to achieve more in a short period. We'll refer to these as "requirement shifts" and "tech debt," respectively.

I believe it's important not to assume that all code degradation you run into is due to tech debt, which is why we'll first take a look at the many ways requirement shifts can make code appear worse over time. We all have those moments when we'll come across some particularly dreadful code and think, "Who wrote this? How could we let this happen? Why has no one fixed this?" If we begin to refactor it immediately, we risk crafting a solution that overemphasizes what we find most urgently frustrating about the code, rather than addressing its truer, core pain points. It's important to build empathy for the code by asking ourselves to identify what has changed since it was written. If we make an effort to seek the initial good, we gain an appreciation for the pitfalls the original solution avoided, the clever ways it might have dealt with a set of constraints, and produce a refactored result that captures all these insights.

Unfortunately, there are times when we simply have to do our best, given very limited resources. When we don't have enough time or money to create a better solution, we start cutting corners and accruing tech debt. While the initial impact of that debt might be minimal, its added weight on our codebases can build up significantly over time. It's easy to dismiss tech debt as bad code, but I challenge you to reframe it. Sometimes the scrappiest solution is the one that gets your product or feature to market the fastest; if getting your product into the hands of users is critical to your company's survival, then the tech debt might very well be worth it.

As you read through the ways in which code can degrade, I encourage you to try to find examples of each of these in the code you work with most regularly. You might not be able to find an example for everything, but the process of searching for the symptoms of code degradation might lead you to develop a new perspective on the pieces of your application you've found most frustrating to work with.

 Once you've pinpointed code you'd like to refactor you will gain valuable insight into the how and why of the original authors' initial solution if you can sit down with them. Oftentimes, they'll be able to tell you immediately why the code degraded. If the authors say something along the lines of, "we didn't know that…," or, "at the time, we thought…," you likely have a case of code degradation due to requirement shifts. On the other hand, if the authors say something like, "oh, right, that code was never any good," or, "we were just trying to meet a deadline," you know that you're probably dealing with a standard case of tech debt.

Requirement Shifts

Whenever we write a new chunk of code, we ideally spend some time explicitly defining its purpose and providing thorough documentation to demonstrate intended usage. While we might try our best to anticipate any future requirements and attempt to design nimble systems able to handle these new demands, it's unlikely we'll be able to predict everything coming down the pipe. It's only natural that the environments around our applications will change unpredictably over time. These changes can affect both code that is in active development and code that has been left untouched to different degrees. In this section, we'll discuss a few ways in which the demands placed on our code might exceed its abilities, using examples from codebases under active and inactive development.

Scalability

One requirement we frequently attempt to estimate is the direction and degree to which our product needs to scale. This laundry list of requirements can get rather lengthy and include a wide range of parameters. Take, for instance, a simple application programming interface (API) request to create a new user entry in a system. We might set some guidelines around the expected latency of the request, the number of database queries executed within the request, the total number of new user requests allowed per second, and so on.

When launching a new product, one of our first assumptions deals with how many users we expect to use it. We craft a solution we think will comfortably handle that number (give or take a safe margin of error) and ship it! If our product is successful, we can end up with exponentially more users than we initially anticipated, and while that's certainly an amazing situation to be in from a business perspective, our original implementation probably won't be able to handle this new, unanticipated load. The code itself may not have changed, but it has effectively regressed due to a drastic shift in scalability requirements.

Accessibility

Every application should strive to be as accessible as possible from day one. We should use color-blind-friendly color schemes, add alternative text for images and icons, and ensure that any interactive elements are accessible via the keyboard. Unfortunately, teams hastening to ship a new product or feature often gloss over accessibility in favor of a more aggressive launch date. While shipping new features might help you retain current users and attract new ones, if these features aren't accessible to a subset of your anticipated user base, you risk alienating them. The second your product becomes inaccessible to some, its perceived utility substantially diminishes.

Although few iterations on official best practices for web accessibility (*https://oreil.ly/r0376*) have been developed by the Web Accessibility Initiative (WAI) since 1999, a number of important revisions have been standardized. With every new iteration, developers of active websites and applications must revisit code sometimes long untouched and implement any necessary changes to comply with the newest standards. Iterations on accessibility standards can decrease the quality of your application.

Device Compatibility

Every year, hardware companies release new versions of their devices; sometimes, they'll even take things a step further and introduce an entirely new class of device. Among smartphones, smart watches, smart cars, and smart TVs, we are constantly playing catch-up, attempting to repackage our applications to work seamlessly on the latest hardware. Users have grown to expect that their favorite applications work on a variety of platforms. If you're a developer for a popular mobile game and a major hardware company releases a new device with a higher screen resolution, you risk losing a significant portion of your user base unless you ship a new version of your game built to handle the larger screen.

Environmental Changes

When changes occur in a program's environment, all sorts of unexpected behavior can begin to manifest. Before the age of modern gaming computers loaded with powerful graphics processing limits (GPUs) and dozens of gigabytes of random-access memory (RAM), we had humble, little gaming consoles housed in arcades and, later, our living rooms. Game developers devised clever ways to use the limited hardware available to them to build classics like *Space Invaders* and *Super Mario Bros*. At the time, it was standard practice to use the central processing unit (CPU) clock speed as a timer in the game. It provided a steady, reliable measure of time. While this wasn't a problem for console games, where the cartridges often weren't compatible with newer, more powerful iterations of the console, it became a rather serious oversight for games running on personal computers. As clock speed on newer computers increased, so did the speed of gameplay. Imagine having to stack Tetris pieces or avoid a stream of Goombas at twice the normal speed; at a certain point, the game becomes wholly unusable. In both of these examples, the requirement was that the code was run on specific physical hardware; unfortunately, the hardware has since changed dramatically, and as a result, the code has degraded.

These types of environmental changes are still a serious concern today. In January 2018, security researchers from Google Project Zero and Cyberus Technology, in collaboration with a team at the Graz University of Technology, identified two serious security vulnerabilities affecting all Intel x86 microprocessors, IBM POWER processors, and some Advanced RISC Machine (ARM)-based microprocessors. The first, Meltdown, allowed rogue processes to read all memory on a machine, even when unauthorized to do so. The second, Spectre, allowed attackers to exploit branch prediction (a performance feature of the affected processors) to reveal private data about other processes running on the machine. You can read more about these vulnerabilities and their inner workings on the official website (*https://meltdownattack.com*).

At the time of the disclosure, all devices running any but the most recent versions of iOS, Linux, macOS, and Windows were affected. A number of servers and cloud services were affected, as well as the majority of smart devices and embedded devices. Within days, software workarounds became available for both vulnerabilities, but these came at a performance cost of 5 to 30 percent, depending on the workload. Intel later reported it was working to find ways to help protect against both Meltown and Spectre in its next lineup of processors. Even the things we believe to be most stable (operating systems, firmware) are susceptible to changes in their own environments; and when these core, underlying systems on top of which we run countless applications are affected, we, in turn, are affected.

External Dependencies

Every piece of software has external dependencies; to list just a few examples, these can be a set of libraries, a programming language, an interpreter, or an operating system. The degree to which these dependencies are coupled to the software can vary. This reliance isn't anything new; many influential programs from the early days of artificial intelligence research were developed in Lisp and Lisp-like research programming languages as they were actively developed in the 1960s and early 1970s. SHRDLU, an early natural language–understanding computer program, was written in Micro Planner on a PDP-6, using nonstandard macros and software libraries that no longer exist today, thus suffering from irreparable software rot.

Today, we do our best to update our external dependencies to keep up to date with the latest features and security patches. Sometimes, however, we either deprioritize or lose track of updates, especially when it comes to code we're not actively maintaining. While allowing dependencies to fall a few versions behind might not be an immediate problem, it does come at a risk. We become more susceptible to security vulnerabilities. We also open ourselves up to potentially difficult upgrade experiences at a later date.

Say we are running a program that relies on version 1.8 of an open-source library called Super Timezone Library. Just a few weeks after releasing version 4.0, the developers of Super Timezone Library announce that they will no longer actively support any versions below 3.0. We now need to upgrade to version 3.0 at the minimum to continue to port security patches. Unfortunately, version 2.5 introduced some backward-incompatible changes and version 2.8 deprecated functionality used widely in our application. What could have been a small, regular investment in keeping the library up to date over the past few years has now turned into a much more complex, urgent investment.

Unused Code

Changes in requirements can lead to unused code. Take, for example, a publicly facing API. Your team decides to deprecate the API and warn third-party developers of the upcoming change. Unfortunately, after you've communicated the intended change, removed the documentation from your website, and ensured that no external systems were still relying on the endpoint, your team forgets to remove the code. A few months later, a new engineer begins implementing a new feature, stumbles upon the decommissioned API endpoint, and assumes, quite naturally, that it is still functional. They decide to repurpose it for their own use case. Unfortunately, they quickly find out that the code doesn't do quite what they intended, simply because the API had been left in the dust and hadn't adapted with the rest of the codebase and numerous iterations of requirement changes.

Unused code can also be problematic from a developer productivity perspective. Every time we encounter code we believe to be unused, we have to determine very carefully whether we can safely remove it. Unless we're equipped with reliable tooling to help us properly highlight the extent of the dead code, we might have a difficult time pinpointing its exact boundaries. If we aren't sure whether we can delete it, usually we'll just move on and hope someone else can figure it out later on. Who knows how many engineers will come across the same piece of code and ask themselves the same question before it's finally removed!

Finally, unused code, if allowed to pile up, can be a hindrance to performance. If, for example, your team works on the client-facing portion of a website, the size of the files the JavaScript files requested by your browser directly translates to initial page load times. Typically, the larger the file, the slower the response. Greedily requesting bloated application code can be quite detrimental to the user experience.

Commented-Out Code

In the case of commented-out code, it's pretty obvious that the code is unused. I always recommend that developers who are tempted to comment-out code instead simply delete it if the code is tracked using version control. If you need it again someday, you can easily recover it by going back through your commit history.

Changes in Product Requirements

Most of the time, it's easier to write a solution for today or tomorrow's product requirements, solving for the problems and constraints we understand and can easily anticipate, than to write one for next year, attempting to solve for unknown future pitfalls. We try to be pragmatic, weighing current concerns against future concerns, and attempting to determine how much time we should invest in solving for either. Sometimes, we simply don't have a good intuition about the future.

Boolean arguments to functions are a great example of the difficulty of predicting future product requirements in action. Most of the time, Boolean arguments are introduced to existing functions to modify their behavior. (We saw one in "Our First Refactoring Example" on page 18, where a Boolean flag was used to decide whether we wanted to know whether each of the grades or the average of those grades fell in a given range.) Adding a Boolean flag is often the smallest, simplest change you can make when you find a function that does almost exactly what you want it to do, with just a tiny exception. Unfortunately, this type of change can cause all sorts of problems down the line. We can see some of those in action in Example 2-1, where we have a small function responsible for uploading an image given a filename and a flag denoting whether the file is a PNG.

Example 2-1. A function with a Boolean argument

```
function uploadImage(filename, isPNG) {
  // some implementation details
  if (isPNG) {
    // do some PNG-specific logic
  }
  // do some other things
}
```

What if, a few months from now, we decide to support a new image format? We might decide to add another Boolean argument to designate isGIF, as shown in Example 2-2.

Example 2-2. A function with two Boolean arguments

```
function uploadImage(filename, isPNG, isGIF) { ❶
  // some implementation details
  if (isPNG) {
    // do some PNG-specific logic
  } else if (isGIF) { ❷
    // do some GIF-specific logic
  }
  // do some other things
}
```

❶ Introduced a new Boolean argument to designate whether the image is a GIF.

❷ An image cannot be both a PNG and a GIF, so we've added an else if here.

To call this function and correctly upload a GIF, we would need to remember to set the second Boolean argument to true. Readers who come across the code calling out to uploadImage would likely be confused and need to refer to the function definition to understand what role the two Boolean arguments play.

> In a language with named arguments, we would be less concerned with needing to reference the function definition to know the role and order of arguments. Regardless of language choice, it remains that while uploadImage(filename=filename, isPNG=true, isGIF=true) may seem nonsensical, it is a perfectly valid function call (and is very likely to cause bugs in the future). Example 2-3 shows an example where it might be difficult for the reader to discern what uploadImage does given the context.

Example 2-3. A function uploading a GIF

```
function changeProfilePicture(filename) {
  // some implementation details
  if (isAnimated) {
    uploadImage(filename, false, true);  ❶
  } else {
    uploadImage(filename, true, false);  ❷
  }
  // do some other things
}
```

❶   Here we are uploading a GIF.

❷   Otherwise, we are uploading a PNG.

Not only is it difficult for developers to understand how `uploadImage` works when reading through functions like `changeProfilePicture`, it's an unsustainable pattern to continue to maintain if more image formats are introduced in the future. The developer who added the first Boolean argument to support `isPNG` was mostly concerned with today's problems rather than those of tomorrow. A better approach would be to split up the logic into distinct functions: `uploadJPG`, `uploadPNG`, and `uploadGIF`, as shown in Example 2-4.

Example 2-4. Distinct functions for uploading different types of files

```
function uploadImagePreprocessing(filename) {
  // some implementation details
}

function uploadImagePostprocessing(filename) {
  // do some other things
}

function uploadJPG(filename) {
  uploadImagePreprocessing();
  // do JPG things
  uploadImagePostprocessing();
}

function uploadPNG(filename) {
  uploadImagePreprocessing();
  // do PNG things
  uploadImagePostprocessing();
}

function uploadGIF(filename) {
  uploadImagePreprocessing();
  // do GIF things
```

```
    uploadImagePostprocessing();
}
```

Now you might be wondering why adding the isPNG Boolean argument is a serious problem if we can just refactor it later. To replace all occurrences of uploadImage properly, we'd need to audit each callsite individually and replace it with either uploadJPG or uploadPNG, depending on whether the Boolean argument is set to true. Because these changes are manual but mundane, the likelihood of us making the wrong replacement is quite high and could lead to some serious regressions. Depending on how widespread the problem might be, and how tightly coupled it might be to other crucial business logic, refactoring what seems like a simple Boolean argument might be a daunting task.

Tech Debt

The most common culprits behind tech debt are limited time, limited numbers of engineers, and limited money. Given that all technology companies are faced with limited resources on one or more axes, each and every one of them has tech debt. Tiny, six-month-old startups; giant, decades-old conglomerates; and every company in between has a fair share of crufty code. In this section, we'll take a closer look at how these influences can lead to the accumulation of tech debt. Although it can be easy to point a finger at the original authors of the code and admonish them for making decisions that appear suboptimal today, it's important to remember that they were operating under serious constraints. We have to acknowledge that sometimes it's just about impossible to write good code under tight pressure.

Working Around Technology Choices

When implementing something new, we have to make some critical decisions about which technologies we want to use. We have to choose a language, a dependency manager, a database, and so on. There's a fairly long laundry list of decisions to make well before the application becomes available to any users. Many of these decisions are made given the engineers' experience; if these engineers are more comfortable using one technology over another, they'll have an easier time getting the project up and running quickly than if they decided to adopt a new stack.

Once the project's been launched and found some traction, these early technology decisions are put to the test. If a problem with a technology choice arises early enough in the lifetime of the application, it might be easy and inexpensive to find an appropriate alternative and pivot to it, but oftentimes the limitations of those choices don't become apparent until well after the application has grown past this point.

One such decision might be to develop an application by using a dynamically typed programming language instead of a statically typed programming language.

Proponents of dynamically typed programming languages argue that they make the code easier to read and understand; less indirection around strictly defined structures and type declarations allow the reader to understand better and more readily the purpose of the code. Many also tout the quicker development cycle they provide due to the lack of compile time.

While there are many upsides to using dynamically typed programming languages, they become difficult to manage when applications grow beyond a critical mass. Because types are only verified at runtime, it is the developer's responsibility to ensure type correctness by writing a full suite of unit tests that exercises all execution paths and asserts expected behavior. New developers seeking to familiarize themselves with how different structures interact with one another might have a difficult time doing so if variable names do not immediately indicate which type it might be. It's not uncommon to end up needing to program defensively, as shown in Example 2-5, where we assert that a value passed into a function has certain properties and isn't unintentionally null.

Example 2-5. Defensive programming in action

```
function addUserToGroup(group, user) {

  if (!user) {
    throw 'user cannot be null';
  }

  // assert required fields
  if (!user.name) {
    throw 'name required';
  }

  if (!user.email) {
    throw 'email required';
  }

  if (!user.dateCreated) {
    throw 'date created required';
  }

  // assert no empty strings or other invalid values
  if (user.name === "") {
    throw 'name cannot be empty';
  }
  if (user.email === "") {
    throw 'email cannot be empty';
  }
  if (user.dateCreated === 0) {
    throw 'date created cannot be 0';
  }
```

```
    group.push(user);
    return group;
}
```

It's very likely the author of the code sample runs into issues regularly with invalid users weaving their way through a callstack at runtime simply due to the dynamic nature of JavaScript. The author just wants to be certain that they are only adding valid users to the group, and that's completely understandable. Unfortunately, now addUserToGroup is primarily concerned with ensuring that the user provided is valid, rather than adding the user to the group. As more decisions are made about what constitutes a valid user, each of these ad hoc validations sprinkled throughout the codebase needs to be updated. There's also an increasing chance we might introduce a bug by simply forgetting to update one such location. Eventually, we end up with lengthy, convoluted, bug-prone functions everywhere.

We can introduce a new function to help mitigate code degradation. Let's say we write up a simple helper to encapsulate all the logic for validating a user object; we'll call it validateUser. Example 2-6 shows its implementation.

Example 2-6. A simple helper function to encapsulate user validation logic

```
function validateUser(user) {
  if (!user) {
    throw 'user cannot be null';
  }

  // assert required fields
  if (!user.name) {
    throw 'name required';
  }

  if (!user.email) {
    throw 'email required';
  }

  if (!user.dateCreated) {
    throw 'date created required';
  }

  // assert no empty strings or other invalid values
  if (user.name === "") {
    throw 'name cannot be empty';
  }
  if (user.email === "") {
    throw 'email cannot be empty';
  }
  if (user.dateCreated === 0) {
    throw 'date created cannot be 0';
```

```
    }
  return;
}
```

We can then update `addUserToGroup` to use our new helper function, drastically simplifying the logic, as shown in Example 2-7.

Example 2-7. Simplified `addUserToGroup` function without inlined validation logic

```
function addUserToGroup(group, user) {
  validateUser(user);
  group.push(user);
  return group;
}
```

Unfortunately, while it's much easier for us to call `validateUser`, replacing all the locations where we previously enumerated each check will be an easy task. First, we have to identify each of those spots. If we're dealing with a large codebase, that might be a daunting task. Second, in auditing each of these locations, we'll probably end up finding a handful of instances where we've forgotten a check or two. In some cases, this is a bug, and we can safely replace the checks with a single call to `validateUser`; in other cases, this might have been intentional, and we cannot blindly replace the existing code with our new helper at the risk of introducing a regression. As such, easing the burden of our defensive programming requires us to plan and execute a sizable refactor.

Persistent Lack of Organization

Maintaining an organized codebase is a little bit like maintaining a tidy home. It seems as though there's always something more important to do than to put away the clothes heaped over the dresser or sort through the stack of mail accumulating on the coffee table. But the more we accumulate, the more time we'll spend combing through it all when we finally get around to it. You might even allow the clutter to build up to the point that it's begun overflowing on to other surfaces. My parents were onto something when they encouraged me to keep things tidy and clean up just a little bit every day; they knew that it was always much easier to take care of a small mess than a massive one.

Many of us fall into the same patterns when it comes to keeping our codebases organized. Take, for instance, a codebase with a relatively flat file structure. Most of the code is organized into two dozen or so files, with a single directory for tests. The application grows at a steady pace, with a few new files added every month. Because it's easier to maintain the status quo, instead of proactively beginning to organize related files into directories, engineers instead learn to navigate the increasingly sprawling code. New engineers introduced to the growing chaos raise a warning flag and encourage the team to begin splitting up the code, but these concerns fall on deaf ears; managers encourage them to focus on the deadlines looming ahead, and tenured engineers shrug and reassure them that they'll quickly figure out how to be productive in the disarray. Eventually, the codebase reaches a critical mass in which the persistent lack of organization has dramatically slowed productivity across the engineering team. Only then does the team take the time to draft a plan for grooming the codebase, at which point the number of variables to consider is far greater than it would have been, had they made a concerted effort to tackle the problem months (or even years) earlier.

Too Many Cooks in the Kitchen

Poorly organized code can lead to even quicker degradation when combined with rapid hiring. Fast-growing companies might be onboarding dozens of new engineers every month. These engineers are eager to dive in and begin committing code, but without a well-defined structure and style, they risk perpetuating existing troublesome patterns deeply rooted in the current codebase.

With too many engineers working in the same codebase, you define ergonomics not necessarily based on what works best for the long-term health of the codebase but rather what works best knowing you'll have to work around other contributors. This can lead to lengthy, defensive code, or suboptimally placed code to avoid potential merge conflicts.

Moving Too Quickly

Rapid iteration and product development can swiftly degrade software quality if not kept in check. When building out new product features under aggressive deadlines, we tend to cut corners: we'll omit a few test cases, give variables generic names, or add a few `if` statements where we could have made a new function. If we do not properly make note of the corners we've cut and allocate the time necessary to correct them immediately after we've met our target deadline, they pile up. Soon, you end up with exceedingly lengthy functions, littered with branching logic and little-to-no unit test coverage sprinkled throughout your codebase. When working in more complex applications, where multiple teams are iterating on distinct features alongside one another, effects of moving too quickly begin to compound. Unless every team can communicate product changes effectively with every other team, the amount of cruft piles up. You can see an example of that compounding effect illustrated in Figure 2-1.

Many of us working on modern applications practice continuous integration and delivery; we merge our changes back into the main branch as often as possible, where they're validated by running automated tests against a new build of the application.

We ensure that customers aren't exposed to half-baked features and partial bug fixes by gating these changes behind feature flags (otherwise known as feature toggles). While these give us a good amount of flexibility during active development, they're easy to forget about once we've successfully introduced the change to all the users.

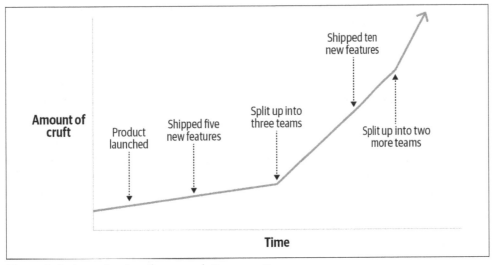

Figure 2-1. A graph of cruft accumulation over time

Every company I've worked for had dozens (if not hundreds) of feature flags still being referenced in the program well after they'd been enabled for all of production. While it might seem benign to leave a few of these checks lying around, there are some distinct risks.

First, it causes added cognitive load on developers reading the code; if the developer doesn't take the time to verify the status of the feature, they might be misled into thinking it is still under active development and only make an important change in the nongated codepath. Second, it can be frustrating to spend time determining whether the feature is active in production, only to find out that it's been live to everyone for weeks. In the severe cases where there are hundreds of essentially defunct feature flags, this can have a very serious performance impact on the application. The cumulative time spent validating each feature-related conditional for a given request or codepath can be significant. We might all see some performance enhancements by cleaning up our obsolete flags.

Applying Our Knowledge

Code degradation is inevitable. No matter how hard we try to avoid them, there will be shifts in requirements our applications will need to adapt to. We can try to minimize development under pressure, but sometimes we need to cut corners to ship quickly and give our business the competitive advantage. If code degradation is inevitable, then refactoring at scale is equally inevitable. There will always be a need for us to address tricky, systemic problems in our codebases. If we think we've reached the point that we think the degradation is just too burdensome and preventing our engineering team from developing as well as it could, then we need to put on our hard hats and figure out both why and how we got to this point.

When we learn to see beyond code's immediate problems and instead seek to understand the circumstances under which it was originally written, we begin to see that code isn't inherently bad. We build empathy and use this newfound perspective to identify the code's true foundational problems and hatch a plan to improve it in the best way possible. Think of this process as just one big exercise in code archaeology!

Now that we've learned how code degrades, we have to learn how to quantify it properly for others to understand. We have to use our hunch that the degradation is at a critical point, our knowledge about why and how it got to that point, to figure out the best way to distill the problem into a set of metrics we can use to convince others that this is, in fact, a serious problem. The next chapter discusses a number of techniques you can use to measure problems in your codebase and establish a solid baseline for your refactoring effort.

PART II

Planning

CHAPTER 3

Measuring Our Starting State

Every spring, I take the time to clean out my closet and reevaluate all of the clothing I own. While some opt for a Marie Kondo–like approach to cleaning out their closets, seeing whether each item "sparks joy," I take a more methodical one. Each year, when I kick off the process, I know that by the end, a number of items will be in the donate pile. What I don't know is which pieces these will be, because it entirely depends on how all of my clothing works together in the first place.

Before I start packing some bags for Goodwill, I take a comprehensive look at the whole. I organize everything by clothing type: sweaters in one pile, dresses in another, and so on, accounting for the practicality of each item of clothing as I go. Which seasons is this dress good for? How comfortable is it? How often have I worn it in the past year? Next, I approximate how many outfits the item can be integrated with. It's only once I have a strong sense of everything I own, and understand the role each item of clothing plays in my closet, that I can start to identify the clothing I can comfortably donate.

The same logic applies to large refactoring efforts; only once we have a solid characterization of the surface area we want to improve can we begin to identify the best way to improve it. Unfortunately, finding meaningful ways of measuring the pain points in our code today is much more difficult than categorizing items of clothing in our closets. This chapter discusses a number of techniques for quantifying and qualifying the state of our code before we begin refactoring. We'll cover a few well-known techniques as well as a few newer, more creative approaches. By the end of the chapter, I hope you'll have found one (or more) ways to measure the code you want to improve in a way that highlights the problems you want to solve.

Why Is Measuring the Impact of a Refactor Difficult?

There are a number of ways to measure the health of a codebase. Many of these metrics, however, might not move in a positive direction as a result of a large-scale refactor simply because they are orthogonal to the pain points the project aims to address. So, in measuring the starting state of our codebase, we want to choose a metric that we believe will summarize the problem well *and* accurately highlight the impact of our refactor.

Measuring the impact of any refactoring effort is tricky, primarily because when executed successfully, refactoring should be invisible to users and lead to no behavioral changes whatsoever. This isn't a new feature we're hoping will drive user adoption or a tweak. We often put a great deal of effort into monitoring critical pieces of our applications to ensure that our users are getting a reliable experience when using our product, but because these metrics capture behavior that our users are likely to notice, most of them remain unaffected when we've refactored correctly. To characterize the impact of a refactor best, we need to identify metrics that measure the precise aspects of the code we want to improve and establish a strong baseline before moving forward.

A Note About Refactoring to Improve Performance

Let's say we operate a small application responsible for tracking customer orders. To ensure that our system is running smoothly, we monitor how long it takes for our service to retrieve the status of an order, given its ID. After a few months, we begin to notice that our response times are slowing and decide to invest some time in refactoring the underlying code. In this scenario, we already have our starting metric: the initial average response time. We can easily measure whether our endeavor was successful by comparing the initial average response time to our new average response time once the rewritten code is deployed. Voila!

Quantifying the impact of refactoring motivated by performance is often the easiest. We generally already have a reliable set of starting metrics readily available. It's also worth noting that performance-driven efforts, unlike refactoring efforts prompted by the desire to increase developer productivity, are one of the only kinds of refactoring that lead to clear, user-facing improvements.

Large refactoring efforts are particularly difficult to measure because they rarely take place in the span of just a few weeks. More often than not, the work involved from start to finish spans far beyond the typical feature development cycle, and unless product development was completely paused while the refactoring effort was ongoing, it might be difficult to isolate its impact from the work of other developers in the same section of the application. Reliance on a handful of distinct metrics can help you paint a more holistic picture of your progress and better distinguish your changes from those introduced by other developers iterating on the product alongside you.

Measuring Code Complexity

Many of us are motivated to refactor as a means of boosting developer productivity, making it easier for us to continue to maintain our applications and build new features. In practice, this often means simplifying complex, convoluted sections of code. Given that our goal revolves around *decreasing* code complexity, we need to find a meaningful way of measuring it. Quantifying the code's complexity gives us a starting point from which we can begin to assess our progress.

Measuring software complexity is easy in two main ways. First, if our code resides in version history, we can easily travel through time and apply our complexity calculations at any interval. Second, a vast number of open-source libraries and tools are readily available in many programming languages. Generating a report for your entire application can be as simple as installing a package and running a single command.

Here, we'll discuss three common methods of calculating code complexity.

Halstead Metrics

Maurice Halstead first proposed measuring the complexity of software in 1975 by counting the number of operators and operands in a given computer program. He believed that because programs mainly consisted of these two units, counting their unique instances might give us a meaningful measure of the size of the program and therefore indicate something about its complexity.

Operators are constructs that behave like functions, but differ syntactically or semantically from typical functions. These include arithmetic symbols like - and +, logical operators like &&, comparison operators like >, and assignment operators like =. Take, for instance, a simple function that adds two numbers together, as shown in Example 3-1.

Example 3-1. A short function that adds two numbers together

```
function add(x, y) {
  return x+y;
}
```

It contains a single operator, the addition operator, +. Operands, on the other hand, are any entities we operate on, using our set of operators. In our addition example, our operands are x and y.

Given these simple data points, Halstead proposed a set of metrics to calculate a set of characteristics:

1. A program's volume, or how much information the reader of the code has to absorb in order to understand its meaning.

2. A program's difficulty, or the amount of mental effort required to re-create the software; also commonly referred to as the Halstead effort metric.

3. The number of bugs you are likely to find in the system.

To illustrate Halstead's ideas better, we can apply our operator and operand counting technique to a slightly more complicated function, which calculates an integer's prime factors, as in Example 3-2. We've enumerated each of the unique operators and operands, along with the number of times they occur in the program, in Table 3-1.

Example 3-2. Operators and operands in a short function

```
function primeFactors(number) {
  function isPrime(number) {
    for (let i = 2; i <= Math.sqrt(number); i++) {
      if (number % i === 0) return false;
    }
    return true;
  }

  const result = [];
  for (let i = 2; i <= number; i++) {
    while (isPrime(i) && number % i === 0) {
      if (!result.includes(i)) result.push(i);
      number /= i;
    }
  }
  return result;
}
```

Table 3-1. Unique operators and operands, with their frequencies

Operator	Number of occurrences	Operand	Number of occurrences
function	2	0	2
for	2	2	2
let	2	primeFactors	1
=	3	number	7
<=	2	isPrime	2
()	4	i	12
.	3	Math	1
++ (postfix)	2	sqrt	1

Operator	Number of occurrences	Operand	Number of occurrences
if	2	FALSE	1
===	2	TRUE	1
%	2	result	4
return	3	<anonymous>	1
const	1	includes	1
[]	1	push	1
while	1		
&&	1		
! (prefix)	1		
/=	1		
Unique operators: 18 Total operators: 35		Unique operands: 14 Total operands: 37	

Given that our prime factorization program has 18 unique operators (n_1), 14 unique operands (n_2), and a total operand count of 37 (N_2), we can use Halstead's difficulty measure to calculate the relative difficulty associated with reading the program with the basic equation:

$$D = \frac{n_1}{2} \cdot \frac{N_2}{n_2}$$

Substituting in our values, we obtain an overall difficulty score of 23.78.

$$D = \frac{18}{2} \cdot \frac{37}{14}$$

$$D = 23.78$$

Although 23.78 might not signify much on its own, we can gradually acquire an understanding of how this score maps to our experiences, working with individual sections of our code. Over time, through repeated exposure to these values alongside their implementations, we become better able to interpret what a score of 23.78 signifies within the greater context of our application.

Each of the three distinct metrics described in this section can be generated at different scales; they can quantify the complexity of a single function or a complete module. You can calculate the Halstead difficulty metric for an entire file, for instance, by summing up the difficulties of the individual functions contained within it.

Cyclomatic Complexity

Developed by Thomas McCabe in 1976, cyclomatic complexity is a quantitative measure of the number of linearly independent paths through a program's source code. It is essentially a count of the number of control flow statements within a program. This includes `if` statements, `while` and `for` loops, and `case` statements in side `switch` blocks.

Take, for example, a simple program with no control flow components, as shown in Example 3-3. To calculate its cyclomatic complexity, we first assign 1 for the function declaration, incrementing with every decision point we encounter. Example 3-3 has a cyclomatic complexity of 1 because there is only one path through the function.

Example 3-3. Simple temperature conversion function

```
function convertToFahrenheit(celsius) {
  return celsius * (9/5) + 32;
}
```

Let's look at a more complex example, like our `primeFactors` function from Example 3-2. In Example 3-4, we reduce it and enumerate each of the control flow points to yield a cyclomatic complexity of 6.

Example 3-4. Operators and operands in a short function

```
function primeFactors(number) { ❶
  function isPrime(number) {
    for (let i = 2; i <= Math.sqrt(number); i++) { ❷
      if (number % i === 0) return false; ❸
    }
    return true;
  }

  const result = [];
  for (let i = 2; i <= number; i++) { ❹
    while (isPrime(i) && number % i === 0) {❺
      if (!result.includes(i)) result.push(i); ❻
      number /= i;
    }
  }
  return result;
}
```

❶ Function declaration is the first control flow point.

❷ First `for` loop is our second point.

❸ First `if` statement is our third point.

❹ Second `for` loop is the fourth point.

❺ `while` is the fifth point.

❻ Second `if` is the sixth point.

When we're reading a chunk of code, every time there is a branch (an `if` statement, a `for` loop, etc.), we have to begin to reason about multiple states with multiple paths of execution. We have to be able to hold more information in our heads to understand what the code does. So, with a cyclomatic complexity of 6, we can infer that `primeFactors` is probably not too difficult to read and understand.

Counting the number of decision points in a program is a simplification of McCabe's proposed method of calculating its complexity. Mathematically, we can calculate the cyclomatic complexity of a structured program by generating a directed graph representing its control flow; each node represents a basic block (i.e., a straight-line code sequence with no branches), with an edge linking them if there is a way to pass from one block to the other. Given this graph, its complexity, **M**, is defined as in the following equation, where **E** is the number of edges, **N** is the number of nodes, and **P** is the number of connection components, where a connected component is a subgraph where the nodes are all reachable from one another.

$$M = E - N + 2P$$

Figure 3-1 shows an example control flow for `primeFactors`.

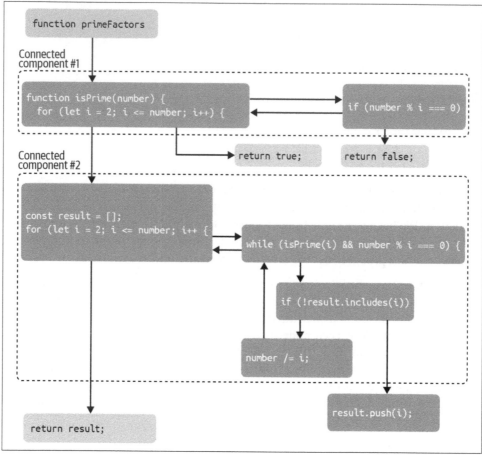

Figure 3-1. Control flow graph for `primeFactors`, with blue nodes signifying nonterminal states and red nodes signifying terminal states. For this example, we have 13 edges, 11 nodes, and 2 connected components.

More Applications for Control Flow Graphs

Control flow graphs (CFGs) can be useful beyond helping us calculate complexity calculations. In practice, when trying to understand particularly complex control flows, I've often taken the time to produce a CFG manually to highlight decision points. While there are more than a handful of tools I could use to generate the CFG automatically, doing this manually requires me to read through the code and helps me cement the flow a bit better.

These data structures can also be used to identify unreachable code effectively. Say we produce a control flow graph from a given set of functions. If within that CFG there is a subgraph that is not connected from any entry point, we can safely assume that it is unreachable and can be removed. On the other hand, if an exit block is unreachable from the entry point, it might indicate the presence of an infinite loop.

NPath Complexity

NPath complexity was proposed as an alternative to existing complexity metrics in 1988 by Brian Nejmeh. He argues that focusing on acyclic execution paths did not adequately model the relationship between finite subsets of paths and the set of all *possible* execution paths. We can observe this limitation in the fact that cyclomatic complexity does not consider nesting of control flow structures. A function with three for loops in succession will yield the same metric as one with three nested for loops. Nesting can influence the psychological complexity of the function, and psychological complexity can have a large impact on our ability to maintain software quality.

McCabe's metric might be easy to calculate, but it fails to distinguish between different kinds of control flow structures, treating if statements identically to while or for loops. Nejmeh asserts that not all control flow structures are equal; some are more difficult to understand use properly than others. For example, a while loop might be trickier for a developer to reason about than a switch statement. NPath complexity attempts to address this concern. Unfortunately, this makes it a bit more difficult to calculate, even for small programs, because the calculation is recursive and can quickly balloon. We'll walk through the calculations for a few examples with if statements to get familiar with how it works. If you'd like to gain a better understanding of how to calculate NPath complexity, given a greater range of control flow statements (including nested control flows), I highly recommend reading Nejmeh's paper.

 Control flow metrics can help you determine the number of test cases your code needs. Cyclomatic complexity offers a lower bound, and NPath complexity provides an upper bound. For instance, with primeFactors, cyclomatic complexity indicates that we would want at least six test cases to exercise each of the decision points.

Our base case for NPath complexity is the same as for our previous temperature converter function in Example 3-3; for a simple program with no decision points, the NPath complexity is 1. To illustrate the multiplicative component of the metric, we'll take a look at a simple function with a few nested if conditions.

Example 3-5 shows a short function that returns the likelihood of receiving a speeding ticket, given a provided speed. Reading through the function, we reach a first if statement, at which point the given speed can either be less than or greater than 45 km/h. There are then *two* possible paths: if the speed is greater than 45 km/h, we enter the code inside the if block; if not, we simply continue. We next need to verify whether the speed is greater than 10 km/h over the supplied speed limit, at which point we again have two possible paths through the code. Eventually, we return our calculated risk factor.

Example 3-5. A short function with two, sequential if statements, with different sections annotated A, B, C, D, E, and F

```
function likelihoodOfSpeedingTicket(currentSpeed, limit){
  risk = 0;  // A

  if (currentSpeed < 45) {
    risk = 1; // B
  } // C

  if (currentSpeed > (limit + 10)) {
    risk = 2; // D
  } // E

  return risk; // F
}
```

NPath complexity calculates the number of distinct paths through a function. We can enumerate each of these paths by calling likelihoodOfSpeedingTicket with a range of values, exercising each set of conditions. We'll walk through one input together, highlighting the path we traverse through the function. All other unique paths are labeled in Table 3-2.

Table 3-2. All unique paths through likelihoodOfSpeedingTicket

Inputs	Path
30, 10	A, B, D, F
30, 50	A, B, E, F
90, 50	A, C, D, F
90, 110	A, C, E, F
Unique paths: 4	

Say we call likelihoodOfSpeedingTicket with a currentSpeed of 30 and limit of 0. Our first if statement will evaluate to true, leading us to B. Our second if statement will also evaluate to true, leading us to D. Then we reach our return statement at F. Repeating this pattern for a variety of inputs, we determine that there are four unique paths through the function. Therefore, our NPath score is 4.

Downsides of NPath Complexity

NPath complexity will always provide an overestimate of the number of execution paths through a section of code. For instance, what would the NPath complexity of our `likelihoodOfSpeedingTicket` function be if we added one final check to see whether the `currentSpeed` is over 135 km/h? We would have three `if` statements, each with two possible outcomes, for a total of 2 x 2 x 2, or 8 total paths through the function. However, it's impossible for the speed to be both under 45 km/h and over 135 km/h, so one of these paths is simply impossible at execution time. It's important to keep in mind that while NPath complexity can be valuable in characterizing how difficult a section of code is to reason out, it is only an estimate on the upper bound.

NPath complexity might better exemplify the behavior of distinct types of control flow statements and effectively capture the psychological load involved with nested decision points, but the values it generates when run on large, legacy codebases can be *massive* (in the hundreds of thousands). This is mainly due to the exponential nature of the metric. Unfortunately, this means that the value itself can quickly lose significance, making small improvements difficult to discern. I recommend that you use NPath complexity to measure constrained sections of the code you are seeking to improve, perhaps taking an average of the individual sections as your starting point.

Some easy forms of refactoring won't have any impact on your CFG metrics. Some complexity is unavoidable simply due to complicated business logic. You *have* to make each of these checks and iterations to ensure that your application is doing what it needs to be doing. When the code you want to refactor involves simplifying unnecessarily complicated logic, then NPath or cyclomatic complexity are great options. If not, then I recommend using a different set of metrics. Do be mindful, however, that even if you are detangling some spaghetti code, NPath or cyclomatic complexity should not be your *only* metrics; you won't be able to characterize the impact of your refactoring effort holistically and properly with only a single data point.

Lines of Code

Unfortunately, control flow graph metrics can be difficult (and sometimes expensive) to calculate, particularly for very large codebases (which are precisely the ones we're looking to improve). This is where program size comes into play. Although it may not be quite as scientific as Halstead, McCabe, or Nejmeh's algorithms, combined with other measurements, program size can help us locate likely pain points in our application. If we're looking for a pragmatic, low-effort approach to quantifying the complexity of our code, then size-based metrics are the way to go.

When measuring code length, we have a few options available to us. Most developers choose to measure only *logical* lines of code, omitting empty lines and comments entirely. As with our control flow metrics, we can collect this information at a number of resolutions. I've found the following few data points to be quite helpful reference points:

LOC (lines of code) per file

Every codebase has the kind of files that look as if you might not reach the end if you started scrolling from the beginning. Measuring the number of lines of code for these would likely accurately capture the psychological overhead required to understand their contents and responsibilities when a developer pops them open in their editor.

Function length

For every endless file, there's an endless function. (More often than not, the endless functions are found in the endless files.) Measuring the length of functions or methods within your application can be a helpful way of approximating their individual complexities.

Average function length per file, module, or class

Depending on how your application is organized, you may want to keep track of the average function or method length per logical unit. In object-oriented codebases, you likely want to keep track of the average length of each method within a class or package. In an imperative codebase, you might measure the average length of each function within a file or larger module. Whatever the greater organizational unit, knowing the average length of the smaller logical components contained within it can give you an indication of the relative complexity of that unit as a whole.

A Note About Counting Lines of Comments

By and large, ignoring comments is good practice when counting lines of code. Docblocks and inlined TODOs do not affect the behavior of our programs, so including them in our size calculations would not help us better characterize a program's complexity. In practice, however, I've noticed that you can easily pinpoint some rather perplexing sections of code by counting the number of inline comments at the function level. In general, developers tend to leave inline code comments when the surrounding logic is difficult to follow. Whether that's because the code is dealing with a complicated piece of business logic or it has just become gradually more convoluted over time, we tend to leave some pointers to others who come after us when modifying exceptionally tricky code. Therefore, we can use the quantity of inline comments within a single function, whether short or long, as a possible warning sign.

LOC might vary wildly, depending on the language of a program or programming style, but if we're comparing apples to apples, we shouldn't be too concerned. When refactoring at scale, we're generally concerned with improving code within a *single, large* codebase. In my experience, the vast majority of developers working with these codebases have invested in establishing style guides, defining a set of best practices, and often enforcing these rules with autoformatters. Some variation is inevitable across teams and components, but broadly speaking, the application as a whole tends to look similar enough that two sets of LOC metrics from distinct sections of the codebase should still be comparable.

Test Coverage Metrics

When we're developing new features, there are a few testing philosophies we can adopt. We can opt for a test-driven development (TDD) approach, writing a thorough suite of tests first and then iterating on an implementation until the tests pass; we can write our solution first, followed by the corresponding tests; or we can decide to alternate between the two, incrementally building an implementation, pausing to write a handful of tests with each iteration. Whatever our approach, the desired outcome is the same: a new feature, fully backed by a quality set of tests.

Refactoring is a different beast. When we're working to improve an existing implementation, whatever the extent of our endeavor, we want to be sure that we're correctly retaining its behavior. We can safely assert that our new solution continues to work identically to the old by relying on the original implementation's test suite. Because we are relying on the test coverage to warn us about potential regressions, we need to verify two things before beginning our refactoring effort: first, confirm that the original implementation has test coverage and, second, determine whether that test coverage is adequate.

Say we want to refactor our `primeFactors` function in Example 3-2. Before we consider making any changes, we need to measure whether it has test coverage and, if it does, whether that test coverage is sufficient. Verifying that the implementation has test coverage is easy. We can just pop open the corresponding test file and take a peek at what it contains. For our example, we find just one test, shown in Example 3-6.

Example 3-6. A simple test for `primeFactors`

```
describe('base cases', () => {
  test('0', () => {
    expect(primeFactors(0)).toStrictEqual([]);
  });
});
```

Determining whether that test coverage is adequate, however, is a trickier task. We can evaluate it in two ways: quantitatively and qualitatively. Quantitatively, we can calculate a percentage representing the proportion of code that is executed when the test suite is run against it. We can collect metrics for both the number of functional lines of code and the number of execution paths tested by our simple unit test, yielding 40 percent and 35.71 percent, respectively. Example 3-7 shows the test output generated with the Jest unit testing framework.

Example 3-7. Jest test coverage output for primeFactors, given our single test case

```
-----------------|---------|----------|---------|---------|-------------------
File             | % Stmts | % Branch | % Funcs | % Lines | Uncovered Line #s
-----------------|---------|----------|---------|---------|-------------------
All files        |  35.71  |      0   |    50   |    40   |
 primeFactors.js |  35.71  |      0   |    50   |    40   | 3-6,11-13
-----------------|---------|----------|---------|---------|-------------------
Test Suites: 1 passed, 1 total
Tests:       1 passed, 1 total
```

Now, we have to decide whether this is adequate test coverage. Neither metric fills me with great confidence that primeFactors is particularly well-tested; after all, this indicates that over three-fourths of the function is not being exercised by our current suite. Test coverage is primarily useful in two ways:

- Helping us identify untested paths in our program
- Serving as a ballpark measure of whether we have tested enough

 If you are looking for strategies for testing legacy software, I recommend picking up a copy of *Working Effectively with Legacy Code* by Michael Feathers. He discusses a bevy of options for how to introduce unit tests retroactively by capitalizing on *seams* in the code, strategic places where you can change the behavior of your program without modifying the code itself.

To improve the test coverage for our example, we can add one more test case, as shown in Example 3-8. If we recalculate our coverage (see Example 3-9), we notice that with just one additional test case, we can achieve near-perfect coverage. Does *this* mean that our test coverage is adequate? Quantitatively it might appear to be sufficient; qualitatively it might not be. Peeking back at our implementation for primeFactors, we can easily identify a few missing test cases, such as providing a negative number, or the number *2*.

Example 3-8. A simple test for `primeFactors`

```
describe('base cases', () => {
  test('0', () => {
    expect(primeFactors(0)).toStrictEqual([]);
  });
});

describe('small non-prime numbers', () => {
  test('20', () => {
    expect(primeFactors(0)).toStrictEqual([2, 5]);
  });
});
```

Example 3-9. Jest test coverage output for `primeFactors`, given our two test cases

```
------------------|---------|----------|---------|---------|-------------------
File              | % Stmts | % Branch | % Funcs | % Lines | Uncovered Line #s
------------------|---------|----------|---------|---------|-------------------
All files         |     100 |    83.33 |     100 |     100 |
 primeFactors.js  |     100 |    83.33 |     100 |     100 | 12
------------------|---------|----------|---------|---------|-------------------
Test Suites: 1 passed, 1 total
Tests:       2 passed, 2 total
```

In my experience, thoughtfully written code generally has between 80 and 90 percent test coverage. This shows that the majority of the code is tested. Be forewarned, however, that test coverage alone is not an indication of how well-tested something is. It's easy to write low-quality unit tests to reach perfect or near-perfect test coverage. If high test coverage is incentivized by management, you will typically find that a significant portion of your unit tests make little effort to assert the corresponding code's important behavior.

From a qualitative standpoint, determining whether test coverage is sufficient is not so simple. There is a great deal of thoughtful writing about this already, most of which goes beyond the scope of this book, but at a high level, I think suitable test quality has been attained if the following points hold true:

- The tests are *reliable*. From one run to the next, they consistently produce passing results when run against unchanged code and catch bugs during development.

- The tests are *resilient*. They are not so tightly coupled to implementation that they stifle change.

- A range of test *types* exercise the code. Having unit, integration, and end-to-end tests can help us assert that our code is functioning as intended with different levels of fidelity.

If we have asserted that the test coverage and test quality is substantial enough, then we should be confident in moving forward with our refactoring effort. If tests are lacking either in coverage or quality, we need to spend the requisite time writing more, and better, tests up front. Measuring the test quantity and quality of each of the sections of code we intend to refactor is an important step in helping us determine how much additional work we need to commit to before we begin refactoring.

Type Coverage

We briefly discussed some of the advantages and disadvantages of dynamically typed programming languages in Chapter 2. Developers working in large, dynamically typed codebases might consider adopting a gradually typed language to enable the introduction of static types. Static types can catch errors earlier in the development process by warning us about mismatched types; they can ease the mental burden of programming by automatically tracking information we would otherwise have to remember. TypeScript for JavaScript, Cython or mypy for Python, Hacklang, and PHP (as of v7.0) are all examples of gradually typed programming languages.

If you are in the process of adding types to your codebase, you will likely want to measure your progress by keeping track of type coverage. We calculate type coverage as the percentage of code that has type information. (This is deliberately vague as it depends on how static typing is implemented in each distinct language. The metric can even differ, depending on the language version.) Similar to test coverage, low type coverage scores can be used to locate code effectively that could benefit from a bit more attention. Reaching 100 percent type coverage is likely impossible, but in my experience working in a gradually typed codebase, I feel most confident working with code that is as highly typed as possible. If you are able to achieve a score of over 95 percent across your application, you're in good shape.

Documentation

Before we start refactoring something, we should take stock of any existing documentation about it. Reading through the documentation may help us gain valuable, additional context on the code. While documentation is not a great source of numerical metrics we can use to measure our starting state, it is a critical source of evidence we can use to describe the current problems we seek to improve. We'll discuss two forms of documentation we should be concerned about when trying to understand and quantify our starting point in anticipation of a large refactoring effort. These are formal and informal forms of documentation.

Formal Documentation

Formal documentation is everything you most likely think of as documentation. This doesn't have to follow any official, industry-level standard (like Unified Modeling Language [UML]). Rather, what makes it formal is that it was deliberately authored (and, in many cases, is actively maintained) to inform the reader about your system. Technical specs, architecture diagrams, style guides, onboarding materials, and post-mortems are a few examples of formal documentation.

We can use things like *technical specs* as evidence that our refactor is necessary or useful by referencing design decisions, assumptions, or other designs considered or rejected. Say, for instance, you work on a subsection of your application responsible for processing all user-related actions within your product. The current implementation requires developers writing new features to remember and enumerate every kind of event that needs to be fired and propagated to sibling subsystems when a user modifies their profile. If your team has a history of writing technical design specs for each of their features, you can locate the original specification document for event propagation. This document describes the current implementation, its limitations, and any alternative approaches.

The limitations section states that while it might be convenient to trigger each required event individually at every location, if the team introduces a substantial number of new events, it might become clumsy and burdensome. Today, your system is experiencing that exact problem. It handles more than a dozen event types and your team is struggling to keep track of the sprawl. With every new feature, your team fears forgetting to trigger a critical event type and potentially introducing a pesky bug. You've done your best to assert the desired behavior with tests but decide that refactoring how these events are handled is the best solution to taming the chaos of repetitive logic.

Technical specs can be very helpful in supporting your hypothesis of exactly what needs to be improved and how. Occasionally, these documents outline alternative approaches considered but not ultimately chosen. You may be able to explore one of these suggestions with your refactoring effort.

Maintainers of *style guides* and *onboarding materials* can sometimes leave traces of their experiences in the documentation they produce. If they've recently made an unexpected discovery about how something works and sought to improve the documentation as a result of that experience, you might be able to catch a glimpse of that in their writing. You might find warnings in large, bolded text of exactly what *not* to do. It's also not uncommon to see a disproportionate amount of content devoted to particularly complex pieces of the codebase in these kinds of documents; more people across the company will have devoted more time to trying to steer readers in the right direction, away from the pitfalls they themselves fell into. If the code you want to refactor is documented in these sources and follows these patterns, it might be good evidence that it can be measurably improved. Think about the ideal tone and content of the documentation for your target code and use that as inspiration.

Postmortems can serve as great supporting evidence. If your team follows the PagerDuty incident response process (*https://oreil.ly/T966e*) and has been doing so for some time, then you likely have access to dozens of postmortem documents detailing the what, where, when, why, and how of every instance where your application wasn't behaving as expected.

When building a case for code that is worth refactoring, I search for postmortems summarizing incidents I believe directly involved that code. Then I read through two sections: "Contributing Factors" and "What Didn't Go So Well?" When I suspect that the complexity of the code had a direct impact on the time to resolution or perhaps even caused the incident in the first place, these two sections will likely confirm it. A count of the number of incidents that list the area you want to refactor as a problem makes a valuable metric.

 It's also important to take note of third-party or publicly facing documentation. While refactoring is not meant to modify the behavior for consumers of your application, this documentation can be particularly useful for bolstering your understanding of the code you're intending to rewrite.

Informal Documentation

Alongside our formal documentation, we produce a wide range of informal documentation. These are the kinds of written artifacts that we don't consider to be proper documentation simply because they don't typically occur in document form. In my experience, I've found more speckled throughout informal sources than in any formal documentation.

Finding these sources is all about thinking outside the box. I'll enumerate a few here but keep your eyes peeled for other sources around you. You just might surprise yourself!

Chat and *email transcripts* can provide insightful information about the code you're seeking to refactor. Best of all, these often grant a good deal of context, both historical and organizational pieces of information. Say, for instance, you want to refactor how asynchronous jobs are structured in your application. The job queue system currently accepts a dynamic set of arguments of arbitrary size to maximize flexibility for its consumers. Unfortunately, this has led to quite a bit of confusion around its actual limitations, putting the system at risk of running out of memory when processing jobs with extremely large argument payloads, or crashing abruptly when it is unable to parse malformed inputs.

You want to be certain that your experience with the system's ambiguity is not anecdotal to you and your team. To measure how troublesome writing new jobs is, you search your company's Slack (or other messaging solution) for a set of keywords that relate to job queue arguments. Unsurprisingly, you come across a number of messages where someone was surprised or concerned that their job didn't work as intended. Developers across the company are asking whether they should provide raw or opaque IDs. Why one over the other? Do we log these job arguments? If so, do we need to be careful about including personally identifiable information? How much data can we send via these arguments? Are we able to serialize entire objects and supply these to the job queue system?

You create a document that points to each of these messages, with a short description of the context around each. (This should be easy to do with a short backscroll through the conversation.) Now you can reference these instances to demonstrate the difficulty that developers are currently running into.

Chat history gives you the unique ability to peek into conversations that occurred long before your arrival. You might be surprised to see people spread across a variety of engineering teams talking about the problems you're eager to fix months or years before your first day on the job. You might encounter others asking the same question at a regular cadence. When this happens, not only is it extremely validating to your endeavor, but you may get some valuable allies by reaching out to the folks on those teams and asking them about their experience with the code you want to improve. Quantitatively, you can use these conversations to approximate how many engineering hours are lost due to confusion about the code you want to improve and answer questions about it.

Depending on your engineering team's project management tools of choice, you may be able to gather some important metrics related to the code you want to refactor by searching for related bugs in your *bug tracking system*. You might also be able to estimate the amount of time other teams or individual developers have spent investigating and fixing bugs or implementing changes related to your target code.

Say the code around a particular feature or feature set has been gaining complexity over time. You want to invest effort in tidying it up so that your team can develop at a quicker pace. If you suspect that your team's velocity has decreased, you can use your *project management software* to confirm it. Note that this is a very coarse metric (and as with all of our other metrics, only quantifies a single aspect of the overall problem). You will probably need intimate knowledge of how your team organizes its development cycles and confidently remove outliers in your data to be able to tease out a compelling metric here, but for some teams, it can be an indisputable one!

Technical program managers at some companies can be a great resource for helping you collect, filter, and disseminate these kinds of metrics. They are often whizzes at navigating project management tools and locating hard-to-find documents. Who knows, you might even make a new friend!

At this point, this may all sound like an excessive amount of investigatory work to quantify a given problem. That's okay! It's up to you to decide which metrics will have the most impact in communicating the severity of the problem and the potential benefit of fixing it. You may not want or need to spend the time digging through hundreds of tasks or postmortems, but if this information is easy to consume and search, it might be worthwhile. These metrics can especially come in handy when trying to convince management and leadership teams that are highly removed from the code that refactoring is worthwhile.

Version Control

We primarily think of version control as a tool to manage changes to our applications. We use it to move forward incrementally, allowing for the development of multiple features at once, and progressive shipment of those features. Sometimes, we use it to refer to previous versions of our code to track down a bug or locate someone who might know about the section of code we're reading. We rarely think of version control as a source of information about our team's development patterns when analyzed in aggregate. Turns out, we can glean quite a bit about the problems our engineering team is facing when we take a look at our commits from a different perspective.

Commit Messages

Although not everyone makes writing descriptive commit messages part of their development method, if you work on a team where a majority of developers do, these short descriptions can provide a glimpse into the issues that they might be running into. We can identify patterns either by searching for a set of keywords or by isolating *commit messages* associated with changes to a set of files we're interested in.

Let's say we're looking at our job queue system problem from earlier. We know that engineers regularly forget to sanitize their arguments before enqueueing jobs, resulting in logging personally identifiable information (PII). We can search through our commit messages and identify commits where the corresponding messages include words like "job," "job handler," or "PII." From this result set, we might find a substantial set of commits that either introduced a new job responsible for leaking PII or fixed a job already leaking it. Alternatively, if our job handlers are conveniently organized into distinct files, we could narrow our search to include only commits with modifications to these files and comb through the derived set for similar patterns.

Some development teams relate their commits or changesets to their project management tools by highlighting bug or ticket numbers in the commit message or branch name. If this information is available to us, we can link the changeset back to our previous collection of metrics on development velocity and bug count. It all comes full circle!

Commits in Aggregate

In his book, *Software Design X-Rays*, Adam Tornhill proposes a set of techniques for teasing out important development patterns from version history. He hypothesizes that these development behaviors can help you identify which sections of your application you should prioritize when refactoring, illustrate how the complexity of certain functions have changed over time, and highlight any tightly coupled files or modules. I highly recommend reading his research to comprehend fully the psychology behind why these measurements are so enlightening, but I'll summarize the basic techniques here so that you might consider them ahead of your next big refactor.

Change frequencies are the number of commits made to each file over the complete version history of your application. You can easily generate these data points by extracting file names from your commit history, aggregating them, and ordering them from most to least frequent. In practice, Tornhill noticed that these frequencies tended to follow a power distribution, where a disproportionate number of changes occur in a small subset of core files. Knowing the files that are committed to most often tells us exactly which files need to be the easiest to understand and navigate for developers and, therefore, which files we should spend the most effort maintaining, from a developer productivity perspective.

We can apply the same concept of change frequencies to files as well. By looking at individual commits, we can carefully attribute changes to respective functions within individual files, producing total frequency numbers for each of them. By combining this data with one of our earlier complexity metrics, lines of code, we can map complexity changes over time across the entire codebase. This information shows us potential hotspots ripe for improvement. We can later regenerate these metrics once we've completed our refactor to confirm that not only the complexity of these hotspots decreased, but hopefully their change frequency had as well.

Tornhill also describes a method for pinpointing tightly coupled modules in your program by looking at sets of files modified within the same commit. To depict this idea, let's say we have three files, *superheroes.js*, *supervillains.js*, and *sidekicks.js*. In a subset of our commits, we have the following changes: commit one modifies both *superheroes.js* and *sidekicks.js*; commit two modifies all three files; commit three again modifies *superheros.js* and *sidekicks.js*; and commit four only touches *superheroes.js*.

From this subset of our version history, depicted in Table 3-3, we notice that of four commits, three of them modified both *superheroes.js* and *sidekicks.js*. This insinuates that some kind of coupling between these two files exists. Certainly not all coupling is bad (as is the case for changes in source code and the corresponding unit test files), but in some cases these patterns can indicate an erroneous abstraction, copy-pasted code, or sometimes both. Once we've pinpointed these problems, we can work to fix them and then rerun the analysis sometime later to confirm that they no longer exist.

Table 3-3. Files modified per commit

Commit #	superheroes.js	supervillains.js	sidekicks.js
1	X		X
2	X	X	X
3	X		X
4	X		

As with each of our quantitative metrics in this chapter, there are some caveats to this kind of measurement. Different developers have different practices around committing changes. Some programmers will make a large quantity of tiny commits; others will make large commits, including dozens of changes across multiple files, into a single changeset. Moreover, it's entirely likely this analysis will reveal some outliers (configuration files frequently changed or hotspots in autogenerated code). We have to be vigilant about these anomalies when poring over the data to mitigate the risk of finding problems where there might not be any.

Code Authorship

Tornhill also derives data about code authorship from version control. Files or modules that have a large number of distinct minor authors are at higher risk of defects. While the research he cites does not explain why that is, he posits that it is likely due to the increased need for coordination among authors combined with inexperience with the implementation. You may be curious to explore the implications of authorship in your own code and derive additional metrics from them.

Reputation

Whether we're aware of it or not, each of the many sections of our software systems have distinct reputations. Some reputations are stronger than others; some are positive, some are deeply negative. Whatever the reputation, however, it is slowly built up over time, spreading across the engineering organization as more and more engineers interact with the code. Word of the most disastrous codebases sometimes even travels outside of your company and into the wider industry, discussed over dinner among friends and on internet forums. Whether these reputations continue to hold true or not, they can tell us plenty about some of the most troublesome pieces of our applications and just how desperately they need our attention.

A simple, low-effort means of collecting reputation data is to *interview* fellow developers. Let's assume you work on an application that charges customers for a monthly service and you want to improve your application's billing code. You set up some interviews with developers that fall into a few categories: those who work directly with the billing code on a regular basis, and those who have worked with it on occasion. For each of these two sets, you'll want to speak to developers who have a range of tenures on their current team and within the company; the experiences of those who have worked integrally with the billing code for years are probably pretty different from those of an engineer who was hired six months ago.

We then derive a set of questions that will help us characterize their experience. We begin with a few questions to frame their background and then delve into their thoughts about the code. A few are suggested in Table 3-4 to get you started.

Given your experience with the billing code, when you were evaluating which files could benefit the most from a thorough refactor, you immediately thought of *charge-CustomerCard.js+*. You decide to ask your interviewees about the file to see what sort of reaction it elicits. If the second you mention *chargeCustomerCard.js*, your interviewee grimaces, whether they have intimate knowledge of the inner workings of that file or not, that's a strong indication that the file could probably use a little bit of love.

If we want to solicit feedback from a larger group of engineers or are tight for time on establishing our starting metrics, we can rephrase our interview questions to fit a standard set of answers. This will make aggregating the responses easier and allow us to derive conclusions from them faster. Be warned, however, that by reducing your fellow developers' thoughts to a set of scores, you'll be stripping away some of the nuance that you might have been able to glean from an in-person (or virtual) interview.

From experience, interviews tend to give you more flexibility to explore ideas and topics that bubble up candidly. It's often the back and forth banter that brings out the best aha! moments. If we sent around a developer survey with long-form interview-like questions, not only would we not be able to ask the respondents in real time to provide more details about their answers, but we would likely get fewer responses. I'm very guilty of opening up a survey, noticing that it is a series of half-a-dozen open-ended questions, and almost immediately setting myself a reminder to do it later. If you want to solicit feedback from engineers in survey form, keep it short; this way, you have a better chance of getting a high response rate.

Table 3-4. Suggested developer interview and survey questions

Interview question	Survey question	Notes
How long have you been working with X code?	Select the option that best describes the amount of time you have spent working with X code: > 6 months; 6 months to 1 year; more than one year.	Note that in the survey question version, you should choose time ranges that make the most sense for your engineering organization. At high-growth, younger companies, the ranges are probably on the order of months; at larger, more established companies, the ranges could be on the order of years.
If you could change one thing about working with X code, what would it be? Why?	If you could choose only one of the listed options to improve your experience working with X code, which one would it be?	For the survey question, choose some options that you think would make the most impact and optionally provide a write-in field. If the code doesn't have any tests, add an option that states that the code is fully tested. If a large proportion of the code is contained within a few functions that are hundreds of lines long, add an option that states that the code is split up into small, modular functions.
Tell me about a bug you recently had to fix that involved X code. What would have made it easier to solve?	Of the Y options listed below, what about X code makes it the most difficult to fix bugs efficiently?	
Have you strategically avoided working in X code before (i.e., fixing a bug at a level above or below the problem area)? Tell me about that experience.	On a scale from 1 to 5, 1 being not likely at all and 5 being very likely, how likely are you to find a way to avoid making changes to X code?	
How does the complexity of X code hinder your ability to develop new features?	With 1 being strongly disagree and 5 being strongly agree, rate the following statement: The complexity of X code is a significant contributor to the time it takes for me to develop new features.	
How does the complexity of X code hinder your ability to test and/or debug your code?	With 1 being strongly disagree and 5 being strongly agree, rate the following statement: The complexity of X code is a significant contributor to the difficulty to test and/or debug my code.	
How does the complexity of X code hinder your ability to review other developers' changes to the code?	With 1 being strongly disagree and 5 being strongly agree, rate the following statement: The complexity of X code is a significant contributor to the time and difficulty involved for me to review other developers' changes to the code.	

Reputation can also hinder a team's ability to hire and retain engineers. Say the billing code is known to be particularly treacherous at your company. While the team probably has a handful of developers who are committed to their roles, working in a frustratingly complex codebase can take a toll on morale. Organizations don't like to admit that they've lost engineers due to code quality and development practices, but it happens all the time. If you're able to collect information on engineers' reasons for leaving the team and tie those back to code complexity, it can be an incredibly compelling metric for dedicating some much-needed resources to refactoring.

Building a Complete Picture

Now that we've familiarized ourselves with a wide range of potential metrics, we have to choose which ones to use. To build the most comprehensive view of the current state of the world, you must identify the metrics that best illustrate the specific problems you want to address. None of these metrics alone can quantify the many unique aspects of a large refactoring effort, but combined, you can build a multifaceted characterization of the problem.

I recommend picking one metric from every category. Find a way to approximate *code complexity* in a way that makes the most sense given the nature of your problem and the tools you have already available to you. Generate some *test coverage metrics* to make sure you start off on the right foot. Identify a source of *formal documentation* you can use to illustrate the problems your refactor aims to solve; back it up with some *informal documentation* as well. Gather information about your hotspots and programming patterns by slicing and dicing *version control* data. Last, consider the code's *reputation* by chatting with your colleagues.

If you find that most of these metrics can help you quantify the current state of the code you are aiming to refactor and the impact it has on your organization, consider choosing the subset that has the greatest chance of showing significant improvements. These are the metrics that will make the most compelling case to your teammates and, ultimately, management. In the end, you'll have to make a convincing argument to those you report to that the time and energy you and your teammates are ready to devote to the refactor will pay off.

We've successfully gathered evidence to help us properly characterize the problem we're experiencing, but setting the stage is only one piece of the puzzle. Next, we have to use the data we've collected to assemble a concrete execution plan.

CHAPTER 4

Drafting a Plan

One day, I plan to complete the 4,500-kilometer drive between Montreal and Vancouver. The drive takes about 48 hours from start to finish, with the fastest route covering most of the length of the border between Canada and the United States. The fastest route isn't necessarily the most rewarding route, however, and if I add a stop to see Parliament Hill in Ottawa, the iconic CN Tower in Toronto, and the Sleeping Giant Provincial Park, I lengthen my trip by a few hours and about 600 kilometers.

Now anyone setting out on this journey knows driving it nonstop from start to finish is both impractical and dangerous. So, before I head out, I should map out a rough outline for the roadtrip. I should figure out how much time I'm comfortable driving on the road-heavy days, and which cities I might want to pop in to do some sightseeing. In total, I estimate the trip might take between seven and 10 days depending on how long I spend sightseeing. The flexibility allows for a few unexpected twists, whether I decide to sightsee an extra day or get stranded on the side of the road and need to call for assistance.

How do you know whether you've had a successful roadtrip beyond actually reaching your final destination? If you set a budget for your trip, you might have achieved your goal if your next credit card bill falls within range. Maybe you wanted to eat a burger at every stop along the way. Probably, you just wanted to see something new, spend some quality time with friends or family, and make a few new memories. As tacky as it might sound, the roadtrip is just as much about the journey as it is about the destination.

Any large software endeavor can look quite a bit like a roadtrip across the country. As developers, we decide on a set of milestones we want to accomplish, a rough set of tasks we want to complete in between each of these milestones, and an estimate for when we think we might reach our destination. We keep track of our progress along the way, ensuring that we stay on task and within the time we've alloted ourselves. By the end, we want to see a measurable, positive impact, achieved in a sustainable way.

We've taken the time to understand our code's past, first by identifying how our code has degraded, then by characterizing that degradation. Now, we're ready to map out its future. We'll learn how to split up a large refactoring effort into its most important pieces, crafting a plan that is both thorough and precise in scope. We'll highlight when and how to reference the metrics we carefully gathered to characterize the current problem state in Chapter 3. We'll discuss the importance of shopping your plan around to other teams and wrap things up by emphasizing the value in continuously updating it throughout the whole process.

Everyone takes a different approach to building out an execution plan. Whether your team calls them technical specs, product briefs, or requests for comments (RFCs), they all serve the same purpose: documenting what you intend to do and how you intend to do it. Having a clear, concise plan is key to ensuring the success of any software project, regardless of whether it involves refactoring or building out a new feature; it keeps everyone focused on the important tasks at hand and enforces accountability for their progress throughout the endeavor.

Defining Your End State

Our first step is to define our end state. We should already have a strong understanding of where we currently are; we spent considerable time in Chapter 3 measuring and defining the problem we want to solve. Now that we've grounded ourselves, we need to identify where we want to land.

On the Road

We're kicking off our roadtrip in Montreal, where we currently live. Of the hundreds of towns and cities speckled along that shore, we have to pick just one to aim for. So, after a bit of research, we decide to aim for Vancouver.

Next, we need to familiarize ourselves with the highways leading directly into the city and decide where we might want to stay upon arrival. We reach out to friends who've either lived in Vancouver or who travel there frequently for recommendations. We land on Yaletown, a neighborhood known for its old warehouse buildings by the water. Now that your trip has a well-defined destination, we can start figuring out precisely how to get there.

At Work

To illustrate the many important concepts in this chapter, we'll be using an example of a large-scale refactor at a 15-year-old biotechnology company we'll call Smart DNA, Inc. Most of its employees are research scientists, contributing to a complex data pipeline comprising hundreds of Python scripts across a few repositories. The scripts are deployed to and executed in five distinct environments. All of these environments rely on a version of Python 2.6. Unfortunately, Python 2.6 has long since been deprecated, leaving the company susceptible to security vulnerabilities and preventing it from updating important dependencies. While relying on outdated software is inconvenient, the company has not prioritized upgrading to a newer Python version. It's a massive, risky undertaking, given the very limited testing in place. Simply put, this was the biggest piece of technical debt at the company for many years.

The research team has recently grown concerned about its inability to use newer versions of core libraries. Given that the upgrade is now important to the business, we've been tasked with figuring out how to migrate each of the repositories and environments to use Python 2.7.

The research team manages its dependencies by using `pip`. Each repository has its own list of dependencies, encoded in a *requirements.txt*. Having these distinct *requirements.txt* files has made it difficult for the team to remember which dependencies are installed on a given project when switching between projects. It also would require the software team to audit each file and upgrade it to be compatible with Python 2.7 independently. As a result, the software team decided that although it was not necessary, it would make the Python 2.7 upgrade easier for them (and simplify the researchers' development process) to unify the repositories and thus unify the dependencies.

Our execution plan should clearly outline all starting metrics and target end metrics, with an optional, albeit helpful, additional column to record the actual, observed end state. For the Python migration, the starting set of metrics was clear: each repository had a distinct list of dependencies, with each environment running Python 2.6. The desired set of metrics was equally simple: have each of the business's environments running Python 2.7, with a clear, succinct set of required libraries managed in a single place. Table 4-1 shows an example where we've listed Smart DNA's metrics.

Table 4-1. Chart to compare the metrics at the start of the project, the goal metrics, and their observed value at project completion

Metric description	Start	Goal	Observed
Environment 1	Python 2.6.5	Python 2.7.1	-
Environment 2	Python 2.6.1	Python 2.7.1	-
Environment 3	Python 2.6.5	Python 2.7.1	-
Environment 4	Python 2.6.6	Python 2.7.1	-
Environment 5	Python 2.6.6	Python 2.7.1	-
Number of distinct lists of dependencies	3	1	-

Feel free to provide both an ideal end state and an acceptable end state. Sometimes, getting 80 percent of the way there gives you 99 percent of the benefit of the refactor, and the additional amount of work required to get to 100 percent simply isn't worthwhile.

Mapping the Shortest Distance

Next, we want to map the most direct path between our start and end states. This should give us a good lower-bound estimate on the amount of time required to execute our project. Building on a minimal path ensures that your plan stays true to its course as you introduce intermediate steps along the way.

On the Road

So, for our roadtrip, we do a quick search to see what the most direct route between Montreal and Vancouver looks like (Figure 4-1). Presuming minimal traffic, it appears to take 47 hours if we were to leave Montreal and drive nonstop westward.

Figure 4-1. The most direct route between our address in Montreal and the Yaletown neighborhood in Vancouver

We can determine a more reasonable lower bound for our trip by deciding how many hours we're comfortable driving per day and splitting that up evenly over the approximate 47 hours. If we want to commit to eight hours of driving, it'll take us just about six days.

Now that we've mapped the shortest possible path between the two points, we can start to pick out any major complications or overarching strategies we want to change. One peculiarity of the direct route is that the vast majority of it travels across the United States, not Canada. If we want to restrict our drive to the area north of the 49th parallel, we'd be adding an extra hour or two to the trip. However, because it does reduce the overall complexity of the trip (no need to carry our passport or worry about time wasted at a border crossing), we'll opt to stay in Canada (Figure 4-2).

Figure 4-2. A slightly slower route restricted to Canadian roads

At Work

Unfortunately, Google Maps for software projects doesn't exist quite yet. So how do we determine the shortest path from now to project completion? We can do this in a couple of ways:

- Open a blank document and for 15 to 20 minutes (or until you've run out of ideas), write down every step you can come up with. Set the document aside for at the very least a few hours (ideally a day or two), then open it up again and try to order each step in chronological order. As you begin to order the steps, continue to ask yourself whether each is absolutely required to reach the final goal. If not, remove it. Once you have an ordered set of steps, reread the procedure. Fill in any glaring gaps as they arise. Don't worry if any steps are terribly ill-defined; the goal is only to produce the minimum set of steps required to complete your project. This won't be the final product.

- Gather a few coworkers who are either interested in the project or you know will be contributing. Set aside an hour or so. Grab a pack of sticky notes and a pen for each of you. For 15 to 20 minutes (or until everyone's pens are down), write down every step you think is required, each on individual sticky notes. Then, have a first person lay out their steps in chronological order. Subsequent team-mates go through each of their own sticky notes and either pair them up with their duplicates or insert them into the appropriate spot within the timeline. Once everyone's organized all of their notes, go through each step and ask the room whether they believe that the step is absolutely required in order to reach the goal. If not, discard it. The final product should be a reasonable set of minimal steps. (You can easily adapt this method for distributed teams by combining all individually brainstormed steps into a jointly shared document. Either way, the final output of the exercise should be a written document that is easy to distribute and collaboratively improve.)

If neither of these options works for you, that's all right! Use whatever method you find most effective. As long as you are able to produce a list of steps you believe model a direct path to achieving your goal, no matter how ill-defined they might be, you've successfully completed this critical step.

The team at Smart DNA gathered into a conference room for a few hours to brainstorm the steps required to get all services using a newer version of Python. On a whiteboard, they started out by drawing a timeline. On the far left was their starting point and, on the far right, their goal. Teammates alternated listing important steps along the way, slotting them in along the line. A subset of the brainstormed steps are as follows:

- Build a single list of all the packages across each of the repositories manually.
- Narrow the list to just the necessary packages.
- Identify which version each package should be upgraded to in Python 2.7.
- Build a Docker container with all the required packages.
- Test the Docker container on each of the environments.
- Locate tests for each repository; determine which tests are reliable.
- Merge all the repositories into a single repository.
- Choose a linter and corresponding configuration.
- Integrate the linter into continuous integration.
- Use the linter to identify problems in the code (undefined variables, syntax errors, etc.).
- Fix problems the linter identified.
- Install Python 2.7.1 on all environments and test.
- Use Python 2.7 on a subset of low-risk scripts.
- Roll out Python 2.7 to all scripts.

We can see from our subset that some can be parallelized, or reordered, and others should be broken down into further detail. At this point in the process, our focus is on getting a rough sense of the steps involved; we'll refine the process throughout the chapter.

Identifying Strategic Intermediate Milestones

We'll next use the procedure we derived to come up with an ordered list of intermediate milestones. These milestones do not need to be of similar size or evenly distributed, as long as they are achievable within a timescale that feels comfortable. We should focus on finding milestones that are meaningful in and of themselves. That is, either reaching the milestone is a win on its own, or it defines a step we could comfortably stop at if necessary (or both). If you can identify milestones that are both meaningful and showcase the potential impact of your refactoring effort early, then you're doing great!

On the Road

For the stretch of the trip between Winnipeg and Vancouver, we ask some friends and family for recommendations of sights to see and things to do. After weighing their suggestions with our own interests, we come up with a rough itinerary, which includes everything from camping to museum visits, tasty pitstops, and a few visits to extended family (Figure 4-3). But at no point do any of these points of interest take us radically off course.

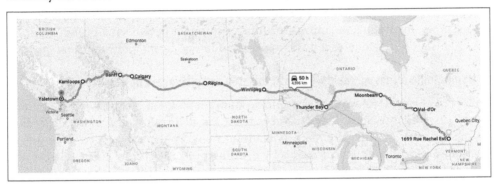

Figure 4-3. Our rough itinerary

At Work

We can apply similar tactics to narrow in on our milestones for our refactoring effort. For each of the steps we brainstormed previously, we can ask ourselves these questions:

1. Does this step feel attainable in a reasonable period?

Let's refer back to our previous example, outlined in "At Work" on page 72. A logical, feasible milestone might be to combine each of the distinct repositories into a single repository for convenience. The software team at Smart DNA anticipates that it'll take six weeks to merge the repositories properly, without disrupting the research team's development process. Because the software team is accustomed to shipping at a quicker pace, and the members are concerned about morale if they set out to merge the repositories too early in the migration, they decide on a simpler initial milestone: generating a single *requirements.txt* file to encompass all package dependencies for each of the repositories. By taking the time to reduce the set of dependencies early, they are simplifying the development process for the research team, taking a substantial step toward enabling the merging of the repositories, and all of that well before the migration to Python 2.7 is complete.

2. Is this step valuable on its own?

When choosing major milestones, we should optimize for steps that demonstrate the benefits of the refactor early and often. One way to do that is to focus on steps that, upon completion, derive immediate value for other engineers. This should hopefully increase the morale of both your team and other engineers affected by your changes.

When scoping out the Python migration, we noticed that none of the repositories used any continuous integration to lint for common problems in the proposed code changes. We know that linting the existing code could help us pinpoint problems we risk encountering when executing it in Python 2.7. We also know that enabling a simple, automatic linting step could promote better programming practices for the entire research team for years to come. In fact, it seems so valuable that under different circumstances, instituting an automatic linting step might have been a project all on its own. This indicated to us that it was a meaningful, significant intermediate step.

3. If something comes up, could we stop at this step and pick it back up easily later?

In a perfect world, we wouldn't have to account for shifts in business priorities, incidents, or reorganizations. Unfortunately, these are all a reality of working, regardless of the industry. This is why the best plans account for the unexpected. One way of accounting for disruptive changes is by dividing our project into distinct pieces that can stand alone in the unlikely event that we need to pause development.

With our Python example, we could comfortably pause the project after fixing all errors and warnings the linter highlighted, but before beginning to run a subset of scripts by using the new version. Depending on how we tackled the refactor, pausing halfway through could risk confusing the researchers actively working in the repository. If the refactor needed to be paused for whatever reason, pausing immediately before we started running a subset of scripts using Python 2.7 would be safe; we would still have made considerable progress toward our overall goal and have a clean, easy place to pick things back up when we were next able to.

After taking the time to highlight strategic milestones, we reorganized our execution plan to highlight these steps and grouped subtasks accordingly. The more refined plan is as follows:

- Create a single *requirements.txt* file.
  - Enumerate all packages used across each of the repositories.
  - Audit all packages and narrow down the list to only required packages with corresponding versions.
  - Identify which version each package should be upgraded to in Python 2.7.
- Merge all the repositories into a single repository.
  - Create a new repository.

- — For each repository, add to the new repository using git submodules.
- Build a Docker image with all the required packages.
  - — Test the Docker image on each of the environments.
- Enable linting through continuous integration for the mono repository (monorepo).
  - — Choose a linter and corresponding configuration.
  - — Integrate the linter into a continuous integration.
  - — Use the linter to identify logical problems in the code (undefined variables, syntax errors, etc.).
- Install and roll out Python 2.7.1 in all environments.
  - — Locate tests for each repository; determine which tests are reliable.
  - — Use Python 2.7 on a subset of low-risk scripts.
  - — Roll out Python 2.7 to all scripts.

Hopefully, after you've identified key milestones, you have a procedure that feels balanced, achievable, and rewarding. It's important to note, however, that this isn't a perfect science. It can be quite difficult to weigh required steps against one another according to the effort they involve and their relative impact. We'll see an example of how we decided to weigh each of these considerations when strategically planning a large-scale refactor in both of our case study chapters, Chapters 10 and 11.

Repeatable Steps

One way that you can break up your refactoring project into meaningful milestones is to choose single, logical portions of the code in which to apply it. This acts as a sort of mini-refactor, where you can illustrate the overarching goal of the refactor on a smaller scale. When taking this approach, you can either choose the part of the codebase that is in most urgent need of the refactor, or one for which your changes will require relatively low effort but model the improvements well.

You can repeat this process, one piece at a time, throughout the target surface area. This gives you the ability to focus on well-defined portions of the codebase one at a time and coordinate with the teams that might be affected by your changes in sequence. With each finished portion, you'll have taken a solid step toward your goal, all while leaving the overall codebase in limited flux. If your codebase is well-sectioned, you minimize the chance that someone working in a single portion of it will be subjected to a refactor in progress for a long period.

For example, the team at Smart DNA could split up the repository merging process into a few individual, repeatable steps for each repository. First, merge the repository's *requirements.txt* file into the global *requirements.txt* file. Next, add the repository to

---

the larger repository using `git submodule`. Finally, test that the scripts are runnable. Simply repeat for all remaining repositories.

> If it's worthwhile, find a way to abstract out your change *first*. Move all the logic that you want to improve behind some sort of abstraction. This will further minimize the risk that other developers will be subjected to multiple implementations (and their details) at any given point. Once you've built the abstraction, you can focus on doing the hard work of changing the necessary logic.

Finally, once we have our end state and our key milestones, we want to interpolate our way through the intermediate steps between our end state and each of our strategic intermediary milestones. This way, we maintain focus on the most critical pieces, all while building out a detailed plan.

This is where we can spend some time figuring out whether certain portions of the refactor are order-agnostic; that is, whether they can be completed at any point, with very few or no prerequisites. For example, let's say you've identified a few key milestones for your project; we'll call them A, B, C, and D. You notice that you need to complete A before tackling B or C, and B needs to be completed before you tackle D. You have three options concerning C: you could parallelize development on C at the same time as D, complete C and then D, or complete D followed by C.

If you have a hunch that B is going to be a difficult, lengthy milestone and D looks just as challenging, you might want to break things up by putting milestone C between B and D. This should help boost morale and add some pep to the team's momentum as you work through a long refactor. On the other hand, if you think that you can comfortably parallelize work on milestone C and D, and wrap up the project a little bit sooner, then that might be a worthwhile option as well.

It all comes down to balancing the time and effort associated with each requisite step, all the while considering their impact on your codebase and the well-being of your team.

Choosing a Rollout Strategy

Having a thoughtful rollout strategy for your refactoring effort can make the difference between great success and utter failure. Therefore, it is absolutely critical to include it as part of your execution plan. If your refactor involves multiple distinct phases, each with its own rollout strategy, be certain to outline each of these among the concluding steps of each phase. Although teams of all kinds use a great variety of deployment practices, in this section, we'll only discuss rollout strategies specific to teams that perform continuous deployment.

Typically, product engineering teams that employ continuous deployment will begin development on a new feature, testing it both manually and in an automated fashion throughout the process. When all the boxes have been checked, the feature is carefully, incrementally rolled out to live users. Before the final rollout phase, many teams will deploy the feature to an internal build of their product, giving themselves yet another opportunity to weed out problems before kicking off deployment to users. Measuring success in this case is easy; if the feature works as expected, great! If we find any bugs, we devise a fix, and depending on the implications of that fix, either repeat the incremental rollout process or push it out to all users immediately.

 It's common practice in continuous deployment environments to use *feature flags* to hide, enable, or disable specific features or code paths continually at runtime. Good feature flag solutions allow development teams the flexibility to assign groups of users to specific features (sometimes according to a number of different attributes). If you work on a social media application, for instance, you might want to release a feature to all users within a single geographic area, a random 1 percent of users globally, or all users who are over the age of 40.

With refactoring projects, while we most certainly want to test our changes early and frequently, and very carefully roll it out to users, it's quite a bit trickier to determine whether everything is working as intended. After all, one of the key success metrics is that *no behavior has changed*. It is much more difficult to ascertain a *lack* of change than to discover even the smallest change. So, one of the easiest ways we can ascertain that the refactor hasn't introduced any new bugs is by programmatically comparing pre-refactor behavior with post-refactor behavior.

Dark Mode/Light Mode

We can compare pre-refactor and post-refactor behavior by employing what we've coined at Slack as the light/dark technique. Here's how it works.

First, implement the refactored logic separately from the current logic. Example 4-1 depicts this step on a small scale.

Example 4-1. New and old implementations, perhaps in different files

```
// Linear search; this is the old implementation
function search(name, alphabeticalNames) {
  for(let i = 0; i < alphabeticalNames.length; i++) {
    if (alphabeticalNames[i] == name) return i;
```

```
  }
  return -1;
}

// Binary search; this is the new implementation
function searchFaster(name, alphabeticalNames) {
  let startIndex = 0;
  let endIndex = alphabeticalNames.length - 1;

  while (startIndex <= endIndex) {
    let middleIndex = Math.floor((startIndex+endIndex)/2);
    if (alphabeticalNames[middleIndex] == name) return middleIndex;

    if (alphabeticalNames[middleIndex] > name) {
      endIndex = middleIndex - 1;
    } else if (alphabeticalNames[middleIndex] < name) {
      startIndex = middleIndex + 1;
    }
  }

  return -1;
}
```

Then, as shown in Example 4-2, relocate the logic from the current implementation to a separate function.

Example 4-2. Old implementation moved to a separate function

```
// Existing function now calls into relocated implementation
function search(name, alphabeticalNames) {
  return searchOld(name, alphabeticalNames);
}

// Linear search logic moved to a new function.
function searchOld(name, alphabeticalNames) {
  for(let i = 0; i < alphabeticalNames.length; i++) {
    if (alphabeticalNames[i] == name) return i;
  }
  return -1;
}

// Binary search; this is the new implementation
function searchFaster(name, alphabeticalNames) {
  let startIndex = 0;
  let endIndex = alphabeticalNames.length - 1;

  while (startIndex <= endIndex) {
    let middleIndex = Math.floor((startIndex+endIndex)/2);
    if (alphabeticalNames[middleIndex] == name) return middleIndex;

    if (alphabeticalNames[middleIndex] > name) {
```

```
      endIndex = middleIndex - 1;
    } else if (alphabeticalNames[middleIndex] < name) {
      startIndex = middleIndex + 1;
    }
  }

  return -1;
}
```

Then, transform the previous function into an abstraction, conditionally calling either implementation. During dark mode, both implementations are called, the results are compared, and the results from the old implementation are returned. During light mode, both implementations are called, the results are compared, and the results from the new implementation are returned. As can be seen in Example 4-3, repurposing the existing function definition allows us to modify as little code as possible. (Though not depicted in our example, to prevent performance degradations as part of the light/dark process, both the old and new implementations should be executed concurrently.)

Example 4-3. Existing interface used as an abstraction for calling both new and old implementations

```
// Existing function now an abstraction for calling into either implementation
function search(name, alphabeticalNames) {
  // If we're in dark mode, return the old result.
  if (darkMode) {
    const oldResult = searchOld(name, alphabeticalNames);
    const newResult = searchFaster(name, alphabeticalNames);

    compareAndLog(oldResult, newResult);

    return oldResult;
  }

  // If we're in light mode, return the new result.
  if (lightMode) {
    const oldResult = searchOld(name, alphabeticalNames);
    const newResult = searchFaster(name, alphabeticalNames);

    compareAndLog(oldResult, newResult);

    return newResult;
  }

  return search(name, alphabeticalNames);
}

// Linear search logic moved to a new function.
function searchOld(name, alphabeticalNames) {
```

```
  for(let i = 0; i < alphabeticalNames.length; i++) {
    if (alphabeticalNames[i] == name) return i;
  }
  return -1;
}

// Binary search; this is the new implementation
function searchFaster(name, alphabeticalNames) {
  let startIndex = 0;
  let endIndex = alphabeticalNames.length - 1;

  while (startIndex <= endIndex) {
    let middleIndex = Math.floor((startIndex+endIndex)/2);
    if (alphabeticalNames[middleIndex] == name) return middleIndex;

    if (alphabeticalNames[middleIndex] > name) {
      endIndex = middleIndex - 1;
    } else if (alphabeticalNames[middleIndex] < name) {
      startIndex = middleIndex + 1;
    }
  }

  return -1;
}

function compareAndLog(oldResult, newResult) {
  if (oldResult != newResult) {
    console.log(`Diff found; old result: ${oldResult}, new result: ${newResult}`);
  }
}
```

Once the abstraction has been properly put in place, start enabling dark mode (i.e., dual code path execution, returning the results of the old code). Monitor any differences being logged between the two result sets. Track down and fix any potential bugs in the new implementation causing those discrepancies. Repeat this process until you've properly handled all discrepancies, enabling dark mode to broader groups of users.

Once all users have been opted in to dark mode, starting with the lowest-risk environments, begin enabling light mode to small subsets of users (i.e., start returning data from the new code path). Continue logging any differences in the result sets; this can be useful if other developers are actively working on related code and risk introducing a change to the old implementation that is not reflected in the new implementation. Continue to opt broader groups of users into light mode, until everyone is successfully processing results from the new implementation.

Finally, disable execution of both code paths, continuing to monitor for any reported bugs, and remove the abstraction, feature flags, and conditional execution logic and, once the refactor has been live to users for an adequate period (whatever that might be for your use case), remove the old logic altogether. Only the new implementation should remain where the old implementation once was. See Example 4-4 for an example.

Example 4-4. New implementation inside the old function definition

```
// Binary search; this is the new implementation
function search(name, alphabeticalNames) {
  let startIndex = 0;
  let endIndex = alphabeticalNames.length - 1;

  while (startIndex <= endIndex) {
    let middleIndex = Math.floor((startIndex+endIndex)/2);
    if (alphabeticalNames[middleIndex] == name) return middleIndex;

    if (alphabeticalNames[middleIndex] > name) {
      endIndex = middleIndex - 1;
    } else if (alphabeticalNames[middleIndex] < name) {
      startIndex = middleIndex + 1;
    }
  }

  return -1;
}
```

As with any approach, there are some downsides to be mindful of. If the code you are refactoring is performance-sensitive, and you're operating in an environment that does not enable true multi-threading (PHP, Python, or Node), then running two versions of the same logic side by side might not be a great option. Say you're refactoring code that involves making one or more network requests; assuming those dependencies do not change with the refactor, you'll be executing double the number of network requests, serially. You must weigh the ability to audit your changes at a high fidelity against a corresponding increase in latency. One trade-off might be to run the dual code paths and subsequent comparison at a sampled rate; if this path is hit very frequently, running a comparison just 5 percent of the time might accumulate ample data about whether your solution is working as expected without compromising too heavily on performance.

We also have to be mindful of any additional load we'll be subjecting to downstream resources. This can include anything from a database, to a message queue, to the very systems we are using to log differences across the codepaths we're comparing. If we are refactoring a high-traffic path, and we want to run the comparison often, we need to be certain that we won't accidentally overburden our underlying infrastructure. In my experience, comparisons can unearth a swarm of unexpected differences (particularly when refactoring old, complex code). It's safer to take a slow, incremental approach to ramping up dual execution and comparison than to risk overloading your logging system. Set a small initial sample rate, address any high-frequency differences as they creep up, and repeat, increasing the sample rate step by step until you reach either 100 percent or a stable state at which you are confident no more discrepancies should arise.

Smart DNA's Rollout

With the refactor at Smart DNA, the greater risk was in migrating each of the repositories' many dependencies to versions compatible with Python 2.7, not with running the existing code itself, using the newer Python version. The software team decided that they would first perform a few preliminary tests, setting up a subset of the data pipeline in an isolated environment, installing both versions of Python, and running a few jobs, using the new dependency file in the 2.7 environment. When they were confident with the results of their preliminary tests, they would slowly, carefully introduce usage of the new set of dependencies in production.

To limit the risk involved, the team audited the jobs that make up the researchers' data pipeline and grouped them according to their importance. Then the engineers chose a low-risk job with the fewest downstream dependencies to migrate first. They worked with the research team to identify a good time to swap the configuration to point to the new *requirements.txt* file and new Python version. Once the change had been made, the team planned to monitor logs generated by the job to catch any strange behavior early. If any problems crept up, the configuration would be swapped back to its original version while the software team worked on a fix. When the fix was ready, the team would repeat the experiment. As part of their rollout plan, the team required the configuration change to sit in production for a few days, allowing for the job to run successfully on a dozen occasions before moving on to a second job.

After the second job was successfully migrated, the software team would opt-in all low-risk jobs to the new configuration. They would then repeat the process for the medium-risk jobs. Finally, for the most critical jobs, the team decided to migrate each of these individually, due to their importance. Again, they would wait a few days before repeating the process for the next job, and so on. In all, the team determined it would take nearly two months to migrate the entire data pipeline to the new environment. While this might sound like a grueling process, both the software and research teams agreed that it was necessary to reduce the risk sufficiently. It gave everyone adequate opportunity to weed out problems by small increments early, ensuring that the pipeline remained as healthy as possible throughout the entire process.

Cleaning Up Artifacts

In Chapter 1, I mentioned that you shouldn't embark on a refactor unless you have the time to execute to completion. No refactor is complete unless all remaining transitional artifacts are properly cleaned up. Following is a short, not-exhaustive list of the kinds of artifacts we generate during the refactoring process.

Feature flags

Most of us are guilty of leaving one or two feature flags behind. It's not *so* bad to forget to remove a flag for a few days (or even a few weeks), but a tangible risk is associated with failing to clean these up. First, verifying whether a feature flag is enabled adds complexity. Engineers reading code gated by a feature flag need to consider the behavior if the flag is enabled or disabled. This is necessary overhead for feature development in a continuous deployment environment, but we should prioritize removing it soon after we are able to do so. Second, stale feature flags can pile up. A single flag won't weigh down your application, but hundreds of stale flags certainly might. Practice good feature flag etiquette; add authors and expiration dates, and follow up with those engineers once those dates have passed.

Abstractions

We can attempt to shield our refactor from other developers by building abstractions to hide the transition. In fact, we might have written one to use the deployment method outlined in "Dark Mode/Light Mode" on page 81. Once we've finished refactoring, however, these abstractions are generally no longer meaningful and can further confuse developers. When our abstractions still contain some meaningful logic, we should strive to simplify them so that engineers reading them in the future have no reason to suspect that they were written for the purpose of smoothly refactoring something.

Dead code

When we're refactoring something, particularly when we're refactoring something at large scale, we typically end up with a sizable amount of dead code following rollout. Although dead code isn't dangerous on its own, it can be frustrating for engineers down the line trying to determine whether it is still being used. Recall "Unused Code" on page 32, where we discussed the downsides of keeping unused code in the codebase.

Comments

We leave a variety of comments when executing on a refactor. We warn other developers of code in flux, maybe leave a handful of TODOs, or make note of dead code to be removed once the refactor is finished. These comments should be deleted so as not to mislead anyone. On the off chance that we come across any stray, unfinished TODOs, we'll be even more gratified that we took the time to tidy up our work.

Unit tests

Depending on how we're executing the refactor, we may have written duplicative unit tests alongside existing ones to verify the correctness of our changes. We need to clean up any newly superfluous tests so that we don't confuse any developers referencing them later. (Redundant unit tests also aren't great if your team wants to maintain a speedy unit testing suite.)

A few years ago, a teammate of mine ran an experiment to determine how much time we were spending calculating feature flags. For the average request to our backend systems, it amounted to nearly 5 percent of execution time. Unfortunately, a great deal of the feature flags we were spending time calculating had already been enabled to all production workspaces and could have been removed entirely. We built some tooling to urge developers to clean up their expired flags and within just a few weeks had dramatically reduced the time spent processing them. Feature flags really do add up!

If there's a common thread for why we should clean up each of the kinds of transitional artifacts we produce, it's to minimize developer confusion and frustration. Artifacts add additional complexity, and engineers encountering them risk wasting a considerable amount of time understanding their purpose. We can save everyone ample frustration by cleaning them up!

As you execute on your refactoring effort, choose a tag that your team can use to label any artifacts you'll need to clean up. It can be something as simple as leaving an inline comment like `TODO: project-name, clean up post release`. Whatever it is, make it easy to search for so that once you're in the final stages of the project, you can quickly locate all the places that could use a final polish.

Referencing Metrics in Your Plan

In Chapter 3, we discussed a wide variety of ways we could characterize the state of the world before we began forming a plan of action. We talked about how these metrics should make a compelling case in support of your project to your teammates and management alike. At the start of this chapter, we also described the importance of using these metrics to define an end state (see "Defining Your End State" on page 72). Now, we need to complement the intermediate steps we identified earlier (see

"Identifying Strategic Intermediate Milestones" on page 76), with their own metrics. These will be useful for you and your team to determine whether you're making the progress you expected to see, and course-correct early if your trajectory appears off.

Execution plans are also one of the first glimpses management (whether that's your team's product manager, your skip-level, or your Chief Technology Officer [CTO]) will have of a project. For them to support the initiative, not only does your problem statement need to be convincing with clear success criteria, your proposal also needs to include definitive progress metrics. Showing that you have a strong direction should ease any concerns they might have about giving the go-ahead on a lengthy refactor.

Interpolating Goal Metrics to Intermediate Milestones

Recall Table 4-1, where we showed our starting metrics alongside our final goal metrics. For each of our milestones, if the start and end metrics are applicable to our intermediate stages, we can add an entry highlighting which metrics we expect to change and by how much if our metrics lend themselves well to intermediate measurements *during* the refactor.

End-goal metrics that might lend themselves better to intermediate measurements include complexity metrics, timings data, test coverage measurements, and lines of code. Be warned, however, that your measurements might trend worse before they trend better again! Consider the approach detailed in "Dark Mode/Light Mode" on page 81, for instance; having two code paths, both of which do the same thing, will definitely lead to a tangible uptick in complexity and lines of code.

Unfortunately, with our Python migration example, the language version remains the same throughout most of the project. Only once the team has reached the stage of rolling out the new version to each of the company's environments can we start to see our metrics change. To measure progress, we will need to come up with a different set of metrics to track throughout development.

Distinct Milestone Metrics

As the previous section showed, not all end-goal metrics will lend themselves well to showing intermediate progress. If that happens to be the case, we'll still need at least one helpful metric to indicate momentum. The metrics we choose might not directly correlate to our final goal, but they're important guideposts along the way.

There are a number of simple options. Say at Smart DNA we've set up continuous integration and enabled the linter to warn of undefined variables. We can use the number of warnings remaining as a metric to measure their progress within the scope of that step. Table 4-2 shows each of the major milestones we brainstormed in "Identifying Strategic Intermediate Milestones" on page 76 with their corresponding metric. (Note that the starting value for the linting milestone is an approximation. The team provided an estimate here by running `pylint`, with the default configuration running across the three repositories and summing up the number of warnings generated.

Table 4-2. Chart of milestone metrics for Smart DNA's Python migration

Milestone description	Metric description	Start	Goal	Observed
Create a single *requirements.txt* file	Number of distinct lists of dependencies	3	1	-
Merge all the repositories into a single repository	Number of distinct repositories	3	1	-
Build a Docker image with all the required packages	Number of environments using new Docker image	0	5	-
Enable linting through continuous integration for the monorepo	Number of linter warnings	approx. 15,000	0	-
Install and roll out Python 2.7.1 on all environments	Number of jobs running on Python 2.7.1 with new *requirements.txt* file	0	158	-

Estimating

After taking the time to associate metrics with our most important milestones, I recommend starting to make estimates. Our plan isn't in its final stages quite yet, so our estimates should not be terribly specific (e.g., on the order of weeks or months rather than days) but, most importantly, should be generous.

Going back to our cross-Canada roadtrip, we've set some general guidelines for when and where we want to stop for food and a good night's sleep along our trip from Montreal to Vancouver. The longest drive we plan to do is the stretch between Regina, SK, and Calgary, AB; just under 800 km of highway for roughly a 7.5-hr drive. By making sure that we're never driving more than eight hours per day, we're giving ourselves plenty of time to pack up in the morning from our starting point and decide how to distribute our day. What's important is that we've given ourselves enough time to enjoy the journey; we still intend to make some serious strides every day, but not so serious that we'll be burnt out by the time we reach Vancouver.

Most teams have their own guidelines and processes around deriving estimates, but if you don't have one already (or don't quite know how to go about estimating a particularly large software project), here's a simple technique. Go through each of the milestones and assign a number from 1 to 10, where 1 denotes a relatively short task and 10 denotes a lengthy task. Estimate how long your lengthiest milestone might take. Now imagine what is most likely to go wrong during that milestone and update your estimate to account for it. (Don't overdo it! It's important to be reasonable with the amount of buffer we add to our estimates; otherwise, leadership might ultimately decide our refactor is not a worthwhile endeavor.) Now, measure each shorter milestone against this lengthier one. If you anticipate that your longest milestone will take 10 weeks to complete, and your second-longest milestone should take almost as much time, then maybe nine weeks is a good estimate. Keep going down the list until you've given everything a rough estimate.

From a refactoring perspective, setting generous estimates is important for two main reasons. First, it gives your team wiggle room for when you run into the inevitable roadblock or two. The larger the software project, the greater the chance something won't go quite to plan, and refactoring is no exception to that rule. Building a reasonable buffer into your estimates will give your team a chance to hit important deadlines while accounting for a few pesky bugs and incidents along the way.

Large-scale refactoring efforts tend to affect multiple teams, so there's a reasonable chance that your project might end up unexpectedly butting heads with another team's project. Setting generous estimates allows you to navigate those situations more smoothly; you'll be more level-headed going into negotiations with the other team, knowing you have sufficient time to hit your next milestone. You're more likely to come up with creative solutions to the impasse. If your team needs to pause work on the current milestone, maybe you can pivot quickly, shifting your focus to a different portion of the refactor, and come back to the current work later.

Second, these estimates will help you set expectations with stakeholders (product managers, directors, CTOs) and teams that risk being affected by your refactor. We'll ask them for their perspective on our plan next, and if we're careful to build ample buffers into the estimates we provide, we'll have some room to negotiate. The next section deals more closely with how to best navigate these conversations.

Remember that you can give the overall project a greater estimate than the sum of each of its parts. Unless your organization is stringent about how to estimate software projects, no rule states that the anticipated project completion date should precisely line up with the completion of its individual components.

Sharing Your Plan with Other Teams

Large refactoring projects typically affect a large number of engineering groups of all disciplines. You can determine just how many (and which ones) by stepping through your execution plan and identifying any teams you think might be most closely affected by your refactor at each stage. Brainstorm with your team (or a small group of trusted colleagues) to make sure you've covered a variety of disciplines and departments. If your company is small enough, consider going through a list of all engineering departments and for each group decide whether they might appreciate the opportunity to provide input on your plan. Many companies put together technical design committees, to which you can submit a project proposal to be critiqued by engineers of different disciplines from across the company. Take advantage of these committees if you can; you're likely to learn a great deal of useful information well before your kick-off meeting.

There are two primary reasons for sharing your execution plan with other teams. The first, and perhaps most important reason, is to provide transparency. The second is to gather perspective on your plan to strengthen it further before seeking buy-in from management.

Transparency

Transparency helps build trust across teams. If you're upfront with other engineers at the company, they're more likely to be engaged and invested in your effort. It should go without saying, but if your team drafts a plan and starts executing on a refactor that affects a number of groups without warning, you risk dangerously eroding that relationship.

You must be mindful of the fact that your proposed changes could drastically change code that they own or affect important processes they maintain. With Smart DNA's Python migration, we're combining three repositories into one. This is a significant change for any developer or researcher working in any of these repositories. The affected teams should be adequately forewarned that their development process is going to change.

The refactor also risks affecting other teams' productivity. For instance, if we're proposing to combine all required packages into a single, global *requirements.txt* file, we may need other teams' help getting their changes reviewed and approved. We might even inquire about borrowing engineers from other teams to help out with the refactor (see Chapter 6 for a more in-depth look at how to recruit teammates).

Similarly, you have to make sure that your plans align with affected teams. If you're planning to modify code owned by another team just as they are planning to kick off development on a major feature (or perhaps their own hefty refactor), you will need to coordinate to make sure you aren't stepping on each other's toes.

Perspective

The second reason to share your plan with other teams is to get their perspective. You've done the research to define the problem and draft a comprehensive plan, but are the teams that risk being affected by your proposed changes supportive of your effort? If they do not believe that the benefits of your refactor outweigh the risks and inconvenience to their team, you may need to reconsider your approach. Perhaps you could convey the benefits in a more convincing manner, or find a way to reduce the level of risk associated with the current plan. Work with the team to figure out what would make them more comfortable with your plan. (You can use some of the techniques outlined in the next chapter to help out.)

If you're working to refactor a complex product, there are likely a number of edge cases you haven't considered. Just getting that second (and third and fourth) set of eyes can make a huge difference. Let's say that while auditing the packages used by the research team at Smart DNA, we fail to notice that some researchers have been manually updating a *requirements.txt* file on one of the machines directly, rather than making their changes in version history and deploying the new code. When we share our plan with the researchers, they'll point out that they typically update their dependencies on the machine itself and that the software team should verify the version there rather than the one checking into their repository. That insight would have saved our software team a great deal of pain and embarrassment had we started executing on the project without consulting the researchers first.

Remember that while it's important to get stakeholders' opinions about your plan before kicking off execution, nothing is set in stone at this stage. Your plan will likely change throughout the duration of the refactor; you'll run into an unexpected edge case or two, maybe spend more time than anticipated solving a pesky bug, or realize part of your initial approach simply won't work. At this stage, we are seeking out other perspectives mostly as a means of ensuring transparency with others and weeding out the blatantly obvious problems early. We'll discuss how to keep these stakeholders engaged and informed as our plan evolves in Chapter 7.

Avoid Scope Creep

While other teams' ideas and outlooks are incredibly helpful in finalizing our execution plan, we have to continue to focus on our ultimate goal so as not to introduce any additional scope accidentally. There might be a handful of small, new steps we need to add to our plan to handle an edge case or two properly that we hadn't previously considered; however, we should be careful to add only what is absolutely necessary to ensure that we can reach our desired end state while maintaining our major milestones.

Be cautious of conversations in which colleagues say something like, "While we're at it we could…" or "I've always wanted X to also handle…". Unless you're well-versed in the art of saying "no," you might end up agreeing to do more than you originally anticipated. We all want our refactor to address as many pain points and please as many engineers as possible. Unfortunately, going into a large refactoring effort with that mindset almost guarantees that it won't be sustainable; there'll always be another problem to address or engineer to appease. We should strive to plan and execute on a refactor we are confident we can deliver on in a reasonable amount of time. It likely won't fix everything, but at the very least it'll fix the *right* things.

Refined Plan

At Smart DNA, the software team worked diligently to build a comprehensive execution plan for its migration from Python 2.6 to 2.7. After stepping through each of the steps we've outlined, defining a goal state, identifying important milestones, choosing a rollout strategy, and so on, the team had a plan it was confident about, as follows:

- Create a single *requirements.txt* file.
  - **Metric:** Number of distinct lists of dependencies; **Start:** 3; **Goal:** 1
  - **Estimate:** 2–3 weeks
  - **Subtasks:**
    - Enumerate all packages used across each of the repositories.
    - Audit all packages and narrow the list to only the required packages with corresponding versions.
    - Identify which version each package should be upgraded to in Python 2.7.
- Merge all the repositories into a single repository.
  - **Metric:** Number of distinct repositories; **Start:** 3; **Goal:** 1
  - **Estimate:** 2–3 weeks
  - **Subtasks:**
    - Create a new repository.
    - For each repository, add to the new repository, using git submodules.
- Build a Docker image with all the required packages.
  - **Metric:** Number of environments using new Docker image; **Start:** 0; **Goal:** 5
  - **Estimate:** 1–2 weeks
  - **Subtasks:**
    - Test the Docker image on each of the environments.
- Enable linting through continuous integration for the monorepo.
- **Metric:** Number of linter warnings; **Start:** approx. 15,000; **Goal:** 0
  - **Estimate:** 1–1.5 months
  - **Subtasks:**
    - Choose a linter and corresponding configuration.
    - Integrate the linter into continuous integration.
    - Use the linter to identify logical problems in the code (undefined variables, syntax errors, etc.).
- Install and roll out Python 2.7.1 on all environments.

— **Metric:** Number of jobs running on Python 2.7.1 with new *requirements.txt* file; **Start:** 0; **Goal:** 158

— **Estimate:** 2–2.5 months

— **Subtasks:**

  — Locate tests for each repository; determine which tests are reliable.

  — Use Python 2.7 on a subset of low-risk scripts.

  — Roll out Python 2.7 to all scripts.

 If you use project management software (like Trello or JIRA) to keep track of your team's projects, I recommend creating some top-level entries for the large milestones. While some of the nitty-gritty details of the refactor might change throughout development, the strategic milestones you defined in this chapter are less likely to shift dramatically.

For the individual subtasks, you should consider creating entries for the first one or two milestones you're planning to undertake. You can figure out smaller tasks your team needs to tackle at a more regular cadence throughout the development process. Later milestones are more likely to be affected by earlier work, and the specifics of their individual subtasks risk changing. Create entries for the subtasks of subsequent milestones only as you kick them off.

We've done the preliminary work required to understand and comprehensively characterize the work involved with our large-scale refactor, and successfully crafted an execution plan we're confident will lead us to the finish line smoothly. Now, we need to get the necessary buy-in from our manager (and other important stakeholders) to support the refactor before we can confidently forge ahead.

CHAPTER 5

Getting Buy-In

By my junior year of high school, I decided I needed a cellphone. Not only did nearly every one of my friends have one, they were no longer interested in having me use theirs to call my parents every time I needed to inform them of my whereabouts. With each text costing roughly 10 cents, and each call costing them precious minutes, I was dishing out dimes and quarters to nearly a half-dozen friends for months. Carrying a pocketful of change wherever I went, hoping I could borrow someone's phone, was no longer my cup of tea.

Because my parents weren't proponents of their daughter having a cellphone, convincing them to get one was going to be an uphill battle. "Everyone else has one" was not going to cut it. My parents would need to be presented with a strong set of evidence-backed arguments. So, I put some together. I formulated an argument around owning a cellphone for safety reasons. Having recently obtained my driver's license, I needed to be able to call someone in case of an emergency. I calculated a rough estimate of the number of hours per week I spent driving to give the argument a bit more weight. Next, I compared device and plan costs, comparing these to the amount of money I'd distributed to friends over the last six months. I'd recently started building websites to make a bit of money on the side and knew I could afford to buy a basic flip phone and pay the monthly bill.

In response to my arguments, my parents said they didn't think it was a necessity. I could borrow my mother's phone when leaving the house. After pointing out that I was spending three to four hours per week driving both myself and my little brother around, they decided that maybe it wasn't a luxury after all. They were sufficiently convinced that the convenience of having a cellphone outweighed its cost. I got a hand-me-down flip phone with a number of my own a few days later.

Today, this experience serves me well when I have to convince others about the benefits of beginning a refactoring project. One of the complaints I hear most often from fellow engineers is that they have a strong desire to refactor something but they simply don't know how to convince anyone to let them do it. They've spent the time identifying the circumstances under which the problem arose, found evidence and metrics to characterize the problem so that they might better understand it, and carefully crafted a plan for how to solve it. They're certain that the problem needs to be solved and are ecstatic about their solution, but are met with skepticism when presenting their ideas to either their manager or tech lead.

This chapter will kick things off by explaining why your manager might not be on board, and help you understand their perspective so that you can craft a compelling argument. Next, we'll cover a few different approaches you can take for garnering the support of your management team, with some specific strategies you can use to get them rallying behind you. Finally, we'll look at some of the forms buy-in can take, and how these can affect both your execution plan and the team you end up putting together.

Why Your Manager Is Not Onboard

Your manager might be hesitant (or outright opposed) to a large refactor for a few distinct reasons. First, they are typically well-removed from the code and unlikely to understand its pain points intimately. Second, they are evaluated on their team's ability to ship effective product features on time. Third, the worst-case outcomes associated with a large refactor are generally much more serious than the worst-case outcomes associated with a new product feature. Finally, large-scale refactors typically require much more coordination with stakeholders outside of your immediate team.

Managers Aren't Coding

Most engineering managers are rarely coding, and hardly partaking in code reviews. In fact, someone hired directly into a management position at a new company might never even see the code their team works on. Because your manager isn't intimately familiar with the problems you and your team are frequently encountering during development, it shouldn't be a surprise that they are skeptical of your proposal. Imagine trying to explain to a dinner guest why you want to replace all of the rickety door knobs in your home; they might be able to understand the frustration logically, but they don't know the extent to which such door knobs are irritating on a daily basis.

Maybe your manager understands the difficulties your refactor aims to improve, but they fail to see why these should be fixed now. After all, if these problems are not new, the company must have been handling them (and is continuing to handle them) just fine. Your manager is weighing the potential upside of building something new against fixing a set of lingering problems.

Managers Are Evaluated Differently

Managers tend to be evaluated on their team's ability to hit deadlines and help achieve business objectives. These tend to include things like building features that help retain and acquire more users, or unlocking new revenue streams. Because managers have these incentives, they're more likely to prioritize work that has a high impact-to-effort ratio—that is, work that is relatively low-effort but offers a high impact. Managers are also more likely to set more aggressive deadlines in hopes of getting these changes out to customers sooner.

These goals are sometimes at odds with those of the engineers on the team. Engineers tend to seek out projects that solve interesting problems and often prioritize building a more robust solution over one that's quick to ship. (Not *all* engineers fit into this mold, but in my experience, this sums up quite a few of them.) A large refactor, while perhaps a meaningful, worthwhile endeavor by you and your teammates, is at the bottom of your manager's potential projects list. At-scale refactors are usually lengthy, and because they are deliberately invisible to users, result in little to no immediate positive impact to the business. If your manager is looking to move up the ladder (or if they're concerned about their upcoming review), they will probably be less than eager to support your plan.

 Even if your manager is convinced that the refactor is worthwhile, they might be risking good standing by giving you the go-ahead. Just as your manager is evaluated on your team's ability to build and deliver on time, their own manager is equally evaluated on the impact that their organization can have on the business. It can be difficult for your manager to convince their *own* manager that a refactor is a valuable investment of engineering time and resources.

Managers See the Risk

There are a handful of ways feature development can go awry. Your team might run into a handful of roadblocks and ship a bit later than initially anticipated, or maybe the feature makes it into the hands of users, only to reveal an abundance of pesky bugs. However, the likelihood of a catastrophic outage during the development of a new feature is relatively low because new features tend to be relatively well-scoped, with relatively well-defined boundaries.

The stakes are *much* greater when executing on a large-scale refactor. The team risks introducing regressions across a large surface area, and the likelihood of a disastrous outage is not nearly as negligible. When untangling old, crufty code, there's a much greater chance your team will unearth unexpected bugs; the risk of being pulled head first into a rabbit hole in an attempt to fix them can significantly delay your deadlines.

Each and every one of the risks we highlighted in Chapter 1 is alarmingly obvious to your manager.

Managers Need to Coordinate

Most companies organize engineering teams around individual portions of their product (or products). Say you work for a music streaming application called Rad-Tunes. RadTunes might have a team responsible for playlist creation, and another for managing search. When a team sets out to build a new feature, it typically is operating within an area of the codebase that it owns. It'd be surprising to see the Search team build a new feature allowing users to create collaborative playlists; the more obvious choice would be for the Playlist team to do so.

Now imagine that you are on the Playlist team and the team is struggling with the song object model. You've come up with a plan for improving it, but it involves modifying code nearly every one of the teams at the company works with regularly. You and your manager will need to coordinate with every one of these teams at the onset to solicit support, and continue to coordinate throughout the refactor to make sure everyone is properly aligned. When you pitch your refactor to your manager, they are seeing the colossal amount of work required to keep everyone organized for the complete duration of the project. It's only normal that they might be hesitant to support it.

What Buy-In Can Look Like

Before we jump into strategies for persuading your manager, we have to understand what buy-in looks like in practice. Buy-in happens on a spectrum. Management can either buy in completely, not at all, or anything between. Most of the time, it ends up somewhere in the middle. The decision to move forward with a large-scale refactor often comes down to two questions:

Is this the right time for the refactor?
> Large-scale refactors can be an expensive investment in terms of development time. Because they can be quite costly (and we want to be certain to budget enough time to see the project to completion), we need to be confident that we're kicking it off at the right time for the company. This means taking into consideration when any ongoing projects are set to complete, and which projects the company (your team specifically) was aiming to ship during upcoming quarters.

> Before pitching the project to your manager, figure out when you believe the team should begin work on the refactor and precisely why that is an optimal time. For instance, is it the right time to fund this project because the problems the refactor aims to solve haven't yet reached a critical point, giving your team ample time to implement an ideal solution? Or perhaps it's the right time because executing on the refactor now could significantly help the team in its upcoming

---

projects. Each of these considerations will be helpful context for your manager when seeking their support.

How many resources (most often in terms of engineers) should be allocated to it?
Refactoring can also be an expensive investment in terms of resourcing. Depending on the level of buy-in you're able to secure from your manager, you may or may not be able to build the ideal team, which we'll take a longer look at in Chapter 6. Note that resourcing can be directly affected by the time at which you anticipate starting the refactor and vice versa.

This chapter assumes your manager is a no-go on all aspects of the refactor. However, if your manager is partially bought-in and you are seeking more support, you can use any of the techniques described to nudge your manager in the right direction.

Strategies for Making a Compelling Argument

Now that we understand why our manager might not be onboard, we can focus on a few helpful strategies for assuaging their fears and constructing a robust case to convince them that the refactor is worthwhile. This section assumes you've already had an initial investigatory conversation with your manager about your project. If you haven't had that conversation yet, "Initial Conversation" on page 101 is a good starting point. This conversation is important for two reasons. First, it helps you understand which factors are weighing most heavily on your manager. Second, it gives you a sense of whether your manager might be more readily convinced by an emotional or logical argument. This conversation will give you the preliminary context you need to choose the most effective strategies to convince your manager.

Initial Conversation

Instead of steamrolling your manager with all of the information you've gathered to date, consider asking them for their opinion first. It can be as simple as kicking off a conversation during your one-on-one with, "I've been thinking about how X is affecting our ability to do Y and I wanted to know whether you had any thoughts about it." By soliciting their opinion, you're indicating to your manager that you value their point of view. You're giving them an important opportunity to be honest with you.

If your manager is familiar with the problem, you can use the conversation to discern early whether they would be supportive of a refactor. If your manager sounds hesitant to pursue a refactor, use what you learned about their perspective as a manager to try pinpointing what they are most concerned about.

If your manager is unfamiliar with the problem, give them a basic, unbiased overview. A good manager will seek to understand why you're concerned and ask the questions they need answered to characterize the problem properly for themselves.

Taking the time to listen during this conversation is absolutely critical. Too many of us spend our time thinking about what we want to say next rather than making the genuine effort to process what someone is saying. Take notes during your conversation. These can either be mental or written; simply choose the medium that works best for you. (I tend to forget in-person conversations quite quickly, so it's important that I write everything down.)

Consider asking a question instead of offering a counterpoint. For example, instead of saying, "That won't work because of X," consider asking, "Have you thought about X?" or, "What's your plan for X?" This continues to show your manager that you care more about their perspective and gives them a welcome opportunity to respond rather than showing them that you care about being right.

 I recommend having this conversation either in person or via video conferencing instead of over email or in chat. Your manager's facial expressions and overall tone when attempting to assess their attitude about a potential refactor are really important.

Once you've had that initial conversation with your manager, you can zero in on the persuasion techniques you might want to use. We'll outline four simple, distinct techniques here, but know that this is not an exhaustive list. Different strategies will work best with different managers, depending on what motivates them the most (e.g., their growth trajectory at the company), or the degree to which they are opposed to the refactor (e.g., they are generally in agreement that the problem exists but are unconvinced it should be fixed imminently). Ultimately, the most effective way to nudge your manager into giving the go-ahead is to use a combination of techniques: opting for those you believe will have the most impact and are most comfortable using. If you are confident and well-prepared, you might just get the "yes" you've been seeking.

Using Conversational Devices

Some of our colleagues can walk into a meeting full of stubborn engineers and within a half hour have everyone persuaded of their opinion. Unfortunately, I am not one of those people. If this isn't you either, not to worry! There are a few easy (and honest) conversational tricks we can use to express ourselves in a more convincing manner.

Compliment their thought process

Very few of us are immune to flattery, your manager included. If at any point during your conversation, you and your manager agree on something, highlight it with a compliment. For example, you and your manager agree that the refactor would be beneficial, but your manager would prefer reevaluating in six months. You can shift the focus back to the benefits of the refactor by saying, "You've made some really great points about the potential benefits of a refactor. It's pretty clear you have a nuanced understanding of the problems we've been experiencing." Your manager will be reminded of the benefits they identified and inclined to weigh them more heavily against the potential downsides.

Present the counter-argument

Not only should you be prepared for any counter-arguments from your manager, you might even consider bringing up the counter-arguments for them. It may sound a bit odd, but a number of psychological studies have shown that two-sided arguments are more convincing than one-sided arguments. There are a few benefits to presenting counter-arguments directly:

- By demonstrating to your manager that you've seriously considered the downsides of a large-scale refactor, you're further demonstrating your thoughtfulness and thoroughness around the effort.
- You're reaffirming your manager's concerns; while you might not be outright complimenting them on their ability to reason about the drawbacks of a large-scale refactor, you are confirming that their apprehension is legitimate. Your manager will be more open to hearing about your ideas if they feel that their own ideas are well understood.

Now the trick to using counter-arguments in your favor is to refute them carefully. Let's refer back to our RadTunes example, "Managers Need to Coordinate" on page 100. Your manager is planning for the Playlist team to spend most of the upcoming quarter building collaborative playlists. You're proposing for the team to spend crucial time rewriting the application's representation of a song before kicking off development on a new feature.

You could tell your manager, "If we began refactoring songs next quarter, we'd have to put off work on collaborative playlists for a few months. That would certainly be disappointing to our customers who have been requesting this feature for the past few years." You can immediately address the issue by following up with a rebuttal: "However, I'm confident that if we rewrite our songs implementation, we'll be able to shave several weeks off of collaborative playlist development and unblock the Search team on surfacing better results by genre."

You can even introduce a counter-argument your manager hasn't brought up yet or one you doubt they'll bring up at all. This sounds counter-productive, but it will boost your trustworthiness and strengthen your stance, assuming you successfully knock down the counter-argument.

 While this is not a book you'd typically find on a programmer's shelf, I highly recommend grabbing a copy of Dale Carnegie's *How to Win Friends and Influence People*. It was published over 80 years ago, but most of its lessons continue to hold true today. The skills it teaches will be helpful to you not only when trying to secure buy-in for your projects, but in all aspects of your life!

Building an Alignment Sandwich

If you are uninterested in playing office politics to your advantage, that's perfectly all right, and you are welcome to skip ahead to "Metrics" on page 123. On the other hand, if you are interested in leveraging the organizational landscape to your benefit, there are a number of levers you can pull to effectively compel your manager into giving the go-ahead on a large-scale refactor. You can build an alignment sandwich, securing the support of your teammates along with the support of upper management, sandwiching your manager between the two.

This approach only works if you have ample support from both sides of the sandwich. If your manager only feels pressure from your team, then they'll still be on solid footing to turn down the refactor, knowing there'll be little flak (if any) from their superiors. If your manager only feels pressure from above, and your team is not vocally supportive (or worse, your team is vocally opposed), they're unlikely to move forward with the project knowing they risk harming team morale.

Be mindful that this strategy can backfire. Given your previous conversation, your manager is aware that you're interested in pursuing this refactor. If they are approached by upper management or other influential individuals at your company about moving forward with the refactor, there's a chance they'll put two and two together and deduce that you've been seeking external influence. If you have a tenuous relationship with your manager, this could lead to some backlash. Regardless of the strength of your relationship with your manager, try being upfront with them about having sought out external opinions; then, instead of having these allies reach out to your manager directly, consider setting up a meeting with the three of you to discuss your perspectives.

Rallying your teammates

Before reaching out to upper management about your refactor, you should take the time get your teammates on the same page. Chances are, you've probably discussed aspects of the refactor with some of your teammates throughout prior investigatory stages (collecting metrics to characterize the problem, drafting an execution plan) to gather their feedback. For the teammates who haven't yet gotten a glimpse of your thought process, take some time to fill them in. This doesn't have to be anything formal; shoot them a message or ask to grab a coffee.

Your ultimate goal is to get them to vouch for the refactor either in a public setting where your manager is present (in a meeting, in a public chat, in an email), or in their own one on one with your manager. You may want to coordinate with your teammates so that not all of them bring it up in their one-on-ones the same week; the trick is to make everyone's interest appear organic, not prepared. Once you've secured sufficient backing from your teammates, you'll have built up the bottom slice of your sandwich.

Skip-level

If your manager isn't interested in pursuing a large-scale refactor, perhaps your manager's manager (referred to as skip-level) will be. Upper-level management tends to have an expansive view of the organization's objectives as well as its current and future projects. Given this broader perspective, your skip-level might be more sympathetic than your manager to a refactor spanning a large surface area because they are better able to visualize the scope of its benefits.

 Some companies have strict hierarchies where going directly to your skip-level is seen as a huge faux-pas. Be mindful of how a conversation with your manager's manager might be perceived before booking time with them. At the very least, be careful not to put down your manager during your meeting; focus on building interest and alignment in your refactor instead.

If you have a preexisting relationship with your skip-level, and you have reason to believe that they would be supportive of your effort, schedule a meeting with them. Your initial conversation should be similar to the one you had with your manager (see "Initial Conversation" on page 101). This exchange should help you discern whether your skip-level is likely to advocate for your proposed refactor. If you determine that they aren't a strong supporter, then you'll want to seek the support of other influential individuals at your company to act as the top slice of bread in your alignment sandwich. If they appear supportive, however, schedule a second meeting. You can discuss the details of your execution plan, align on the resources you'll need, and determine how they can help you get the approval of your manager.

Having a strong relationship with your skip-level can be quite beneficial regardless of refactoring aspirations. In fact, I highly recommend holding quarterly (or even monthly) one-on-ones with your skip-level if at all possible. Upper management can be a valuable resource if you're looking to expand your reach as an engineer; if you need to grow your skills by leading an effective project in your part of the organization, they'll be able to identify the right project for you. If you're seeking mentorship, they can connect you with other senior engineers at the company. Having an established relationship with your skip-level can also help you navigate difficulties in your relationship with your direct manager, if they ever arise.

Departments

Within every company, there are typically a handful of departments that have considerable authority over the business. When their input is required, their decision is the final say, whether that's a decision on how a new feature should be designed, a new process should operate, or a bug should be resolved. In many industries (the financial services industry, healthcare, human resources), this is the legal and compliance department. If you've been at your current company for several months, you likely have an inkling of which department that might be. If you're not quite certain, ask your peers; they might have a story or two about the security department's involvement with an incident or the sales team's input on a new feature.

In some cases (not all), these departments might have a vested interest in your refactor. Take, for instance, the compliance team at Smart DNA, our biotechnology company from "At Work" on page 72. Above all else, the team is responsible for ensuring that the sequenced DNA of its customers remains safe at all times. Having most of the company's systems using an outdated version of Python would likely be an area of concern for them, given that security patches can no longer be applied. If the research team at Smart DNA had not been in support of updating their Python dependencies, the software team could have reached out to the company's compliance team and enumerated the many ways running an unsupported version of Python is a vulnerability. The compliance team would then put pressure on the necessary engineering managers to prioritize the migration, giving the software team its top slice of bread for a completed sandwich.

Tapping into influential engineers

Every company has a handful (or two) of highly influential engineers; these engineers are a combination of extremely senior members of your technical staff (think principal and distinguished engineers), have been at the company for a significant length of time, or, in some cases, both. Many of them, if not most, are still knee-deep in the code. If they're familiar with the surface area you want to improve, not only will they immediately understand the problems your refactor addresses, but they'll also have valuable insights to contribute to your plan to date. Securing their support can be crucial in legitimizing your effort to your manager. At some companies, there is no greater stamp of approval than that of a senior engineer. If you can garner their thumbs-up, your alignment sandwich will have a sturdy top slice.

If you can rally the support of multiple upper-level influences (your skip-level, critical business departments, highly influential engineers), that's even better! Your alignment sandwich doesn't need to be perfectly balanced; leaning a little bit top-heavy only makes the approach more powerful.

Rewarding Refactoring

If you have healthy relationships with management (middle management and upper management alike), and you want to ensure that refactoring and other software maintenance work is prioritized at your company, you can leverage these relationships to build systems that reward it. At an individual contributor level, no engineer should be told that refactoring is equivalent to career suicide; instead, work with engineering promotion committees and human resources to include (and encourage) code maintenance. At a managerial level, no manager, regardless of their position in the hierarchy, should elicit a culture of generating tech debt. Some companies have had success reducing tech debt by requiring managers to include maintenance efforts in their quarterly planning, even going so far as highlighting code quality and upkeep on their management career ladders. After all, management is not just about making sure your team is efficient, happy, and shipping quality features on time; it's also about doing the unglamorous work of maintaining and improving existing code, so that it continues to scale to accommodate changing circumstances.

Relying on Evidence

If your manager is partial to logical arguments, then you should use the evidence you gathered in Chapter 3 to bolster your position. Set up some time with your manager to continue your initial conversation. Tell them that you've given the refactor more thought, and that you've spent time characterizing the problem so they might better appreciate its value (and, hopefully, its urgency).

Ahead of your meeting, prepare your evidence. If you've gathered an abundance of evidence, focus on the two or three most startling pieces. Some metrics are better communicated in visual form, so consider putting together a graph or two to better illustrate the points you want to emphasize. Taking the time to synthesize this information into a medium that's easy for your manager to consume is beneficial for a few reasons. First, it'll give you a comprehensive document you can circulate to other interested individuals at the company. This can be useful when garnering support cross-functionally or recruiting teammates, which we'll cover in Chapter 6. Second, you'll have something you can reference during your meeting. For those of us who aren't confident in their ability to persuade others, having a clear set of topic points you can reference throughout your discussion can make all the difference.

 For engineers who are a bit more timid and haven't yet built the social capital necessary to lean on influential colleagues or play hardball with their manager, I recommend relying heavily on the metrics argument. Facts are easy to prepare, easy to memorize, and usually difficult to refute.

Playing Hardball

If you are exceedingly confident that your refactor is critical to the business and your manager is unwilling to budge, there are a few more severe options you can consider. Presenting these severe options is often referred to as playing hardball. A word of caution: either of these approaches can seriously jeopardize your relationship with your manager and fellow colleagues. When successful, however, they can be really effective, and, if your refactor proves successful (which it most definitely will be, given you are reading this book), can catapult your career forward.

It's important to note that not everyone is in a strong enough position (either in their role at their current company or financially) to play hardball with their manager, and that's okay! You need to have built up quite a bit of clout and established a long history of good performance in your current role to be able to pull this off.

One final note before we dive in: with both of these tactics, you must be willing to follow through. If your manager calls your bluff and remains unconvinced, not only does it risk eroding your relationship, it diminishes your ability to take a similar approach successfully when another important project comes along.

Stop doing unrewarded maintenance work

When there is a serious need to refactor something at a large scale, it usually indicates that there is an amount of nontrivial work going on behind the scenes to keep things operational. Management is typically unaware of this work, or, if they are, they do not recognize its importance. If you are actively, regularly finding ways to mitigate the problem your refactor aims to solve, you can warn your manager that you no longer plan to do this work. The idea is to stop doing any invisible work that is preventing management at your company from seeing the problem your refactor aims to solve.

Take our Python migration at SmartDNA, for instance. Before Python 2.7 was rolled out to all environments, whenever a security patch was was made available, your team needed to spend valuable time porting the patch to the outdated Python 2.6 systems. Because security patches cannot be anticipated, any time a new vulnerability was discovered, your team had to pause all feature work and divert its energy to porting the patch. This kind of maintenance work was extremely time-consuming and high-risk, but necessary under the circumstances. Unfortunately, management was unwilling to recognize this operational cost of running outdated software.

In this scenario, you could put pressure on your manager to prioritize the Python upgrade by suggesting that the team would no longer port any new security patches as they become available. Tell your manager that you are trying to set appropriate boundaries for the team; given that your team is primarily focused on feature development, you can assert that supporting legacy software run by the research team is not strictly a responsibility. If during your quarterly or yearly planning process, your manager does not properly account for the work involved with porting a new patch on a regular basis, make a point to highlight that.

Yes, you are drawing a hard line. You might even feel guilty for no longer doing important maintenance work (which most developers believe is a critical part of their job). That's completely normal. I've made this argument before and worried about being irresponsible, letting the company down. What I came to realize was that by holding my ground, I was doing just the opposite; I was showing the business where it had an important blindspot, and the significance of that blindspot. By redefining expectations with your manager, you are shedding light on the pervasiveness of the work involved to keep your systems operational without a substantial refactor.

Giving an ultimatum

If all else fails, you can suggest to your manager that if they continue to oppose the refactor, you'll either transfer to another team or outright quit the company. If you want to stay at the same company and are able to switch teams, identify a team you are interested in joining before bringing it up with your manager; better yet, try to find a manager who is supportive of the refactor elsewhere at the company and is interested in having you join their team. If switching teams isn't on the table, you might threaten to quit. You should thoughtfully consider this decision, and seriously examine whether you have the necessary financial stability to do so before speaking to your manager.

This is not an easy conversation to have with your manager. First, bring up that you're concerned that the company isn't taking the problems you've identified more seriously. If your manager is eager to keep you on their team, they might reassess and allow the refactor to move forward.

Buy-In Shapes the Refactor

Even though securing buy-in happens well before a single line of code is written, it can be one of the most difficult aspects of refactoring at scale. Managers can be apprehensive to kicking off a lengthy, engineering-focused endeavor with good reason; they have their own sets of constraints and incentives within an engineering organization. That said, each of us has the ability to learn and master techniques to convince them that the effort is worthwhile despite any misgivings. We can discover how to lean effectively on our teammates and colleagues in the broader organization to give us the additional support we need.

After the dust has settled, depending on the degree of buy-in you've obtained, you may or may not be able to execute on your refactor. If your manager remains skeptical, consider shelving the project for now. You can continue to accrue supporting evidence, waiting for a more opportune moment to reintroduce the subject. For instance, if your company suffers from an incident caused by a problem your refactor seeks to solve, this might be a good time to revive the conversation with your manager. The next time your team enters its long-term planning phase, consider proposing the refactor once more. Keep a watchful eye and an ear to the ground for any opportunities to shed new light on your refactor.

If you've acquired buy-in, whether that's an enthusiastic yes or a lukewarm nod, you'll need to leverage that support to garner resources for your project. You'll need to determine which engineers are required to give the refactor its greatest chance of success, and at which stages their expertise will be needed. We'll discuss everything you need to know to make these decisions in Chapter 6.

Building the Right Team

Ocean's 11 is one of those heist films that shows up on everyone's list of favorites. It starts off with Danny Ocean getting released from prison. He meets up with his partner in crime and friend Rusty Ryan to propose a heist. The plan is to steal $150,000,000 from three Las Vegas casinos: the Bellagio, the Mirage, and the MGM Grand. The two thieves know they can't pull off the heist alone, so they start gathering a crew of criminals, including a former casino owner, a pickpocket, a con man, an electronics and surveillance expert, an explosives professional, and an acrobat.

The team splits up into two groups: the first group gets to know the ins and outs of the Bellagio, learning the routines of the staff and gathering details on how the casino operates; the second group builds a replica of the casino vault to practice maneuvering past its challenging security system. Within a few days, the group hatches a plan. High jinks ensue, hurdles are dodged, and (spoiler alert!) the team eventually escapes with the cash.

Ocean and Ryan could never have robbed the Bellagio alone. Not only would they have needed months to gather the financial resources required to prepare for the heist, it's unlikely that they could have concocted a reasonable plan to bypass the casino's defensive measures by only the two of them. By assembling a team just the right size with just the right skills, they cut down on their execution time *and* increased their chances of success.

To execute on a large refactoring effort successfully, we need our own Ocean's 11. Danny spent months iterating on his heist while locked up in New Jersey; from his blueprint, he derived a list of skills and expertise he needed, along with the names of potential candidates with these abilities. In this chapter, we'll learn how to assemble different kinds of teams, depending on the kind of expertise we require to execute on our refactoring effort most effectively. As technical leads, we'll learn how to narrow our list of potential teammates and convince them to join us on our journey. Finally, we'll discuss how to make the best of an unfortunate situation: needing to execute on the project alone.

Identifying Different Kinds of Experts

In Chapter 4, we learned how to draft an effective plan of action. We learned how to capture and synthesize the important complexity of our refactoring effort in a few concise, top-level milestones with a handful of critical subtasks.

Because most of us work on a team with a few other engineers, there's a strong likelihood that our plan was derived cooperatively and we intend to execute it as a team. When executing a large-scale refactor, however, we almost always need some help from colleagues on different teams across the company. On the other hand, there are times when we scope out and plan a refactoring effort either alone or with just one or two other engineers. In either case, we can use our plan to figure out precisely which engineers we'll need and when.

We can start by rereading our plan. As we go through each step, we try to visualize the code we'll need to interact with. Can we conjure it up easily? Can we confidently identify the changes we need to make and reason through the potential impact or downstream effects of those changes? Do we understand the pitfalls we might run into in the given area of the codebase? Do we understand the potential product implications of the changes we want to make? Are we deeply familiar with the technologies we'll either be directly or indirectly interfacing with? If so, great! We're probably in a good position to make those changes ourselves. If not, then we'll need someone else's help. We can enlist someone for help in one of two ways, either as an active contributor or as a subject matter expert.

An *active contributor* is heavily involved with the project, ideally from day one. They are actively contributing to the effort by writing code alongside you. Active contributors should be consulted for input on the execution plan early and through each of its revisions.

Subject matter experts, or SMEs for short, are not active contributors to your effort. They've agreed to be available to talk through solutions with you, answer questions, and maybe do some code review. While their contributions can be very meaningful, their time commitment to the project is minimal. Their primary focus remains on other projects distinct from yours.

Let's make this a bit more concrete by working through an example project. Your company's monitoring and observability team is migrating from one metrics-collection system to another (maybe StatsD to Prometheus). They've built up the infrastructure, provisioned some nodes, and are now ready to start accepting traffic from your application. The team needs one or two developers who are intimately familiar with how the application uses StatsD to help with the transition. Being one of those people, you've decided to lend a hand by writing a new internal library to interface with the new solution and ultimately replace the current library. You'll need to ensure that the Prometheus library offers feature parity with the current one and a clean, intuitive API. Your final task will be to establish best practices for using the new library and encourage its adoption across the engineering organization.

You don't need to have intimate knowledge of how the new metrics-collection system works to do your job proficiently. You can lean on the monitoring team when needed and it can lean back on you if it notices something odd about the integration process with your application. In this example, you're an active contributor collaborating with the monitoring team.

While auditing uses of the StatsD library, you notice that another product development team is using it in a way that is distinct from most other teams. You want to understand why the team is using the library in this way, and whether this behavior absolutely needs to be replicated in the new system. If this behavior is necessary, you have to make sure that Prometheus can accommodate it. You reach out to a few folks on the team to see whether they might have time to answer your questions. One team member, let's call them Frankie, eagerly agrees to meet with you. After a quick chat, you come to the conclusion that the behavior should be supported in the new Prometheus library, and Frankie's agreed to review your code as you build out the functionality. Frankie, in this scenario, is a SME.

You might need a number of *types* of expertise to execute your refactoring effort successfully. With our metrics-collection example, we needed the monitoring team's technology expertise with StatsD and Prometheus, Frankie's product expertise with a specific set of use cases, and our own expertise with how the codebase uses the metrics-gathering libraries at large. We might even want to consult with someone from the security team to confirm that no sensitive customer data ends up flowing through the new system (and if it does, we have measures in place to contain it swiftly).

When enumerating each of the kinds of expertise you'll likely need, keep an eye out for a range. Refactoring at scale typically affects a large surface area, so it shouldn't be surprising if you end up with a lengthy list. Don't worry, we'll learn just how to narrow that list down next.

Matchmaking

We've now successfully drafted a list of types of expertise we want available to us while we execute our refactoring effort; for our metrics-collection refactor, we need a technology expert, a product expert, and, finally, a security expert. Alongside each of the kinds of expertise, we denote the major project milestone at which point that expertise will be needed; if the expertise is needed throughout multiple milestones, simply note the earliest milestone when that help will be needed. Our final step before beginning to brainstorm potential experts is to label whether we think we'll need an SME or an active contributor for each expertise. We can pencil this in for now, because the role we anticipate the expert to have might change as we meet with potential candidates and work out their involvement with the project.

Finally, we have to match each expertise with one or more people. Start from the beginning of the list and, for each item, write the first few names of either individuals or teams that come to mind.

If you work at a large company or haven't gotten to know folks across different engineering teams, you may have a difficult time coming up with experts for each expertise. That's okay! You can start off by identifying a department. If you have access to an updated organization chart, use it to try to locate the best team within the department you identified. Do not be afraid to leverage your manager to help you generate and subsequently reduce the list of experts. Part of their job is to make sure that the team has all the resources it needs to execute projects efficiently, and they likely have much better insight about which teams across the organization are well suited to help out.

 If you don't have access to an updated organization chart but your engineering team has on-call rotations and uses a service like PagerDuty to alert engineers about incidents, you might be able to find the right experts by referencing these rotations. Look for the feature or infrastructural component for which you're seeking an expert and find the team with the corresponding on-call rotation. Voila!

Continue to jot down names until you've run out of items. Table 6-1 shows an example list we came up with for the metrics-gathering migration.

Table 6-1. A list of expertise types and potential experts

Knowledge area	Milestone	Role	Expert
Understand how the order fulfillment code uses StatsD (distinct from most other product features)	1	SME	Frankie, Mackenzie, Order Processing Team
Automated end-to-end testing between library and Prometheus	2	active contributor	Jesse, Automated Testing Team
Monitoring application traffic to Prometheus as teams begin to adopt it	3	SME	Monitoring Team
How our application deployment pipeline will affect Prometheus nodes	1	SME	Jesse, Release & Deploy Team
Security implications of gathering metrics about customers; security-conscious customers we should be particularly careful about monitoring	1	SME	Product Security Team

Experts of Many Trades

Next, highlight any names that pop up more than once. There isn't much overlap in our example set, but we notice that Jesse might be a good candidate for two of the five items. Your company may have a number of senior engineers with a wide breadth of expertise that could be helpful to your refactor. Conferring with someone who happens to be an expert on multiple relevant topics can be helpful on many fronts.

First, it can help us decrease the total number of people we'll need to coordinate with to complete our project. Coordinating a large project with a single team can be difficult, never mind coordinating a large project involving multiple developers across a number of teams. Each contributor not only has to be pitched on the effort and brought up to speed, but they must also adapt to your team's development process (i.e., weekly or daily stand-ups, monthly retrospectives, etc.). It can take a considerable amount of time and effort before everyone is well-aligned and operating at a good pace.

Second, experts who happen to have a deep understanding of multiple important aspects of the project likely have a strong perspective on how these pieces work together. This can be valuable insight shared by few other engineers at the company. Given our sample list of experts in Table 6-1, Jesse is likely one of those individuals. From our conversations with them, we know that they've worked closely with the release & deploy team over several months to help it build a percentage-based release system for two important services at the company. We also know that after that project Jesse moved to the internal tools team, where they worked to improve the availability of automated testing environments. Jesse is just one of those engineers who's been at the company for a while, worked on a laundry list of projects, and has keen insight into how each of these pieces works together.

Unfortunately, people like Jesse can be quite busy (probably because they're providing input on a number of projects as an SME, in addition to leading a few of their own). If they are not available to help in a regular capacity but you believe their unique knowledge is critical to the refactoring effort, offer to have them review your execution plan. I've found their input particularly helpful in verifying my least-confident time estimates. If you're looking for an expert to be actively involved in your project, they'll be able to suggest another expert or two to replace them.

If very few names (or none at all) overlap and your list of required types of expertise is quite lengthy, not to worry! You can still successfully execute a large-scale refactor with just a handful of resourceful individuals.

Revisiting Active Contributors

For me, a good rule of thumb is to limit the number of active contributors to the size of team you've been most comfortable working with in the past. If you've been on successful product engineering teams of six, then limit your team to six active contributors. Everyone's experience working with different teams at different companies is a little bit different; you know yourself and your preferred working conditions best, so go with what you know to be most effective. Large refactoring projects are plenty complex enough from both process and technical standpoints; don't let your team be yet another potential curveball.

If your list of active contributors feels too long, review your list and see whether there is any expertise for which you can instead seek out the help of an SME. Coordinating with SMEs comes at a much lower coordination cost because they are only consulted on an ad hoc basis. We'll cover some strategies for effectively communicating with SMEs in Chapter 7.

Biases in Our Expert List

If we happen to know someone who could be a valuable expert on one or more of the items on our list, we might ask them for their help directly. Chances are, they'll be more than happy to help out. After all, asking someone you know is probably the most convenient option. If you've worked together previously, you'll be able to establish a cadence that works well for both of you pretty quickly and begin making some salient progress early.

Asking a colleague for help directly can have its drawbacks, however. Software engineers are notoriously bad at estimating how much time and effort a task will take. This is often a consequence of the relentless optimism that being a software engineer requires. When something seems like a small request, sometimes our colleagues can be a little *too* quick to say yes, not taking much time to scope the commitment properly. They may only realize well after the project's kicked off that they've said yes to a few too many things and are now struggling to juggle it all. (I've been that person and trust me when I say that saying yes to too many things is just as unhelpful as saying no to everything.)

Another problem with asking a colleague for help directly is that you might overlook others who are better suited for the role. We all suffer from a number of biases we must consciously work to counteract. One such bias is *recency bias*, when we tend to recall things we've seen more recently more quickly. We are more likely to list a colleague as a good potential expert if we've heard their name or spoken to them more recently. We need to be mindful of that bias before we finalize our expert list, and take a minute to question whether each expert truly is the best one for the job or if we just happened to see their name copied on an email a few days ago. If we think a more qualified candidate might be available, we should do our research and consider contacting a team rather than an individual. Managers of expert teams can vet your request for help to each of their developers and gauge interest. Great managers will identify those on their team who could contribute meaningfully but also would benefit the most from the visibility and career growth of contributing to your refactoring effort.

It's also important not to confuse expertise with seniority. Frankie might not be the engineer with the most industry experience or have the longest tenure at the company, but they've made significant contributions over the past few months and you're confident they can answer your questions and offer valuable insights in code reviews. Sometimes, the most senior person might not be the best collaborator; oftentimes these developers are very busy leading demanding projects of their own and their time is more valuable elsewhere. Your project might also be a prime opportunity for someone to get valuable exposure and visibility beyond their immediate team. Refactoring (particularly refactoring at scale) can be a tricky endeavor, but it's not one that engineers with just a year's (or even some months') experience can't meaningfully contribute to and learn from.

 If you've highlighted a team as being a good set of expert candidates, I recommend talking with their manager directly so that they can vet your request to their team, gauge interest, and help identify a number of potential candidates. Asking the manager for their input in choosing one or two experts from their team can help you minimize the biases you bring to the recruitment process.

Types of Refactoring Teams

We've spent quite a bit of time in this chapter talking about forming a team. But what about your existing team? Are you the best-suited group to take on the proposed refactoring effort? To set yourself up for success as a technical lead for your team, you have to understand why your team is best positioned within the context of your organization to take the project on. There are generally three kinds of teams that undertake large-scale refactoring projects.

Owners

This kind of team owns a particular piece of the product and is refactoring code that it primarily owns or is responsible for. This code interfaces with other teams' code at some number of boundaries. At those boundaries, they must figure out whether to make the changes themselves or coordinate with the engineers whose code they are interfacing with to make the necessary changes.

Say, for instance, you work at a company with three broad engineering groups: developer productivity, infrastructure, and product engineering. You are on the team responsible for testing libraries and tooling for your application in the developer productivity group. While it's always great that engineers across the organization are writing more unit tests, you're worried that the amount of time required to run them all has begun to hinder everyone's ability to ship code quickly. With performance in mind, you start tracking timings for individual unit tests, gathering metrics on how long certain operations like setting up a complex mock state take. Your team decides to kick off a refactor, focusing their efforts on speeding up the mock setup process. Although benchmarks for the new version show a drastic improvement, existing unit tests will need to be migrated to use the new setup logic to benefit from the speedup. There are two main ways to go about the migration:

Option 1: One team migrates all tests

The first option is for your team to migrate everyone's tests for them. This approach has some distinct advantages. Your team is the most familiar with how best to migrate a test from the old to the new mocking logic; you know which kinds of tests lend themselves to easy migrations, the pitfalls to avoid with trickier tests, and how to maximize usage of the new mocking system to reap the most performance improvements. Your team is likely also the most motivated to execute the migration. As owners of the testing framework, you've decided that this is a top priority. You've likely set some quarterly objectives around decreasing the amount of time required to run the full testing suite. Knowing you'll be evaluated on whether your team achieved that goal is *very* motivating (especially when nearing the end of the quarter).

On the flip side, there are thousands of tests to migrate. Your team might develop a clever way to use code modification tools to migrate some of the easiest migration automatically, but that would only get you a small percentage of the way to completion. If you divvied up the remaining callsites evenly across your team, it might still take you weeks of manual, repetitive work to move everything over to the new system. Your team is also not intimately familiar with what each of these tests is actually testing. As much as we'd like to assume that the tests treat the current mocking system as a black box, we can't always predict how tightly coupled the tests might be to the behavior of the existing implementation. There is a strong chance that we will eventually need some context for what (and how) the test is attempting to test functionality to adapt it to use the new mocking system properly.

Option 2: Teams update their own tests

The second option is for the teams in the product engineering group to migrate the tests related to the features that they own themselves. With this approach, your team no longer needs to tackle thousands of tests alone. By distributing the work across the engineering organization, there's a strong chance that the positive impact of the migration will be experienced much more quickly. Engineers on your team also don't need to worry about deciphering how some of the trickier tests work on their own. With each team tasked with updating its own tests, it can do a much more effective job of retaining the intended behavior of the test. (As an added bonus, teams participating in the effort are given a great opportunity to review their current test coverage critically and maybe even improve it beyond shedding a few seconds at runtime.)

This approach comes with a few drawbacks of its own. While you should produce documentation for how to best upgrade a test, regardless of which option your team chooses, the initial quality of (and timely updates to) the documentation becomes much more important with this approach. Engineers actively migrating their tests will rely heavily on your team to answer questions and be available for code reviews. Even if you have an exceedingly thorough document of frequently asked questions readily available, you'll probably still have to answer the same handful of questions more than once.

Although you hope to convince enough engineers that the performance improvements of the new system are worth the effort, there will probably be a number of teams that fail to take the bait. A few teams might commit to the migration but ultimately fail to complete it because building new features was of higher priority. When encouraging other teams to participate in a refactor, even when everyone agrees that the benefits are tangible and significant, be mindful that unless these teams have committed equally, setting quarterly objectives for its completion, your project will be one of the first to be pushed aside.

Striking a balance

Neither option is perfect, but the one you choose will have an impact on your ability to achieve your team's short- and long-term goals as well as on your relationship with other engineering teams. If possible, I recommend mixing the two strategies to minimize the downsides of either approach and maximize your chances of completing the refactor successfully. With our test scenario, for example, here are a few steps I would recommend.

Proposed Approach

1. Have your team identify a few simple tests that might benefit the most from the migration. Reach out to the product engineering teams to get additional context on which tests they deem to have the most impact.

2. Start with Option 1 (see "Option 1: One team migrates all tests" on page 118). Begin migrating the tests manually and document the process thoroughly. (If the tests are clearly owned by a specific team, either give that team a heads up or work with it to complete the migration.)

3. For the migrated test files, run benchmarks to demonstrate the performance impact clearly. Document those, too.

4. Develop a code modification tool to migrate a few simple cases automatically. Run the modification tool on small, logical subsections of the testing suite until all candidate tests have been migrated.

5. Kick off Option 2 (see "Option 2: Teams update their own tests" on page 118). Evangelize the new mocking system by highlighting the benefits and pointing engineers to sample migrations. Spin up office hours to answer questions and troubleshoot with engineers in person. Consider organizing regular jam sessions, when engineers across the organization can join with your team to crank out a few migrations.

6. Work with teams to set quarterly objectives for improving the performance of their tests; if they've committed to being evaluated on their participation in the effort, the chances are better that the tests will get done.

Cleanup Crews

Some larger engineering organizations have teams dedicated to improving developer productivity. The range of the kind of work that these teams take on can be quite wide: they provision and manage development environments; they write editor extensions and scripts to automate repetitive tasks; they build tooling to help developers understand the performance implications of their proposed code changes better; they maintain and expand upon the core libraries all product engineers depend on (including logging, monitoring, feature flags, etc.). More often than not, the developer productivity teams that continue to work alongside product developers within the boundaries of the application end up taking on the role of the cleanup crew.

Cleanup crews take on the important (but often thankless) work of identifying and shedding cruft and antipatterns from a codebase and establishing better, more sustainable patterns in their stead. These teams are usually made up of engineers who care deeply about code health and want their fellow product engineers to have an easy time developing, testing, and ultimately shipping new features. Seeing other developers at the company use (and appreciate) their libraries and tools is what gives them the greatest satisfaction.

Typically, these teams take on hefty refactors for two reasons. First, the teams' breadth of knowledge of the codebase is unparalleled. Because these crews are owners of core, functional libraries, they tend to have at least some exposure to almost every corner of an application. This is especially true of teams that work inside monolithic codebases. Second, the teams value developing ergonomic solutions that are accessible to everyone, regardless of team or seniority; they have valuable experience thinking about what kinds of interfaces strike the right balance between extensible and practical. If the main driving motivation behind the project is to boost developer productivity (and keep it there), then this is the perfect team. A third, implicit reason, is that by having the cleanup crew map out and execute the refactor, product development teams can continue to focus on feature development relatively undisturbed.

Unfortunately, cleanup crews are not sustainable. When these groups are productive, other engineering teams, typically feature-development teams, feel less of a responsibility to commit to doing important maintenance work. Over time, the cleanup crews accrue an insurmountable amount of work, slowly burning out their team members. As a result, these teams are usually short-lived or have high turnover. Furthermore, the teams shirking maintenance work gradually lose the muscle memory associated with supporting features long term. Throwing another large-scale refactor their way might not be a viable option.

Tiger Team

A *tiger team* refers to a team of technical specialists, selected for their experience and energy, assigned to achieve a specific goal. (Just like Ocean's 11!) The term was first coined in a 1964 paper titled *Program Management in Design and Development*, in which tiger teams were suggested as an effective method for improving the reliability of aeronautic and spacecraft systems. One particularly well-known tiger team was assembled after the Apollo 13's service module malfunctioned and exploded in an effort to return the astronauts safely to Earth. The group later received the Presidential Medal of Freedom for their efforts in the mission.

When engineering organizations encounter crises (a sudden, lengthy outage; serious performance problems for an important customer; a sharp decrease in reliability), leadership might ask a cross-functional set of expert engineers to drop whatever they're currently working on and go all-in to solve the problem at hand. Generally, these groups work under some sort of time pressure, whether it is "we need this fixed before X happens" or "we need this fixed as soon as possible," so they tend to be short-lived. Because the focus tends to be on brainstorming and developing a minimum viable solution, large-scale refactoring efforts are not usually the focus of tiger teams, but there are always exceptions. If you're able to make a convincing case to management that your effort solves a problem that is critical to the success of the business, and the scale of the work that needs to be completed is relatively large in comparison to the amount of time available before the problem becomes dire, then a tiger team could be your best option.

The Pitch

Now that we've gained context on the kind of relationship our team has with our refactoring project, determined the expertise we'll need, and brainstormed a list of corresponding experts we hope to recruit, we come to the hard part: convincing them to help us. While we might not be able to offer one eleventh of the 150 million dollars contained inside the Bellagio safe, we can try to make a convincing argument that contributing to the refactor is well worth their time and effort. Different individuals respond differently to a number of techniques, so we'll outline a few here.

Do not be afraid to deploy multiple tactics for a single expert (whether that's a team or an individual). The busiest or the most skeptical experts will likely need more than just a single reason to agree to embark on the journey with you, and rightfully so! As a collaborating expert in any role, you are agreeing to allocate a (maybe significant) portion of your valuable time and energy to the project. If the refactor comes with significant risks (and most do), you are opening yourself up to involvement with incidents. If it's likely to drag on for a while, you may have to pass up other opportunities as they arise. Getting involved with a sizable refactor does not come without its risks. You should not try to minimize those risks; instead, aim to make the experts see that the benefits decisively outweigh them.

Finally, persistence can be a technique on its own. If you've spoken to each of the potential experts for a given expertise on your list and haven't gotten anyone to bite, loop back around. The first few candidates will have had more time to consider the opportunity and you'll probably have a few more tricks up your sleeve from the many other conversations you'll have had to date.

Appealing to an engineer is a different experience from appealing to a team's manager. Engineers are much closer to the code; they experience the pain points your refactor wants to address much more concretely, acutely, and frequently. In my experience, you very rarely have to spend considerable (if any) time convincing engineers that the problem you perceive is an actual problem; they often know exactly why the pain points you're seeking to fix are so important to fix because they've experienced the exact pain on multiple occasions themselves. With engineers, you'll probably be able to use most of the pitching techniques outlined in the upcoming sections successfully (maybe combining a few).

Managers, on the other hand, might only feel the pain from a secondary perspective; for example, they might notice a gradual increase in time estimates suggested by engineers during sprint planning due to an equal increase in complexity of the code. In one-on-ones, some engineers might express frustration with frequent incidents due to brittle, poorly tested code. Managers also often have no incentive to prioritize refactoring over feature development. This is usually because managers are measured on their team's productivity in shipping net new product innovations at a regular cadence. Spending a quarter or two improving the code the team is responsible for so that they can subsequently speed up their development velocity in future quarters is a difficult sell for upper management, so managers don't put up a fight unless there is a dire need for code cleanup. Of the techniques proposed next, I recommend leaning heavily on the metrics and bartering pieces.

 You can ensure that managers are motivated to prioritize code health and quality on their team(s) by explicitly evaluating them on their ability to define measurable goals around it and supporting the team in achieving those goals. It's not always easy to get upper management to buy into adding this as an important evaluation metric, but if you can, it can make a world of difference in how your engineering organization builds and maintains software.

Metrics

In Chapter 3 we explored a variety of ways in which we could quantify the current state of the application before embarking on our refactoring journey. Chapter 4 discussed how to develop a thorough plan of action, complete with a solid set of success metrics determined from the initial measurements taken using the methods outlined in Chapter 3. These metrics can help you build a convincing argument for getting help with your refactoring endeavor.

Typically, these kinds of pitches are most effective with the more skeptical experts and those who are most data-driven in their regular work. These are the engineers who are always asking questions; they actively monitor the p95 response times of APIs their team is responsible for maintaining; they're the first ones to notice an uptick in the average number of database operations hitting a specific shard. Appeal to their analytical side with your own metrics and you might secure yourself a new expert.

First, articulate why the metrics you've chosen are good indicators of the problem. Take the time to explain the relationship carefully among the problems you hope to fix, how you choose to quantify them, and the initial statistics you've gathered. Choose simple metrics first, and then augment your case with additional supporting data points. If you've acquired or generated any visuals that help illustrate the problem, reference them; even those coworkers we think of as numbers people appreciate an explanatory graph or chart every so often.

Juxtapose the starting metrics with your defined success metrics, starting with the desired end state. Afterward, you can walk the expert through the evolution of the metrics throughout the effort, from start to finish. Emphasize that your success metrics decisively show that the refactor would be successful and that they are sufficiently ambitious but achievable.

Generosity

There's an odd cognitive dissonance known as the Benjamin Franklin effect: you have a better chance at getting someone to like you if you ask them for a favor than by doing a favor for them. To give an example, say Charlie asks a favor of Dakota. Dakota happily obliges. The phenomenon follows that Dakota is more likely to do another favor for Charlie than if Charlie had done one for them. The idea is that people help others because they like them, even if they actually don't, because their minds struggle to maintain logical consistency between their actions and perceptions.

Engineers working closely with the code you aim to improve are more likely to understand its pain points. They probably know at least a handful of other engineers (either on their immediate team or in the organization at large) that experience these same pain points regularly. If this expert is the kind of coworker that has a finger on the pulse when it comes to the health of the codebase and the engineering morale surrounding it, there is a strong chance that they have a great deal of empathy for their teammates and you can successfully appeal to their inner altruist.

Ask the expert about the things they've heard their teammates complain about. Make a mental (or written) note of the specific pain points that the refactor intends to fix. Once you've commiserated on the difficulties of the code in its current state, list each of the problems they mentioned and walk through your proposed solution. There might be a few problems that you don't yet have an explicit solution for, and that's perfectly all right! In fact, this is precisely why you reached out to this expert; you seek their perspective on the problems you're trying to solve. Make it clear to them that these are the kinds of insights that they could provide to the project. Finally, emphasize that their contributions would concretely make their coworkers' lives (at least a little bit) more pleasant and more productive. Point to the expected benefits of the refactor and summarize the success metrics (because a multifaceted pitch is ultimately a stronger pitch).

Opportunity

If the expert you're pitching is looking for a good career advancement opportunity or a chance to be more visible to other parts of the engineering organization, a large-scale refactoring project can be the perfect line item on their resume. Earlier in the chapter, we mentioned that some managers might want to identify team members who might both be an asset to the project and gain valuable visibility within the broader engineering organization; if they've provided you with a few names, make sure to have a conversation with them about what kind of growth and visibility these individuals need to get to the next level.

When you sit down with the expert, have a conversation about what types of growth opportunities they're looking for. Hopefully the engineer and their manager are aligned on what behaviors they need to exemplify or projects they need to drive to grow in their career, but that is not always the case. If you want to convince the engineer decisively to join you, all the while setting them up for success, taking the time to coalesce the manager's expectations with those of the engineer is the best approach. From the combined input, take the time to identify a few key portions of the refactor that this expert could contribute to in a way that demonstrates the key characteristics they're looking for. When you meet with them, walk them through each of the milestones and highlight the contributions they can make. Describe how you hope each of these contributions can help them achieve their goals. Be careful to keep an open dialogue, and be open to their input. You're not in their shoes, nor are you their manager, so their perspective on how they can best be set up for success might differ from your own.

Bartering

If all else fails, be ready to barter. Bartering can be a great way to acquire the resources you need to finish your project successfully, with some sort of commitment in return. Typically, bartering doesn't happen between you and another engineer but rather between your own manager and the manager of the team you're seeking help from. The promise you make in return can vary; it's all about finding what the other manager values most and finding an adequate alternative you're happy to provide in exchange. Here are just a few examples:

- Say your team has an open headcount and the team you want to recruit experts from is in desperate need of additional headcount. If your organization allows it, and you are comfortable giving up some of your available headcount, you could provide the team with the headcount it needs in exchange for one or two engineers to contribute actively to the refactoring effort.

- On the off-chance that your teams have compatible feature ownership, you could barter taking additional ownership of some components the other team has been wanting to shed. Oftentimes when teams have unclear or debated boundaries, areas tend to become entirely unowned or tossed between the two teams frequently (which essentially leads them to be unowned). In exchange for help, your team could agree to own those features or components decisively for a set period of time (a few quarters or a year).

- If your engineering organization has communal responsibilities (completing a certain number of hours of customer support or participating in interviews), you can offer for your team to take on some (or all) of the expert team's responsibilities for a defined period after the refactoring effort has wrapped up. (Ideally, you agree for the exchange to kick off only after the project has finished or when it is near completion, because any time taken away from it will only make it drag on, to the detriment of everyone involved.)

When bartering takes place between two engineers, normally it's an exchange of subject matter expertise; that is, the expert you're recruiting as an SME wants you to contribute as an SME on an ongoing or future project. I've also seen engineers agree to trade code review, take on additional on-call shifts if they share a rotation, or agree to document and facilitate a certain number of post-mortems on the expert's behalf.

Be aware that with bartering, either party can fall through on their promise if priorities shift within the duration of the refactoring effort. Reorganizations at companies of any size can render these agreements void due to shifts in management or feature ownership. Managers or engineers leaving the company or switching teams can also have an impact on any prearranged agreements. The longer the refactor goes on, the greater the chance the agreement might fall through for whatever reason.

Repeat

If you cannot convince the first name for each type of expertise, don't worry! This is why brainstorming multiple names early on is important. Ideally, you can secure an expert for each kind of expertise, and if you have trouble coming up with more candidates, consider reaching out to those who've turned down the opportunity for any additional recommendations; they might be able to give you a name or two.

If you cannot secure an expert for a skill that you won't need initially, consider pausing the search and picking it back up once you reach the stage when it becomes necessary. Experts who were previously on the fence might be convinced to join if they see sufficient progress and maybe the hint of a positive shift in the initial metrics. Refactoring can be a little bit like snowballs rolling down a snow hill; as it gains momentum, it affects greater and greater surface area, gathering up more and more resources as it nears completion.

A Few Outcomes

If all the stars align, we might manage to convince everyone we've pitched and assemble the absolute best team for the job. Congratulations! Unfortunately, the ideal outcome is quite unlikely. There's a strong chance you won't be able to assemble your perfect dream team, and that's all right. We can figure out a way to work effectively with the resources we can secure and deliver a quality refactor! Before we close out the chapter, we'll spend some time exploring what a realistic scenario might look like and how to make the most of it. We'll also briefly discuss how to handle the worst-case scenario: having to go it alone.

Realistic Scenario

The most realistic scenario is one in which you end up with a small handful of committed experts and teammates. At smaller companies experiencing a great deal of growth, everyone wears more than one hat and every engineer has a full plate, so it's unlikely you'll be able to get an expert to fill each of your desired kinds of expertise. At larger, more stable companies, you might have a difficult time getting folks from other teams to commit to helping you out simply due to organizational boundaries and priorities; just because someone is an expert in something you'll need context on to complete your refactor successfully doesn't mean that it is that expert's or that expert's management chain's top priority.

Regardless of who you were able to convince before kicking off development, you're in a good spot if you've managed to gather a core team of at least a few engineers for the earliest portions of the project. After all, the team you start with might not be the team you end with, because the support and expertise you need to complete the first few milestones aren't necessarily the support you'll need for the remainder of the project. You might very well be able to encourage others to join you once you've shown some tangible progress and the benefits of the refactor become more visible to fellow engineers.

Worst-Case Scenario

The absolute worst-case scenario is if you aren't able to secure any additional help and need to execute the project alone. Now before we start exploring how to make the best of this situation, I want to take a moment to acknowledge that if your only option is to execute a large, cross-functional refactor alone, you may want to consider not doing it at all. If the engineering organization is not sufficiently convinced by your proposal to allocate staffing properly, and the expert engineers you've reached out to are unconvinced as well, maybe it's time to go back to the drawing board and strengthen your case. Otherwise, maybe it's time to consider that perhaps now is not the right time to execute on this project.

In the event that your manager, teammates, and a number of other engineers believe in the importance of the effort, but there simply aren't enough resources to go around, you may consider moving forward alone. Be forewarned, however, that it is not an easy path. Working alone can be terribly isolating. Because it's just you, slowly making progress one step at a time, it can feel like you aren't making significant progress. You rarely have the chance to bounce ideas off other people who have substantial context on the state of the project and don't need to be brought up to speed every time you need a second opinion.

On the plus side, you don't have to coordinate with anyone else; you hopefully know the sequence of steps you need to take, and you can execute them serially. Not needing to coordinate with anyone else can also be a serious downside. You have to keep very, very good track of everything you are doing and make that information available publicly so that others who are invested in your effort but unable to contribute can gauge where you are on the project.

One or two incidents are nearly inevitable when making expansive changes to a codebase. While postmortems should be blameless, when there is only a single individual responsible for a given project, it can feel as though the burden of responsibility and subsequent remediation falls solely on you instead of on a group of folks.

 I highly recommend taking a look at Etsy's postmortem process (*https://oreil.ly/DFSh_*) developed by John Allspaw if you haven't already. Their approach to incident response is quite thorough and promotes deliberate, focused growth within an engineering organization, all the while preserving individual engineers' psychological safety.

I recommend that you find a buddy, maybe someone else who has also been tasked to be the sole owner of a significant project. This person is there to keep you accountable and motivated, similar to how you might regularly meet up with a friend for yoga: you know that they'll be there because you'll be there, and vice versa. You can establish a regular cadence for meeting up and talking through the progress you've made to date on your respective projects. You can help each other brainstorm solutions to the tough problems, and, on occasion, review each other's code. Either way, having someone there to keep you company on the tough road ahead is absolutely critical to staying on track.

Fostering Strong Teams

You'll need to hone one important skill throughout the entire team-formation process to build an effective team: communication. The best communicators can assemble the best teams by convincing the right engineers to join and setting clear expectations of their involvement from day one. Each contributor, whether they are an active teammate or a subject matter expert, is well aware of their role and responsibilities within the larger effort and feels confident in their ability to deliver on the stated expectations.

Communication continues to be of utmost importance throughout the remainder of your refactoring effort, especially as you begin to make changes to your codebase. In the next chapter, we'll discuss the importance of frequent, thorough updates and explore techniques for establishing and maintaining a free flow of information between your team and those affected by your changes.

PART III

Execution

CHAPTER 7

Communication

A friend of mine, we'll call her Elise, recently embarked on a house-building journey. Over a period of several months, Elise became intimately involved with every step of the process. She coordinated with plumbers, electricians, carpenters, tile-layers, and countless crews cycling in and out of her build site. Each of these professionals worked in tight-knit teams, bringing her home to life, piece by piece.

Every so often, some of Elise's friends, like me, would ask her how the house was coming along. She'd launch into an epic tale about the bathroom tiles, pulling out pictures of samples she considered, detailing the many phone calls required to replace the original batch when most of them arrived cracked. Then she'd realize she hadn't told me about the plans for the second bathroom and pivot to a new set of anecdotes.

I did love hearing about how her house was coming along, but Elise's nonlinear story-telling, coupled with the grueling detail, was a bit too much for me (and many of her other friends). So, after a few conversations, we asked her to start a blog. There, she could document the progress, complete with pictures and arduous detail, and we could periodically check in and casually browse at our leisure. We'd found a way of keeping up with the construction in a medium that worked for everyone.

Elise has a direct, detail-oriented approach in her everyday communication with the construction crews, and more of a big-picture approach in her blog. With a large refactoring project, you have to manage communication hurdles from two distinct perspectives as well: first, within your own team (Elise with her construction crew), and second, with external stakeholders (Elise with her friends). In this chapter, we'll discuss communication techniques you can use to keep both groups informed and aligned. We'll look at important habits you should establish for your team, and some tactics for fostering a productive team. Then we'll look at what measures you should be taking to keep individuals outside of your team in the loop. We'll also discuss some strategies for coping with stakeholders that are either too hands-on or not hands-on enough.

The ideas in this chapter are meant to give you a blueprint for developing strong communication habits on your team. Your company might already have well-established practices around the way large, cross-functional software projects are coordinated, tracked, and reported on. Your manager, product manager, or technical program manager may also have their own ideas of how best to set up your team for success. I recommend listening to these individuals, reading the ideas that follow, and piecing together something that you believe will work best for everyone. Hopefully by the end of this chapter, you'll have a new set of tools ready to use for your next large refactoring project.

Within Your Team

Communication within your team is hopefully already low-friction and frequent. If so, your team is probably participating in a number of exchanges during a regular workday. You're pair-programming, reviewing each other's code, and debugging together. Your team might also have daily stand-up and weekly sync meetings. Many of us don't think about how we're communicating when we're partaking in these interactions. They simply feel like a routine part of our job, as they should. However, some of these interactions could be made a little bit more deliberate to support longer-term, technically complex projects better (like a large-scale refactor.)

A Note About Regular Communication

If your team is not already communicating effectively on a frequent basis, maybe you should consider delaying a large refactoring project until after your team has taken the time to iron out its difficulties. Your team might be suffering from a number of problems. Maybe you're working with a team with conflicting egos, or teammates who spend more time talking than listening. Whatever you're struggling with, your team won't be able to execute well (if at all) on a crucial project without addressing its communication issues. Quite a few resources are available on how to improve team communication, but I recommend picking up a copy of Marshall Rosenberg's *Nonviolent Communication*.

If your team is relatively new or has been formed for the explicit purpose of executing a refactor (as is the case for most tiger teams), spend some time doing one or two team-building exercises first. It's important for the team to feel comfortable with one another going into this sort of project for a few reasons. First, everyone will likely ship one or two bugs at some point. You want your team to be supportive and help you rectify the mistake quickly rather than criticize you for your mistake. Second, you will need to be able to solve tricky problems together; being able to check your ego at the door will help you reach a good solution faster if you aren't worried about which

---

one of you has the best idea. Third, large-scale refactors can drag on for a while. You'll need to be able to give your fellow engineers honest feedback throughout the project so that you can continue to work together effectively. No one wants to grow increasingly irritated with a teammate to the point that they can no longer work with them. Trust me, I've made that mistake.

To keep your team moving forward, free from misunderstandings and other mishaps, there are a few communication habits you should consider implementing from the very start. Some of these concepts will be familiar to those who practice Agile, even minimally. We'll look at both high-frequency habits (i.e., on a daily or weekly basis) and low-frequency habits (i.e., on a monthly or quarterly basis) that are important for taking a critical look back at what you've accomplished to date and what still lies ahead.

 If possible, I recommend instituting a policy of no laptops and minimal phone usage during meetings. Ideally, the only people who should be using a laptop during a meeting are those actively participating by either taking notes, or sharing content on their screen. If a meeting attendee is on call or actively contributing to incident remediation, having a laptop out is more than fine. This policy might sound a bit rigid, but I truly believe that it can benefit everyone. I find that I maintain much better focus during meetings I attend without my computer; I listen more attentively, offer better ideas, and more often leave the meeting feeling that it was productive. If you're curious to give it a try, start out by instituting the policy for just one or two meetings. You might find that they're more productive and, on occasion, end earlier!

Your team is probably communicating pretty frequently in a number of unique ways. During your typical workday, you're probably chatting, pair-programming, reviewing code, and debugging together. There are some more regular, structured means of communication that can be meaningful to make sure that everyone is checking in at a good cadence. We'll outline a few here and describe how they can be valuable.

Stand-Ups

Stand-ups are a great habit for keeping everyone on the team aligned at regular intervals. They can be a good forcing function for you and your teammates to update the status of your tasks within your project planning tool. Stand-ups are also a great opportunity to reflect back on the past 24 hours; have you made sufficient progress or should you reach out to a teammate for a helping hand? Given what you learned yesterday, what do you plan to do today?

Every team has a different approach to stand-ups. Some folks prefer an in-person meeting where everyone gathers around their desks and recites their progress from the day prior. Requiring everyone to be present for stand-ups at a regular time every day has its advantages. They provide engineers with a daily anchor point around which they can plan their work.

When working on large software projects, having a designated time when you can take stock of the progress you've made, however small, is crucial. Sometimes the scope of the effort can seem overwhelming, and being able to focus on incremental steps forward can make it feel more achievable. Daily, in-person stand-ups also provide a forum for everyone to get important face time with one another. As monotonous as stand-ups might seem, if the majority of your team spends a significant portion of its time programming independently, daily stand-ups might be one of the few face-to-face interactions it has.

 When I use the words "in-person," I'm referring to any face-to-face medium. That can be physically in person in the same office or scattered throughout the world and meeting over video conference. The important piece is that everyone is taking the time to see and listen to one another away from distractions.

Other teams prefer an asynchronous way of catching up, relying instead on their main collaboration platform (whether that's Slack, Discord, or a similar tool) to post a summary of their previous workday. One downside of in-person stand-ups is that they require everyone to be available at precisely the same time every day. For highly distributed teams, in-person stand-ups are either very inconvenient or nearly impossible amid a wide array of time zones. They can also awkwardly break up engineers' mornings or afternoons and diminish the amount of time they have to focus deeply on a task at hand.

Effectively refactoring code usually takes acute concentration; you are trying to decipher what the current implementation is doing (by reading through it or running the corresponding unit tests) and then, from that understanding, determine the best way to improve it, and then, finally, craft the improved implementation, replicating the precise behavior of the initial solution. Most programmers need several consecutive hours of uninterrupted time to get into the headspace required to make measurable progress toward a difficult task. If an engineer gets into work at nine o'clock only to be interrupted by a stand-up at 10:30, they might not even bother to start on a task, knowing that they won't make much progress.

To best simulate a stand-up meeting, asynchronous stand-up usually requires the participants to provide an update by a certain time. Say, for instance, your team provides updates asynchronously by 10:30 a.m. every weekday. If you're an early bird and typically get in to the office at 8 a.m., you might provide your update immediately and dive headfirst into your next task. Your fellow teammates submit their updates as they begin working. By 10:30 a.m., if anyone on the team hasn't written anything yet, they might get a gentle nudge from your manager until everyone's given an update.

You can continue to hold daily stand-ups when working on a large-scale refactor, but you may want to revisit their frequency throughout its execution. For example, if your team has entered a milestone with highly parallelized workstreams, updating one another on these distinct, loosely related streams on a daily basis might not be a good use of time. If your updates are highly technical and detail-oriented, most of your teammates won't have the granular context needed to appreciate them. Instead of a daily stand-up, you could consider providing more comprehensive updates twice a week or during a weekly sync.

Weekly Syncs

Daily stand-ups are meant to convey a quick snapshot of everyone's progress; they are not a one-size-fits-all means of regular communication with your team. Think about the half-hour stand-up. If your team members are spending a considerable amount of time discussing at great depth their tasks and the problems they're solving during the stand-up, you should consider two options. The first is to ask them to continue their discussion after the stand-up; if the conversation does not involve a significant portion of your team, that should work just fine. Your second option is to begin hosting a weekly sync. This forum should give your team more dedicated time to dig into the topics most top of mind for them.

With large refactoring efforts, because the affected surface area can be quite substantial, a range of engineers from across the organization will typically be involved. When the team is highly cross-functional, with not all members devoting 100 percent of their time to the refactor, a weekly sync is usually a better option than a daily stand-up. With a weekly half-hour or one-hour meeting, the team members can focus on discussing only the updates that are pertinent to the refactor.

I would recommend budgeting about an hour for a weekly sync. You can structure a weekly sync as you would a stand-up, with a few tweaks. For the first half of the meeting, have everyone take turns sharing what they've accomplished in the refactor over the previous week. If you expected to make more progress, you should hypothesize about why that is: Did you run into roadblocks? Did other, nonrefactor work take center stage? It's just as important for the team to know what's holding up the project as it is to know what everyone's working on. This way, if work needs be redistributed to keep the project moving forward, the team can spot it right away and pivot accordingly. As you go around the room, make note of any topics that folks might want to discuss at greater length.

For the second half of the meeting, take the time to discuss any important topics. You can gather these topics throughout the week and come to the weekly sync with a complete agenda. Maybe, for example, a teammate discovered a new edge case during testing. Although this was probably discussed in a stand-up at some point, you may want to discuss the edge case further during the weekly sync and give the team a chance to amend the rollout approach to make sure similar edge cases are properly handled.

You can also gather discussion topics during everyone's updates, keeping an ear open for any intriguing subjects. For instance, a teammate might have mentioned spending time prototyping a way to automate the more repetitive portions of the refactor. Others on the team might benefit from learning more about this prototype and how they can leverage it themselves. As always, practice good meeting etiquette and make sure that everyone has an opportunity to share their thoughts.

Strong teams are built through strong connections, and strong connections are built through meaningful in-person interactions. Weekly syncs are the perfect forum for solidifying your relationship with your teammates. Why is building a strong team so important? Having a team that supports one another can be particularly helpful when the going gets tough. For example, if someone on the team ships a change that causes a serious regression, knowing that the team has their back and one or two teammates will be happy to jump in to help resolve the issue can substantially reduce their anxiety and, in the long run, prevent burnout. Being able to show up for one another is also really important when the work starts to drag.

Most large-scale refactors have sizable milestones consisting of tedious, repetitive work. (All of the examples in this book to date have one or two lengthy, monotonous steps.) These milestones tend not to be exceptionally challenging or engaging; they're dull but necessary. When the team needs to execute these stages, usually the project starts to feel as though it has slowed to a crawl. Teammates can be more prone to burnout during these stages, but having a group of individuals you can lean on, with which you can share your frustrations, can make a world of difference. If someone on the team is having a difficult time finding the energy to continue, maybe someone else with a bit more capacity can step in and lend a helping hand.

Be certain to take notes during your weekly sync so that you have a record of everything that was discussed (and any conclusions drawn by the team). These notes, combined with the tasks you've been tracking in your project management software, will be helpful when you need a quick reference of everything that's been achieved by the team for your next retrospective.

Weekly syncs can be combined with stand-ups, or replace stand-ups entirely. In my experience, I've found that even with daily or twice-a-week stand-ups, having a weekly team sync is incredibly beneficial because it gives everyone an open forum to discuss the week's most important topics in greater depth. I would especially recommend holding a weekly sync if your team opts for asynchronous stand-ups; this way, everyone has an opportunity to interact in person on a regular basis. Try out different variations of stand-ups (asynchronous or in-person, daily or every other day), combined with a weekly sync, and see what works best for your team.

Retrospectives

Retrospectives are just as beneficial to teams executing on a large-scale refactor as they are to Agile product development teams. They give your team an important opportunity to reflect on the latest iteration cycle, highlight opportunities for improvement, and identify any actions you can take moving forward. Setting time aside to discuss what went well, what could have gone better, and what you plan to change is an essential part of growing a team as a unit and as individuals.

The vast majority of Agile development teams participate in regular retrospectives at different cadences. Some product-focused teams will hold a retrospective (a retro) after the launch of a new feature or after a set number of development cycles. Teams working on longer-term projects might hold a retro once a month or once a quarter. Large, at-scale refactors typically benefit most from retrospectives at the end of major milestones. These are usually lengthy enough to have substantial content to consider, but not so large that the team has trouble remembering everything that's unfolded since the last retrospective. On occasion, smaller subtasks within a single milestone may feel notable enough to justify a retro of their own; there is no perfect, one-size-fits-all answer for all teams and all refactors. If you're inclined to think a retrospective is worthwhile, simply ask your team whether it agrees. If it does, schedule one; if it doesn't, simply wait until the team's completed the next substantial set of work.

If you aren't confident in your ability to run a good retrospective, there are plenty of publicly available resources to help you. Atlassian (*https://oreil.ly/kgz9y*) has quite a few articles and blog posts on its website, outlining best practices and exploring original ideas for spicing up your retros.

Outside Your Team

As with any large-scale software project, a fair share of individuals outside your team will have an interest in your progress. This could include upper management, engineers on affected teams, or senior technical leaders. Upper management will want to check in on the project to ensure that the refactor is progressing at the expected pace and producing the expected results. From its perspective, large refactoring efforts can easily turn into money pits: valuable, expensive engineering time is spent rewriting functionality that already exists, and if the project strays, the time and financial investment only increases. There's also the matter of opportunity cost, as we discussed in Chapter 5, when managers have to weigh the refactor against further feature development. Upper management will want to be reassured regularly that its decision to invest in the refactor was a good one, and if at any point it determines otherwise, it will likely hatch plans for either pausing or stopping the refactor altogether. You can make sure that it continues to support your effort by honing your communication skills when providing updates outside of your team.

Managers and engineers on teams affected by the refactor will want to keep track of each stage of the project to gauge when they risk bearing its effects. They'll want to know precisely when the team expects to roll out relevant changes and how long it anticipates it will take. Meanwhile, senior technical leaders will be on the lookout for any setbacks as an opportunity to help steer the project back in the right direction. Typically, these individuals play an important role in shaping the company's technical vision and are responsible for ensuring that complex, important technical endeavors succeed, including any large-scale refactors.

In this section, we'll discuss how you can ensure that all your external stakeholders stay up to date with the latest progress on your refactor. We'll first look at some work you can do upfront to set good habits early, and then we'll look at how you can keep up with external communication throughout the project's execution.

When Kicking Off the Project

There are some important preliminary decisions you'll want to make about how you plan to communicate with your external stakeholders when you kick off your refactor. By making these decisions early, you'll help your team save valuable time when coordinating with colleagues outside of your team and decrease the overall likelihood of any miscommunication with external parties.

Choosing a single source of truth

Even the smallest companies use a number of tools for the same set of tasks. Your company might use both GSuite and Office 365, with some departments preferring one product over another. Even within your own engineering organization, you may have documents speckled across GSuite, GitHub, and an internal wiki. As someone searching for information about a product feature or in-flight project, having to search half a dozen platforms for disjointed pieces of information is aggravating. It can be even more frustrating when pertinent information is in more than one location, and the information doesn't agree.

When you kick off your refactor, choose a platform your team enjoys using to collect all documentation related to the project. Because you'll be regularly creating new documents and updating existing ones, you'll want to choose the solution that has all your favorite bells and whistles. If you're annoyed every time you need to add something new, you'll be less likely to do it, and the documentation will fall out of date.

Within your chosen platform, create a directory to house all pertinent documentation; this will serve as your single source of truth. Documentation can include technical design specifications, the execution plan you developed in Chapter 4, meeting notes, postmortems, and so on. Wherever other engineers look for documentation, either link to your directory or, better yet, link to a specific document within it. If your colleagues have muscle memory from searching GitHub for technical documentation but you prefer writing in Notion, create an entry for your documentation in GitHub and link it directly to your Notion entry. This way, not only will your documentation be easy to find, you'll be certain that there aren't any outdated copies floating around.

As your team generates documentation throughout the execution of the project, make sure that it all lands in your project directory (with updated external links from other widely used document sources).

Setting expectations

Next, you'll want to set expectations with external stakeholders. Many of these stakeholders will regularly check in with you, polling for new information. Unfortunately, this model can become quite bothersome the more stakeholders you have. If you or your manager receives an email or message every time someone in upper management has a question about how the refactor is progressing, before long, you'll end up spending quite a bit of time answering these requests. On the other hand, there may be some stakeholders that you wish would check in periodically but unfortunately do not. When this is the case, your team must push information out. Consistently needing to propagate information proactively out to numerous stakeholders can get irritating, particularly if the receiving party doesn't acknowledge that they've read the information you provided.

Instead of either answering each request or contacting each stakeholder individually, spend some time determining how you intend to communicate progress and setting up expectations with your stakeholders early about where and with what frequency they should expect these communications. When stakeholders break from the patterns you've established (e.g., you get a ping from your skip-level), instead of providing the information directly, simply reply with a gentle reminder of where they can find what they need.

When you kick off the refactor, take some time to draft a rough communication plan. This plan should include information about the following:

Where stakeholders can find information about the current stage of the refactor
There are a number of places where you can make this information easily accessible to external parties. If your team uses Slack, you can create a channel to house conversations pertinent to the refactor and set the channel's topic to a short description of the current stage of the project. At the end of the week, post a weekly round-up message detailing the progress made over the past few days. (If you hold weekly sync meetings, you can draft this message immediately afterward and link to your meeting notes.) If your team uses JIRA, provide a link to the project board. For stakeholders who need regular, high-level updates, consider adding a summary field that the team updates weekly on the top-level project.

Where stakeholders can find a high-level project timeline
You can include a high-level project timeline at the root of your project documentation directory, directly within the communication plan itself, or as a subsection to your execution plan. Make sure to keep this timeline updated if any dates end up shifting as the project progresses.

Where engineers can expect to find technical information about the refactor
Here, you can link to the directory where your team intends to draft documentation related to the refactor. Provide a short summary of the kinds of documents the team plans to aggregate there.

Where stakeholders can ask questions
There will be instances when individuals across the company will either not be able to find the information they need in the provided resources, or prefer asking the question directly rather than locate the information for themselves. When that happens, you'll want to make sure that they know where to go. If your team uses Discord, either direct them to the project channel or set up a channel exclusively for questions. If your team relies on email and it has an email group, have the members send an email to the team as a whole rather than to an individual. If your team is cross-functional, set up an email group for everyone involved and direct questions to that group.

When affected teams should expect to hear from you
When coordinating with teams that risk being affected by the refactor, you want to maintain a high level of transparency. You want to make sure that no one on these teams is surprised or set back by the work your group is doing. To make

sure that everyone is on the same page, provide a list of guidelines you intend to follow when interacting with other teams' code. This could include tagging one or more individuals from that team for code review when modifying code for which their team is responsible or attending their stand-up to provide updates on the refactor when pertinent to their team.

During Project Execution

There are a few communication habits your team should consider adopting during the project's execution. These strategies can help everyone at the company stay informed of your progress while minimizing the amount of proactive outward communication your team needs to do. We'll also discuss how best to engage with engineers external to the team when seeking out their expertise about the project.

Progress announcements

Progress announcements are not only important to let everyone know that you've completed another milestone (and unlocked any number of benefits as a result), they are also crucial in continuing to make your team feel productive and boost their morale. Large-scale refactors can feel daunting for teams, even for teams accustomed to working on lengthy projects. Celebrating each milestone as it wraps up helps everyone feel a sense of achievement throughout the duration of the project.

However your company announces the launch of new features, whether that's a department-wide email or a message in a Slack channel, inquire about providing important progress updates for the refactor. Your team will get important recognition for their hard work and demonstrate to a wide audience that refactoring is a valued engineering investment.

Execution plan

In Chapter 4, we learned how to draft an effective execution plan for our large-scale refactor. We can go beyond using this plan as a simple road map and use it as a place to document our work throughout the project's progression. Make a copy of the original execution plan. The original version should remain relatively untouched beyond light updates to estimates and milestone metrics as necessary. The copy will serve as a living version of the original document and should be progressively updated as the project develops. (Enabling version history will give you the ability to easily go back in time and compare your initial values with your latest updates.) This could include anything from strange bugs encountered, unexpected edge cases uncovered, or diversions in the plan. This second version of your original execution plan should give any stakeholders a much more nuanced view into your progress and help your team keep better track of the work it has achieved to date.

For instance, in our example from Chapter 4, the software team at Smart DNA was tasked with migrating all Python 2.6 environments to Python 2.7. We've copied over the first milestone of the team's execution plan as follows:

- Create a single *requirements.txt* file.
  - — **Metric:** Number of distinct lists of dependencies; **Start:** 3; **Goal:** 1
  - — **Estimate:** 2–3 weeks
  - — **Subtasks:**
    - — Enumerate all packages used across each of the repositories.
    - — Audit all packages and narrow list to only required packages with corresponding versions.
    - — Identify which version each package should be upgraded to in Python 2.7.

As the software team begins making progress on the migration, it might start filling in the copy of its original plan with more context on its findings. We can see some of those additional details in the plan that follows:

- Create a single *requirements.txt* file.
  - — **Metric:** Number of distinct lists of dependencies; **Start:** 3; **Goal:** 1
  - — **Estimate:** 2–3 weeks
  - — **Subtasks:**
    - — **Enumerate all packages used across each of the repositories.** When we started combing through all of the packages used by the first of the three repositories, we were surprised that the code relied on six additional dependencies that weren't explicitly listed in the respective *requirements.txt* file. The researchers were able to provide an updated list for the first repository as well as in the 10 other dependencies missing from the *requirements.txt* files for the other two repos.
    - — **Audit all packages and narrow list to only required packages with corresponding versions.** Thankfully, 80 percent of the packages used by the three repos were the same. Of that set, only eight of those packages had different versions that needed to be reconciled.
    - — **Identify which version each package should be upgraded to in Python 2.7.** This was tricky for seven of the packages in the final, combined set. For these packages, their 2.7-compatible versions deprecated a number of APIs and features that the researchers actively used in two of the three repos. We worked with the research team to gradually migrate away from using these deprecated features before continuing with the refactor.

Updating the execution plan as you go means that others can reference it throughout the project's lifetime to get more context on the specific work the team is doing during each of its many stages. Any SMEs joining the project at a later milestone (or any new teammates being onboarded partway through the refactor) can ramp up on everything the team's worked on to date just by reading through the execution plan. If you're anything like me, sometimes you forget why you made a certain decision several months ago; by keeping a verbose account of everything you've encountered and the conclusions you've reached along the way, you can easily go back and remind yourself of precisely what happened and why.

A detailed account of the team's experience can also be helpful for engineers and managers referencing the refactor well after it's completed. Engineers seeking to understand how the codebase has evolved over time may want to read your detailed plan. For the engineers involved with your refactor seeking a promotion, having concrete documentation pointing to the highly technical problems they solved at each step can be incredibly valuable. Elsewhere at the company, engineers looking to kick off their own large-scale refactor might look to your documentation for an example of how to execute a substantial refactor successfully.

Seeking feeback from senior engineers

All of us seek advice from peers and experienced colleagues when solving difficult problems. While we might be eager to request feedback from senior engineering leaders (and benefit greatly from it), getting and retaining their attention can be notably difficult. Whether they've been engaged with the refactor from day one as SMEs (see Chapter 6), or are just getting up to speed, they'll likely be slower to respond to your inquiries simply because they are unusually busy with many responsibilities across a multitude of projects. Ideally, if you are able to communicate your expectations appropriately, none of these individuals should become bottlenecks.

 The term "senior engineer" here refers to the most experienced individual contributors within a team, department, or company at large, not to be confused with the title, Senior Engineer, held by many professionals in the industry. These are usually the folks with much bigger titles like Senior Staff, Principle, or Distinguished Engineer. Sometimes, these are simply the folks who have been at the company the longest.

When soliciting feedback from these senior engineer leaders, we must first decide the scope of the feedback we're looking for. This is helpful for two main reasons. First, explicitly defining which aspects of the problem or solution we want our colleague to evaluate ensures that we won't get unexpected, frustrating feedback on pieces we've already nailed down. Second, they'll be able to focus immediately on just the essential pieces, saving them a great deal of time and energy they would have otherwise spent assessing a much greater problem.

Next, we have to determine how crucial their feedback is to the momentum of the project; that is, can you continue to make progress without their input? If you believe you can continue to make progress without their opinion, be explicit about it. This way, the engineer can properly prioritize giving you the feedback you need against similar requests they might be juggling from other engineers across the company. If you believe their input is required for your team to continue making progress, letting them know that they are now a blocker should give them adequate urgency to get back to you quickly. Regardless of the urgency, you should set some clear expectations for when you need their feedback by so that no one is left twiddling their thumbs.

If you've let a senior engineer know that their insights are a blocker, set expectations for when you'd like to have heard from them, and if you are still waiting for a reply, it's time to get assertive. If their calendar isn't flooded with meetings, book some time with them one on one to discuss the item at hand. (Be certain that your meeting description has all the pertinent details!) If you just need a few minutes of their time, try stopping by their desk and seeing whether they're available to chat, or catch them on their way out of a meeting. It's much more difficult to put off talking to someone when you're face to face.

We also need to consider how crucial the senior engineer leader believes their own feedback is to the momentum of the project. If you both agree that their input is not a blocker, great! But if there's a chance that they'll be surprised and disgruntled if you move forward without taking their opinion into consideration, you need to be aware of it so that everyone's expectations are properly aligned.

To illustrate this in action, let's say you're working on a prototype for a new library you're building as part of a large refactor. Your prototype defines some basic interfaces, with a handful of temporary, incomplete implementations. You put up your changes for code review, complete with a short description and links to a design document your team developed. You want some feedback from a senior engineer, so you tag them and a few other teammates for review. Unfortunately, you forget to tell the senior engineer that you're looking for feedback on the interfaces (not the implementations) and are hoping to merge these changes within the next week.

A few days pass with comments from your teammates but nothing from the senior engineer. You send them a message asking whether they've had a chance to take a look at the code review. They assure you that they saw the request and that they intend to get to it by the end of the week. After some back and forth with your teammates, you decide to merge the prototype and continue iterating on it in subsequent code reviews.

A day later, the senior engineer opens up your code review and begins to read through it. They immediately begin commenting on the implementation details, becoming increasingly alarmed as they realize that the code has already been merged. Now everyone's irritated: you're irritated that the senior engineer took too long to review your changes and ultimately focused on the wrong aspect of the code; they're irritated that they left comments on what turned out to be temporary code and that you've merged your changes without waiting for their input. All of the disappointment and miscommunication could have been avoided had the right expectations been set from the start.

Working Alone

In the unfortunate circumstance when you've been tasked with executing a refactor alone, you need your external communication to be much more frequent and deliberate than if you were working with a team. Why? When you're working by yourself, it's far too easy to forget that others are concerned with your progress. You might forgo using any project management software, relying instead on a series of sticky notes strewn across your desk. You might still be required to participate in broader team rituals such as a daily stand-up or weekly sync but feel a strong disconnect when engaging in these tasks, given that your colleagues have limited context on your work.

Even if your manager is supportive of your work, you need to find a way to make it accessible to a broader set of colleagues; this includes fellow teammates, engineers in other parts of the organization, and upper management. To put it bluntly, everyone but you is an external stakeholder. You should consider using all the techniques outlined in "Outside Your Team" on page 138 and modifying the techniques from "Within Your Team" on page 132. Here are a few ideas:

- If you are still required to participate in daily stand-ups with colleagues not engaged with the refactor, consider jotting down your updates somewhere that is easily accessible to external stakeholders. If not, you could host your own asynchronous stand-up, writing about what you achieved yesterday and what you hope to achieve today; if you find project management tools useful, you might use this time to update your tasks, using whatever lightweight process works best for you.

- If your team is still hosting weekly syncs and encourages everyone to submit agenda items, hold yourself to adding at least one topic every week. This will help keep everyone on your team aware of the work you're doing and will hopefully give you some exposure to different perspectives on the problems you're solving. If you don't have weekly syncs, consider blocking out an hour regardless. You can use this time to review your work to date and update any documentation. (I find

---

that I have a much easier time keeping documents up to date when I specifically allocate time for it.) You might also consider writing a weekly summary and posting it somewhere others can readily consume it.

- Host office hours when any external stakeholders (including engineers from affected teams) can come ask questions about the refactor or talk through a problem with you. The best cadence for these will depend on how often you're making changes to others' code and how engaged these engineers are with the refactor; you can probably start off with twice a month and decrease or increase the frequency as needed.

Always Iterate

If there's only one thing you take away from this chapter, it should be this: there is no single correct communication strategy. Every refactor needs different communication strategies, and these strategies can change throughout the lifetime of the project. The habits you establish should be molded by each of the facets that makes the refactor unique: the team you've gathered, the engineering groups affected by the changes, and the level of involvement of external stakeholders.

If at any point you find that your habits are no longer serving you well, shake things up! In the best case, great communication habits can keep your team working effectively at a sustainable, steady pace. In the worst case, bad communication habits can hold your team back and actively prevent the project from moving forward. If something isn't working, you're much better off attempting to change it than sticking with habits that could slow you down.

Our next chapter continues with the theme of establishing patterns that help you and your team execute in a productive way. We'll highlight an assortment of ideas (both technical and nontechnical) your team might want to try throughout the refactor's development.

CHAPTER 8

Strategies for Execution

Opened in 1904, the New York City subway is among the world's oldest and most-used public transit systems, serving just under six million riders on an average week-day. Those of us who are intimately familiar with the sprawling network have developed dozens of tiny optimizations that make riding the subway second nature. We listen for announcements to changes in service late at night on a Tuesday. We know the precise force and angle with which to scan our MetroCards through the turnstiles. For newcomers to the city, we can share some of these small but mighty tips to make their first few trips a bit less hectic.

Think of this chapter as like the friendly New Yorker giving you advice as you set out to navigate the city's subway system. It contains a medley of tips for promoting smooth execution throughout a refactor. We'll first touch on good team-building practices. There are a handful of ways we can go beyond establishing regular communication habits to keep our teammates productive and happy. Next, we'll cover a few items you should be keeping track of during the refactor to make sure that you're staying on course and know precisely what to attend to when you've reached the final stages of the refactor. Finally, we'll discuss a few coding strategies to keep sturdy reins on the refactor as you're implementing it.

Team Building

In Chapter 6, we examined a few reasons having a strong team is important within the context of large software projects, including ambitious refactors. We mostly focused on the benefits of having reliable teammates during difficult times (e.g., when the project reaches a mundane stage or hits a new roadblock). What we didn't mention is that teams that work well together are more creative, learn more from one another, and ultimately solve problems better and faster. To that goal, it's vital for you and your teammates to prioritize regularly participating in team-building activities.

The options outlined here are not exhaustive, but I believe that they are some of the most useful habits to develop to strengthen your relationship with your teammates. Once you've built up the muscle memory around them, they'll become second nature and will surely make the refactor fly by smoothly.

Pair Programming

Pair programming is a great team-building tool. Working on a problem together gives the participants a great opportunity to learn each other's strengths (and weaknesses) in a collaborative, low-stakes environment. If your team hasn't had much experience working together yet, consider encouraging them to pair upon a handful of tasks at the onset of the project. Starting early is important; not only does a new project give you the unique opportunity to set good habits from the very start, understanding your teammates' abilities early can help the project start off on the right foot and continue to make forward progress efficiently.

More practically, pair programming can also be a great way to transfer knowledge from one teammate to another. Engineers who are alone in understanding one or more pieces of a given system are a liability to your project and, not infrequently, your company as whole. In many cases, these engineers may feel that they are unable to take time off or completely disconnect from work for a few days out of fear that they'll be needed in the event of an emergency with the part of the system only they know. To ensure that no single developer on your team is a knowledge island, you can set up pairing sessions as a means of transferring their expertise to others on the team. Evenly distributing knowledge across each of your team members lightens the load on any single developer if problems arise with any aspect of the refactor.

Pairing can also be a great way to debug or solve a difficult or abstract problem. We say two heads are better than one for a reason: by having two engineers thinking through the same problem, you're more likely to come up with a greater variety of solutions, landing on one that works well sooner. The active back and forth helps you address disagreements head-on, refining your solution more effectively. As you navigate through the problem together, you'll end up making fewer mistakes; in fact, research out of the University of Utah (*https://oreil.ly/yA75W*) shows that code written in pairs results in about 15 percent fewer bugs. Finally, you're less likely to get distracted; because you're both committing the time and energy to solving a problem together, reasoning through the problem out loud, the temptation to check your email or shoot someone a message decreases.

Refactoring in pairs can be particularly effective because while one person is typing, the other is freer to think about the bigger picture. When refactoring, it's easy to get stuck in the weeds trying to untangle what often tends to be confusing, legacy code. Your pair can help you regain focus on the greater goal and, by thinking through the problem a few steps further, point out any pitfalls you may run into earlier in the development process.

Pair programming isn't without its downsides, however. When it comes to scoping out a problem or learning something new (e.g., using a framework, adopting a tool, learning a programming language), some engineers, including me, prefer to do so on their own. I find that I'm able to retain important concepts better if I stumbled through learning them the first time around. For problems that are well-defined and relatively straightforward to solve, pairing isn't a particularly productive approach; while there is a slight chance you might solve the task more quickly and produce a less buggy outcome, tying up two engineers' time on a simple task is not always the best use of resources on your team.

Pairing can also be a draining task for the duo. Needing to articulate your thinking process over a sustained period of time takes up quite a bit more energy than quietly working on your own, reasoning through the problem internally. By the end of a pairing session, you might need to take a break and switch gears to recharge. For developers who aren't great verbal communicators, pairing can be especially challenging, making any pair programming exercise feel like a chore. This is why it's important to be mindful of every one of the team's abilities and preferences when advocating for pairing.

In being mindful of drawbacks, here are a few recommendations for how to institute pairing on your team:

Encourage pairing, but do not make it mandatory
There's a strong chance that some members of your team are great proponents of pair programming and others are not. By highlighting its benefits and underscoring your support for the practice, you'll hopefully convince those who are on the fence (or have never tried it before) to give it a go. (And hopefully, after having tried it, they'll be eager to repeat the exercise.) On the other hand, forcing those who are uncomfortable to pair can be a recipe for disaster; they may grow to resent the team and the project, leading them to seek a way out.

Pair engineers with similar levels of experience
Unless you're using pair programming as a tool to teach something specific to someone more junior, you're better off pairing like-skilled engineers. When working through a difficult problem or debugging an issue, developers who are at a similar level are less likely to be frustrated by the other's lack of experience. You'll more effectively bounce ideas off of one another if you're at comparable levels in your technical ability.

Timebox the session
Because pair programming can be taxing, it's important to give the session a well-defined cut-off (with breaks as needed). Start with an hour, and if you come to

the end of the time and you have the energy (and time) to keep going, extend your session by another hour. Give each other an opportunity to call it a day; you don't want the pairing to stretch beyond either of your capacities and risk needlessly decreasing the efficiency of the session.

Keeping Everyone Motivated

In Chapter 4, we discussed building a focused, properly balanced execution plan that gives the team enough flexibility to prevent exhaustion. We can further ensure that our teams stay motivated throughout a long at-scale refactor by taking the time to recognize our teammates and celebrate our achievements along the way. Your team doesn't need a massive budget for branded mugs or access to coveted off-site activities to build meaningful connections across the team or highlight the group's contributions. There are a number of simple but effective ways to keep everyone's morale up.

Motivating individuals

First, we'll consider how we can keep individuals motivated. One of the more compelling ways we can boost a teammate's drive is by giving them the opportunity to contribute to the refactor in a way that best leverages their unique skills and abilities. Your teammates will be much happier (and likely more productive) if they are working on pieces of the refactor that they find to be the most rewarding. If your teammates are looking for opportunities to grow, whether by developing a new technical skill or by overseeing a more significant portion of the project, do your best to make these opportunities available to them. Remember how you pitched this teammate the idea of joining your effort in Chapter 6 by offering them the opportunity for greater visibility or responsibility (and perhaps even a promotion.)

If possible, give your teammates the flexibility to choose when, where, and how they work. Not everyone is cut out to work from 9 a.m. to 5 p.m. with a half hour for lunch at noon every day. Some might prefer to come in to the office at the crack of dawn and head out in the early afternoon. Others might only log on midmorning, pick up their children midafternoon, and wrap up after dinner. If you can accommodate your teammates' assorted schedules while continuing to maintain good communication practices (see Chapter 7), they will be not only be thankful, but likely even more productive overall!

Recognizing individual teammates for their distinct contributions is a great way to keep them motivated. By showing them that you and the rest of your team appreciate their hard work, you're reaffirming that they are doing the right thing, encouraging them to keep going, and fostering a sense of belonging on the team. Recognition can take just about any shape: it can be through a formalized department- or company-wide program, or can be as simple as crafting a handwritten note. Be mindful of your teammates' preferred way of being recognized. Although some enjoy hearing their name called out at an all-hands, others shy away from public praise. Recognition in the wrong form is at best not very effective, and at worst a total fiasco. Sometimes, a thoughtful email or glowing peer review is more than enough.

 Your manager can be a great asset for helping you set up ways to recognize your team as a whole. (You'll probably need their support if you're hoping to get a budget for whatever you're planning to put together.) That said, there is unique value in having the team recognize its peers.

You could, for example, put together a lightweight "Win of the Week" tradition. To kick it off, the team acquires a small trophy (or any item clearly visible from a teammate's desk) and chooses someone to recognize for excellent work done over the previous week. This could be anything from stepping in to help resolve a tricky bug, or crafting a great description for a given patch. The following week, the winner chooses the next winner, passing on the trophy. The tradition continues until the project wraps up or until the team chooses to retire it.

Motivating teams

Next, we'll take a look at helpful methods for keeping your team motivated as a whole. A near foolproof way to get everyone excited about doing great work is to turn it into a game. By gamifying the more mundane portions of the refactor, you may find your teammates eager to complete tasks and progressing toward milestones more quickly. A good example might be a simple game of Bingo. Identify small but important contributions your team can make during the refactor's current milestone and plop them into a Bingo game sheet generation tool. These can be as simple as pairing with someone on a difficult problem or completing 10 code reviews. You can print out the boards and distribute them to your team and offer a small prize for winners.

When gamifying any number of tasks, be mindful not to incite too much competition. While it can be a great motivator, if it gets out of hand you'll risk sparking conflict and seeing morale and teamwork deteriorate. Incorporate aspects of teamwork into the game deliberately; this will encourage everyone to pull up those around them and further solidify your team. With a large-scale refactor, there is very little room (if any) for sloppy execution, so you'll also want to be careful to chiefly incentivize the quality of the work rather than its completion. If you put emphasis on reaching the finish line, your teammates might cut some corners in an attempt to get there faster.

When planning estimates for smaller subtasks within larger project milestones, consider gamifying part of the process. Have each member of the team submit their best guess of when you'll hit a target metric, following *The Price is Right* rules (i.e., closest without going over). When you reach the metric, recognize the winner with a drumroll reveal at your next team meeting. Everyone will get a kick out of trying to hit the nail on the head and your estimates might get better over time!

Finally, remember to celebrate your team's achievements with a gathering or two speckled throughout the project, particularly after concluding significant milestones. Moments of celebration help create sustained engagement and maintain good morale. If the team never has the opportunity to hit pause and commemorate each other's efforts, your refactor will begin to feel like an endless rat race. Carve out some time to bring everyone together whichever way works best, whether that's a team potluck lunch or a midafternoon coffee toast. You'll all be thankful to have taken a moment to reflect on your accomplishments.

Keeping a Tally

As you're executing your refactor, it's important to check on your progress frequently and maintain a running tally of important findings. By measuring and reflecting often, you'll be more confident that the project is headed in the right direction and decrease the likelihood that your team forgets something important in the final stages of the refactor. Be certain to continue to update the living version of your execution plan, discussed in "Execution plan" on page 141, with your midproject updates.

Intermediate Metric Measurements

In Chapter 3, we examined a number of distinct ways to characterize the problems we aim to fix with our refactor. We later used those metrics to inform our execution plan, and further broke down the project into individual milestones, each with its own set of metrics. We shouldn't lose sight of these goals while actively executing the refactor at the risk of veering off course. With every ambitious software project, there is a significant and dangerous opportunity for scope creep at every turn.

By measuring the team's progress toward each intermediate metric on a weekly (or biweekly) basis, you are holding yourselves responsible for moving the needle forward on the goals you've identified as the most important. With frequent check-ins, the team is less likely to give in to the temptation to embark on any tangential side quests, allowing for the project scope to increase. Periodic check-ins also give you the ability to assess your velocity. If everyone is focused on the right tasks, but there is little positive change in the metrics for several weeks in a row, something is clearly amiss. Perhaps the team is struggling to make substantial progress because it continues to encounter a number of difficult bugs, or the metrics are not ideal candidates for conveying your team's contributions. Whatever the underlying dilemma, you'll know you successfully solved it when you begin to notice a good change in your metrics once more.

Unearthed Bugs

Regardless of whether your refactor is motivated by the desire to surface and fix systemic bugs, you are bound to encounter a handful of defects throughout the endeavor. For each bug, no matter what you decide to do about it (fix it or not), you should document when in the project it was uncovered, the conditions under which it arises (for easy reproduction), and what actions were taken as a result. There are typically two options when confronting a bug within the context of a refactor; the first is to fix the bug, and the other is to reimplement it.

Consider the case in which your team fixes the bug. If the fix is easy and clean as a result of the refactor, having an example you can quickly reference to demonstrate its efficacy is convenient to show it to stakeholders or share it with peers. Sometimes, just one or two thorny, well-documented bugs can convince anyone who was initially on the fence about the refactor that it is well worthwhile. On the other hand, if your team ports the bug into the refactor, you'll need to know precisely where to find it and how to reproduce it either to fix it or to hand it off to the appropriate team to patch.

To Fix or Not to Fix

There are a number of factors to consider when deciding whether to fix a bug encountered during a refactor. First, it is far easier to verify that the refactor accurately replicates the original behavior if it is copied exactly, bugs and all. By fixing a bug while refactoring a section of code, we are decisively deviating from the reference behavior. Not only do we now have to consider the fixed bug when doing thorough regression testing of any kind, we also open ourselves up to introducing entirely new bugs or unexpected behaviors as a result of the bug fix.

When refactoring at scale, we often find ourselves knee-deep in unfamiliar code. What we might consider to be a bug might very well not be. Even if we consult with the team responsible for the feature, and it confirms that there is a defect, we may not have the necessary context to fix it, and the team responsible may not be comfortable diving headfirst into the refactor. That said, fixing the bug now brings joy to your users sooner and makes your refactored solution more correct. There is a certain amount of convenience that comes with actively fixing issues as they arise.

My recommendation is to write failing unit tests highlighting the bug. Get in touch with the team responsible for the affected feature and share your tests with them. Talk to the team about the conditions for reproducing the bug. If the team believes it is

---

expected behavior, scrap the tests and continue with the refactor. If the defect is legitimate, have the team decide the priority of the fix. If it's of high priority, have the team fix the bug *first*, using the unit tests you wrote to confirm that the behavior now works as intended. Then, once the bug fix has landed and the unit test now passes, incorporate the fix into the remainder of the refactored code.

Clean-Up Items

In "Cleaning Up Artifacts" on page 87, we looked at the importance of including a distinct phase in our execution plan for cleaning up artifacts produced during the refactor. Every refactor should prioritize leaving the codebase in an orderly state for other developers; after all, usually a substantial motivation for a large refactor is to improve the ergonomics of your codebase. While we might have a modest intuition about the kinds of artifacts we'll be generating throughout the project well before we write our first line of code, there will undoubtedly be an assortment of them we create on the fly.

Keep track of everything that'll need tidying, whether you plan to tackle the clutter at the end of your current milestone or only in the final stages of the project. Updating your list immediately as you render a section of code obsolete is critical; this way, you'll be certain to remove each relevant artifact once you've reached the cleanup phase. The engineers who interface with the newly refactored code will be grateful for an orderly experience.

 Just as a cook would recommend cleaning pots and pans as you use them when preparing a meal, I recommend continually cleaning up as a refactor progresses. It is far easier (and safer) to remove pieces of code soon after rendering them unnecessary. At this stage, the myriad of interactions between the newly obsolete code and the remainder of the refactor is fresh in your mind, and you risk making fewer mistakes extricating it.

Out-of-Scope Items

Nearly every engineer on your team will encounter a few opportunities to add scope to the refactor during its lifetime. Obviously, your project will have a better chance at hitting its important deadlines if everyone resists the temptation, but these opportune extensions should not be outright ignored. Consider keeping a list of the opportunities you encounter to expand on the project. Having a succinct set of spin-off projects can demonstrate the versatility of your refactor; if there is a broad number of distinct ways to capitalize on the project's momentum to continue to improve the codebase, your stakeholders (and peers alike) will be more likely to believe the refactor was a valuable endeavor. If your own team (or any other team at the company) wants to build upon the foundation established by the refactor and continue making incremental improvements to the codebase following its completion, they could scope out a few projects from this list and kick them off immediately.

Programming Productively

There is a handful of useful strategies you can adopt to make a lengthy refactor much more pleasant for both yourself and your team members. Large software projects are not always tricky to develop; in fact, when writing something entirely new, there might be only a handful of difficult maneuvers, most of which are necessary only when embedding the feature into the existing codebase. On the other hand, when a significant amount of code needs to be written for a refactor, the majority of it a copy of existing behavior, it needs to be carefully designed and delicately integrated with its original implementation. There are considerably more opportunities for the painstaking process to fail. Hopefully, you can learn to navigate the refactoring development process successfully by following the techniques described in this section.

Prototyping

When we set out to draft a plan for our refactor in Chapter 4, we aimed to strike the right level of detail. We wanted the plan to be approachable for important stakeholders who might not be intimately familiar with the technical details, but sufficiently specific that we could properly inform a team about the project and begin execution without ambiguity. Where the plan remained deliberately vague is a perfect opportunity for prototyping.

Prototyping early and often helps your team ultimately move faster if you abide by two important principles:

Know that your solution will not be perfect
> Focus on crafting a solution that works well overall, being mindful about not spending too much time perfecting the details. Remember that even if we spent hours attempting to devise the ideal solution, a future change in requirements might render it obsolete. (We saw a few concrete examples of this in Chapter 2.) A great solution is one that solves the most important problems well and allows for a fair amount of flexibility down the line.

Be willing to throw code away
> If we spend a week or two writing a solution that simply doesn't deliver, take the pieces that work, throw the rest away, and start again. Prototyping is all about trying something, learning from that experience, and starting again.

Let's consider a refactor in which your team wants to split up a bloated class into a few distinct components. Your team came up with a preliminary design that divides its primary responsibilities into three new classes, but there are a number of minor, albeit important, responsibilities that have yet to be assigned to any one of them. Instead of committing wholeheartedly to a solution early in the process, you decide to prototype a few options, trying out the ergonomics of the new classes in just a few illustrative sections of the codebase. Given the prototypes, your team is able to decide what works and what doesn't, and iron out a solution that should integrate well with the remainder of the codebase.

Keep Things Small

When making sweeping changes across a large surface area, it's easy to get carried away. Say, for instance, we need to migrate all callsites of one function, `pre_refactor_impl`, to a new one, `post_refactor_impl`. There are about 300 instances of `pre_refactor_impl` throughout the codebase, spanning just over 80 files. You could do a simple find and replace, lump the changes into a single commit, and put the patch up for review by a teammate. If the migration is fairly straightforward, although creating just a single set of changes might appear to be more convenient, there are a few severe disadvantages.

First, committing small, incremental changes makes it much easier to author great code. By pushing bite-sized commits, you can get relevant feedback early and often from your tooling (e.g., integration tests running on a server through continuous integration). If you push a wide breadth of changes infrequently, you risk needing to wade through and fix a heap of test failures. More modifications per commit leads to a greater likelihood of cascading test failures; fixing one error only reveals another. Keeping tight commits ultimately enables you to understand their impact better and fix any failing tests faster. The same applies when manually verifying changes.

Second, reverting a small commit is much easier than reverting a big one. If something goes wrong, whether during development or well after the code has been deployed, reverting a small commit allows you to carefully extract only the offending change.

Third, because concise commits tend to be sufficiently focused, you'll also be able to write better, more precise commit messages. With better commit messages, not only will you be able to locate a specific set of changes faster, your teammates will understand them better when scanning through the version history at a later date. (Tiny commits typically get reviewed and approved much, much faster, too!)

Finally, it is nearly impossible for a teammate to review the entirety of the modified code adequately. Although organizations should not rely on code review to catch bugs (relying instead on thorough and earnest testing), if there is insufficient test coverage, the burden of catching potential mistakes falls to the reviewer. Superficially, the changes may seem easy to verify, but after auditing just a few of them, unless we retain a steadfast focus, our ability to spot discrepancies wanes. Large changesets are far easier to review if split up into logically organized, pithy commits.

When refactoring, you want to maintain the original version history as much as possible. Consider using operations like `git mv` to move files around rather than deleting them and adding them back. Make it clear in your commit descriptions that the change is part of a larger refactor, so that engineers know to dig deeper into the commit history when looking for a potential code owner. Be a thoughtful teammate when writing descriptions for your teammates reviewing your code. Write a thorough description, outlining what the review should expect to find in the changeset, along with any necessary context.

Test, Test, Test

Because refactors involve gradually reimplementing existing behavior, we need to ascertain that the changes are not modifying the intended behavior. In practice, it is typically much more difficult to verify that nothing has changed than the opposite, making it particularly important to test incrementally and repeatedly when refactoring. By frequently rerunning unit tests, integration tests, or walking through manual tests, we can either confirm that everything has remained unaffected or pinpoint the precise moment at which the behavior diverged.

Before you begin modifying any section of code, verify that there are neat, distinct unit tests for it. There might already be a handful of tests to assert the behavior, but you should take the time to determine whether any additional cases are missing. If the tests are too coarse (e.g., only testing the flow for a top-level function, without any tests for any of the individual helper functions), split them up. Granular tests, just like granular commits, will help you narrow down issues early.

Asking the "Stupid" Question

We've all been in that meeting: the meeting where we sit with a bunch of senior engineers, talking about a technology or a product feature we don't understand very well. At first, it seems as though everyone's following along, nodding as a select few lead the discussion. We're confused, but we're too worried that we'll look unprepared to ask any clarifying questions. There are two directions this meeting usually ends up taking. The first is the one in which we continue to sit quietly and spend the rest of the meeting trying to piece everything together, unable to contribute meaningfully to the conversation. The second is the one in which someone else interjects, politely asking the very same question we were too embarrased to ask. We're thankful for our teammate's curiosity (thankful we weren't alone), and we're able to get back on track with everyone else pretty quickly.

We can't always count on our inquisitive teammates to have the same questions, nor should we be content to waste time sitting in a meeting or reading an email thread, continuing to wonder what is being discussed. So, I propose a third direction, in which you stand up and simply ask the "stupid" question. By prioritizing clarity over maintaining an illusion of omniscience, you are modeling important behavior for your team. You're affirming that no question is, in fact, a stupid question, and that above all else, it's important to make sure that everyone is on the same page. You'll have more productive discussions and fewer misunderstandings, and get to work solving the right problems more quickly.

When refactoring something at scale, because the surface area of the changes can be quite vast, there is a distinct chance that you will come in contact with portions of the codebase you're unfamiliar with. Being unafraid to seek out the experts in these areas and ask for guidance is crucial. Whether you need a short explanation or a more in-depth walkthrough, it's imperative to build a strong understanding of the code you're seeking to modify. Not only will you save on development time, and introduce fewer bugs as you refactor it, you'll also have the insight necessary to refactor it in a way that best suits the code.

Conclusion

Once you've pushed the final few commits and tidied everything up, you're ready to take on one last, vital task. You need to find ways to make all your efforts persist long-term. Our next chapter will take a look at a few important steps your team can take to ensure that your codebase does not slowly regress to its previous state.

CHAPTER 9

Making the Refactor Stick

A little over a year ago, a friend of mine named Tim decided to stop consuming sugar altogether to help him shed a few pesky pounds and regain more energy. The first week was tough; he felt lethargic and craved anything sweet, but by the end of the third week, the sugar withdrawal had abated and he began to feel peppy again. Shortly afterward, the benefits of the new diet began to creep in: he felt more alert throughout the workday, and he lost a few pounds.

After that, sticking to the diet was his biggest challenge. Tim had seen his friends try and fail to stick to a diet, so he knew that he needed to set realistic expectations for himself. To eliminate the temptation, he banished any sweet food from his apartment. He kept a regular food journal to keep himself accountable, but allowed himself the occasional treat when meeting up with friends. Two months into his journey, his partner joined him on the sugar-free journey, and together they were able to better support and encourage one another. Today, Tim is in much better health and his energy levels are only rivaled by his puppy.

Refactoring is a bit like taking up a new diet and sticking with it. Although it might seem like the greatest challenge is figuring out the change to make and implementing it, equally significant effort is required to ensure that the change lasts. In this chapter, we'll look at a variety of tools and practices we can adopt to ensure that the improvements we made with our at-scale refactor are as long-lasting as possible. We'll examine how to encourage engineers across the organization to embrace the patterns established by the refactor and how to use continuous integration to continue to promote their adoption. We'll talk about the importance of educating fellow engineers by doing a post-refactor roadshow. Finally, we'll touch on how to integrate incremental improvement into the engineering culture so that, hopefully, fewer large, at-scale refactors are needed in your near future.

Fostering Adoption

Quite often, a large number of engineers will need to interact with your refactor. You need these engineers' support for the refactor and the patterns it established for two reasons.

The first is to ensure that the changes it introduced persist long-term. Expansive refactors can be polarizing; frequently, within any company of more than just a few individuals, there are both avid supporters and opponents of the chosen design. If the opponents of the design refuse to write new code following the new design/patterns, they'll find ways to avoid doing so and generate new cruft at the boundary between the changes made by your team and their own code. Ultimately, this build-up could render nearly all the benefits of the refactor meaningless.

Even if you plan and execute a quality refactor, not everyone will understand or agree with your vision. For newcomers to the engineering team, the problems the refactor attempted to solve may not be abundantly clear. When fellow engineers do not have the necessary context to properly appreciate the outcome of a refactor, they may struggle when working at its perimeter. They risk incorrectly implementing the new patterns it introduces, or fail to use them at all in situations when the code would greatly benefit from them.

The second reason you need engineers' support is to enable the further permeation of the patterns established by the refactor throughout the codebase. You not only want the changes you introduced to remain, you also want them to inform future decisions made by engineers working in the codebase for months, perhaps years to come. Consider a simple analogy: a refactor is just like weeding an overrun vegetable garden, turning over the soil, and planting a few scallions. Maintaining the scallions would be our first goal, and encouraging our family members to plant other vegetables of their own into the newly replenished soil would be our secondary goal.

For example, a team refactoring the primary logging library used throughout its extensive codebase, after more than a few mishaps with engineers accidentally leaking personally identifiable information (PII) into their data processing pipelines, rewrote the library's primary interface to refuse arbitrary strings. If developers wanted to log a new field or create a new log type, they now had to register it in the logging library and then use it accordingly. Instead of replacing each individual callsite in the existing logging library, the team decided to scope down the refactor and simply modify the logic of the existing library to call into the new one.

Some engineers at the company were reticent to lose the flexibility that comes with being able to log arbitrary strings. Engineers coming from previous companies with more flexible logging might also be confused about why a new logging framework would purposefully introduce these limitations. Without properly communicating your motivations to these engineers, and working with them to address their frustrations, you risked them finding inventive ways of working around the safe-guards built into the new logging library, thus further increasing the risk that PII would be leaked into your data processing pipelines once more.

Even if engineers accept the changes brought about by the refactor, they may not be in favor of actively converting existing callsites to use the new library directly. They may also be apathetic about adding new log fields and types to the new library, choosing instead to use existing fields and types for a broader range of logs, thereby diminishing their specificity. By making it extremely easy to extend the logging library, and then teaching engineers how to do so, you'll ease their transition and, hopefully, increase overall usage of the new library throughout the codebase.

While there a number of ways we can encourage adoption of the refactor across our engineering organizations, the following methods are the ones that work best in my experience. The first is to *build ergonomic interfaces* for engineers to use when interacting with the newly refactored code. These interfaces should be defined early in the project's execution and be further refined throughout development. You should be gathering feedback from both your teammates and trusted peers across the engineering organization on how the boundary between the refactor and the remainder of the codebase could be made more ergonomic. If you've wrapped up the refactor and haven't sufficiently vetted your interfaces with their future users, set up a workshop with a few engineers from distinct product areas and work with them to iterate on the interfaces.

The methods we'll look at more closely in this chapter are most effective post-refactor. These include *teaching* engineers about the refactor using the documentation you've crafted, and finally, carefully *reinforcing* usage of any new patterns introduced by the refactor to encourage continued adoption.

Education

There are two primary methods of educating others about your refactor. The first is active; this includes planning and leading workshops or similar training to engage actively with engineers. The second is passive; this includes step-by-step tutorials engineers can walk through on their own, or short online courses through your company's learning platform.

Active Education

An active educational component is most important when the refactor affects a critical portion of the codebase that is used frequently by other engineers from a range of teams. Engineers who are accustomed to an existing set of patterns will need to familiarize themselves with a whole new way of doing things.

Workshops

One of the best ways to ensure that engineers can work effectively with the refactored code is to engage with them in a forum that requires them to work interactively through code samples and ask questions as they learn how to interface with the refactor. A significant advantage of holding workshops is that it encourages busy engineers to deliberately set aside time to get up to speed; some of us are involved in so many different tasks that we would otherwise never manage to prioritize informing ourselves about the refactor.

The time to educate engineers actively about how to interface with the refactor is once it's been newly completed. You don't want engineers coming in to learn new code and patterns when there's a risk that it might still be in flux or it hasn't yet been fully cleaned up and prepared for use by individuals who aren't intimately familiar with the details of the refactor. Take the time to verify that everything is in order before scheduling your first workshop. Better yet, do a dry run of the workshop with your team to iron out any kinks before opening it up to your peers.

These sessions shouldn't be held in perpetuity. Ideally, within a few months, most of the engineers most significantly affected by the refactor should be well acquainted with it. At that point, the refactored code becomes the new normal, and demand for help understanding it should dramatically decrease. Consider holding just two or three workshops, and keep an eye on the interest level and subsequent attendance. Live trainings, as engaging as they might be, are incredibly time consuming for your team and should be held only a handful of times. If demand continues after more than just a handful of sessions, you may want to invest in improving your documentation and leaning on it more heavily.

In practice, because just about every engineer uses logging in their regular workflow, our previous example would a perfect candidate for a training session. Here's how it could be structured:

1. Give a quick overview of the goals of the refactor. To communicate its impact effectively and excite your coworkers to take advantage of it, talk through the most compelling examples. With the logging library, for instance, you might show a few misleading log statements responsible for leaking PII over the past few months; then, demonstrate how to use the new logging library to prevent this information from being leaked altogether.

2. Next, to cement these concepts, pair up the attendees and ask them to migrate the same simple log statement to use the new library. Answer any questions as they arise. There may be more than one solution here; if there is, have the pairs explain their distinct solutions.

3. Finally, have the pairs choose a more complex log statement to migrate, ideally one that requires extending the log library (by either adding a new log type or field type). Check in with each group and answer any questions they might have.

Office hours

Office hours can be an equally helpful forum for actively educating your colleagues. They give engineers an open opportunity to drop by and ask you and your team questions about the refactor and its adoption in their specific use cases. Not everyone who will interact with your refactor will have time (or interest) to attend a workshop; having office hours when they can have your team's undivided attention will make them more likely to have a positive experience adopting the changes implemented by the refactor. Furthermore, previous workshop attendees can drop by and get additional guidance if necessary.

One of the advantages of hosting office hours is that it enables your team to time-box the amount of time they spend answering questions pertaining to the refactor. Your team may start to get bombarded with requests from colleagues across the company as soon as the refactor wraps up. If you aren't judicious with your time, these questions could easily monopolize your attention (not to mention disrupt your day with frequent context-switching.) By diverting all nonurgent requests to your office hours, you are protecting your team's time and focus.

Keep track of the questions and concerns your team addresses during these office hours and use these to write an FAQ. This document will help save your team valuable time repeatedly answering the same questions both during office hours and beyond.

Engineering gatherings

Many engineering groups host regular open forums (e.g., Thursday afternoon Drinks and Demos, or bi-weekly Lunch and Learn) where engineers can present about the work they're spearheading. Large refactoring projects often come with a number of interesting stories: the mind-boggling, load-bearing bug the team uncovered, the terrifying encounter with code last modified 15 years ago, the deploy gone wrong. Most of us genuinely enjoy hearing one another's stories about our experiences in the code we share, and we tend to vividly remember the particularly good ones.

Sign up to give a short talk to your peers about a compelling portion of the refactor to make them aware of the project and curious to learn more about its motivations and how they might benefit from it in their areas of the codebase. Sometimes, a little bit of great storytelling is all the publicity you need to garner the support of your fellow engineers.

Passive Education

In Chapter 7, we discussed the importance of documentation: not only the importance of producing thorough documentation throughout the refactoring process, but also the importance of choosing a medium and organization scheme that works well for your team. Once you've reached the final stages of the refactor, your team should prioritize crafting documentation describing the intent of the refactor and how it can benefit fellow engineers working within the same codebase. Per our discussion in Chapter 7, any documentation you or your team produces should be added to your source-of-truth directory.

This documentation can take a number of forms: it can be an FAQ, a short README providing a high-level summary of the project's goals, or a tutorial. Having documentation you can point curious engineers to helps your team save time answering questions. As previously mentioned in "Office hours" on page 163, your team will likely need to answer a multitude of questions from peers throughout the company. Instead of answering everyone individually, your team can instead point them to prepared documentation.

If you intend to write a how-to guide on navigating the codebase post-refactor, I recommend writing it from a historical perspective; that is, ground it in the story of the refactor, starting from the very beginning and concluding with the current state of the world. By discussing the refactor from such a perspective, you can prevent your documentation from immediately becoming outdated. Whenever possible, add dates to give readers appropriate context (even something as broad as a year may suffice). Let's illustrate this, using our logging example.

1. Start by giving readers the insight that you and your team acquired by spending the time understanding why the code had degraded before you sought to improve it (see Chapter 2). In the case of our logging library, begin by giving an overview of the initial design and the decisions that informed that design. Talk about how the authors wanted the library to be lightweight and easy to use, and allow anyone to (carefully) log just about anything conveniently.

2. Discuss how that as the product became more complex, and more engineers joined the team, the risk of leaking PII increased. List recent, serious instances when leaks occurred, demonstrating a growing frequency in recent months.

3. Describe your solution and how it inhibits PII from being leaked. Compare and contrast the same log statement, using both the previous and new logging libraries. Try to avoid using words like "now," "currently," or "today." Although you may be outlining how the code presently functions from your perspective, there is a strong chance that the code will continue to evolve. By prefacing your explanations with something like "as of September 2020," instead of "today," you are future-proofing your documentation.

Reinforcement

Positive reinforcement is a powerful tool. Regardless of proximity to the project, developers across the company will need to be reminded of the patterns established by it (and probably more than once). Here, we have two broader options. You can employ many of the motivational tactics we described in "Motivating individuals" on page 150 to recognize engineers who are doing a great job of adopting the patterns established in your refactor. Seeing your coworkers being publicly praised for their contributions can lead to a rapid increase in adoption by developers far and wide.

A second option is to automate reinforcement in the development process with continuous integration. With continuous integration, we can kick off a number of processes when an author pushes a new commit, indicates that their code is ready for review, or prepares to merge their changes with the main development branch. A typical setup will verify changes by running a series of tests alongside lints and code analysis tools. We'll look at both linting and code analyzers and then consider the ways in which you can configure these tools to effectively free your team from needing to actively encourage and monitor adoption.

Progressive Linting

Progressive linting allows you to improve a codebase gradually by only enforcing rules on newly written or modified code. This enables developers to address problems slowly as they arise rather than requiring one or two engineers to patch every instance where the rule would be violated. If your team is replacing one pattern with another, writing a new (progressive) linter rule is an easy way to nudge developers to use the newer pattern and prevent propagation of the deprecated pattern.

For example, as part of the logging library refactor, your team wants to eradicate references to `logEvent`, which allows for arbitrary strings to be ingested, in favor of `logEventType`, which only logs specific, non-PII pieces of data. Your team could write a new linter rule that bans any new usage of `logEvent`, with an error message informing engineers that the function is deprecated and encouraging them to use `logEvent Type` instead.

Some engineers are very sensitive about encountering unexpected linter failures. Be certain to adequately communicate the goal of the new linter rule and when it will come into effect so that no one is surprised. Add as much context to the error message as possible so that engineers hitting the error don't need to pull up any additional documentation to fix it.

Not all languages have extensible linters that allow for developers to write custom rules, and even fewer have progressive linting capabilities built in. Some engineering teams invest in building these tools internally (and, in some cases, later open-source their solutions). If you are using an extensible linter, and are able to write custom rules, a quick way to introduce progressive linting is by running the linter either only on modified files in a given commit or only on the code difference itself.

Code Analysis Tools

Many of the metrics covered in Chapter 3 can be monitored over time, using out-of-the-box code analysis tools triggered at integration time. There is a wide range of both free and paid open-source solutions that will automatically calculate code complexity at different scales (individual functions, classes, files, etc.) and generate test coverage statistics. Many of these solutions are easily extendable so that your team can develop and hook in its own metrics calculations and assert new rules as time goes on.

For example, say your team wants to ensure that no function in the codebase exceeds 500 lines. Your team could configure your chosen code analysis tool to warn or throw an error whenever a change causes a function to cross that threshold. If an engineer comes along and adds a few lines to an existing function, increasing its line count from 490 to 512, they'd be nudged to split up the function into smaller subfunctions before merging their changes.

Gates Versus Guardrails

Each verification step configured in our integration flow can either be a gate, preventing the changes from continuing to move forward, or a guardrail, producing a warning for the code author to consider before proceeding.

Too many gates can be detrimental to an engineering organization: they slow down development and can frustrate engineers (especially if they are unexpected). Say your organization has configured 10 blocking test suites. When a developer is ready to put their code up for review, the test suites kick off in parallel. Unfortunately, about half of these suites take just over 10 minutes to run, and a few of them regularly produce flaky results. Engineers are spending valuable time waiting for their code to clear each of these 10 gates.

Now suppose that instead of setting up gates, the organization instead institutes guardrails; that is, instead of having each of these test suites block progress, the team decides which two or three are truly business-critical premerge, and labels the others as optional. Engineers are now responsible for determining which suites they believe to be most important to their changes, and if the results are flaky, they can choose to ignore them. Of course opting for more guardrails comes with its own risks, and perhaps more bugs may make it out into production, but by and large, I'm of the opinion that we should be trusting our fellow engineers more.

Ownership

Many engineers at larger companies (including me) are often pinged with questions about code they are listed as having last modified. As someone who has refactored a significant breadth of code as a result of multiple large-scale refactors, I try to maintain version history as much as possible, but my name often pops up via `git blame` deep in the depths of functions I'm only vaguely familiar with. As a result, I've been brought into incidents, tagged on JIRA tickets, and assigned to code reviews with very little context, only to disappoint the individuals seeking my help. Fortunately, we can frequently correctly identify the team responsible for the code at hand. Unfortunately, every so often, the code is not owned by anyone, and no one is eager to claim it.

Unowned code is a thorny problem that nearly every company with a sizable engineering team faces. We will not attempt to solve it here, but I do want to provide you with some defenses in case you or your team is pulled in by virtue of a `git blame`. While you might be happy to help, be careful not to set a precedent of cordially accepting to solve problems pertaining to unowned code. Before you know it, not only will you have cemented yourself as the de facto owner of that code, but others may come knocking, requesting your help with unrelated instances of unowned code.

Let the individual reaching out to you know that your team is not responsible for the given code. Offer to work with them (or ask your manager work to with them) to identify a better candidate. If the ask is short-term (e.g., a simple bug fix) and relatively urgent, you may have better luck identifying someone who has the time and sufficient context to prioritize it. Hopping through version history to find a viable temporary owner prior to your own changes or identifying the developer (and from there, the team) with the most recent commits in the same file are both good options.

Once you've identified someone who is able to handle the immediate request, ask your manager to work with their peers to locate a longer-term home. These conversations may result in a long, frustrating game of hot potato, but hopefully, at this point, you've successfully exfiltrated yourself from the equation.

Integrating Improvement into the Culture

There will always be a need for large-scale refactors, as long as none of us can predict how shifts in technologies or requirements will continue to affect our systems. However, I do believe that some large-scale refactors *are* avoidable, and that we should do our best to prevent them when possible. As we conclude this chapter, I want to leave you with some thoughts on how to build a culture of continuous improvement. By perpetually pinpointing and taking advantage of opportunities for tangibly improving our code, we can hopefully ward off ambitious, disruptive refactors for a while longer.

First and foremost, one of the best ways to maintain a healthy codebase is simply to continue deliberately refactoring small, well-contained portions of code as you encounter the opportunity. We do not want to become drive-by refactorers (see "Because You Happened to Be Passing By" on page 16), but instead focus on incrementally improving areas of the codebase owned and maintained by our own team. There are always plenty of opportunities for us to tidy up in our own neighborhood. When we encounter an opportunity for another team to improve their code, we can reach out, leaning toward asking questions to understand their problems better, rather than immediately proposing a solution. Work together to craft a cleaner implementation.

We should encourage and facilitate design conversations on our team frequently, seeking others' feedback early rather than forging ahead on our own. Code reviews are not only an opportunity for someone to double-check our work, but also a chance for an open discussion about how we can make our solution just that much better. As code authors, we should consider annotating our code reviews with specific questions for our reviewers. As reviewers, we should be just as analytical when reviewing our peers' code as we are when we are writing code ourselves.

Finally, hold inclusive design reviews early in the feature development process. This means inviting engineers from all backgrounds to evaluate your designs and ask questions. Your reviewers should span all experience and seniority levels; they should include individuals from a wide range of backgrounds. The more diverse perspectives you are able to gather, the more likely you'll be able to spot fatal flaws early and, ultimately, the more likely you'll be able to architect a far superior solution.

Whenever you next sit down to work, think critically about how what you do today might or might not lead to a large-scale refactor later. Sometimes, all we need is a little reminder of the potential long-term consequences of our decisions to steer us back in the right direction.

PART IV

Case Studies

Before I dive into our case studies, let me set the stage by telling you a little bit about Slack: the history of the product, the company, and its early influences.

Slack was developed as an internal tool at a small gaming company based out of Vancouver called Tiny Speck. The team, a mash-up of engineers, designers, and product people from Flickr, sought to build a fantastical, massively mulitplayer online game focused on community building. They called it Glitch.

Because everyone was distributed across North America, Tiny Speck began to rely heavily on internet relay chat (IRC) to communicate. Before long, the team realized that it needed something a bit more powerful: a tool that enabled it to keep in touch asynchronously, search through message history, and send files. The members set out to build it.

The game ultimately shut down in 2012, and the company laid off most of its employees, but Tiny Speck had one final trick up its sleeve. In an unlikely pivot, the few remaining employees chose to commercialize their internal communications tool. They polished the experience and branded it Slack: searchable log of all conversation and knowledge.

The Tiny Speck crew contacted friends and past colleagues to test out its new tool. With each new batch of users, the team collected feedback, fixed bugs, and built new functionality. By May 2013, the product was ready for a preview release, available to a select few who requested invitations. Just nine months later, Slack launched publicly.

Usage skyrocketed. Within a year, the tool went from having just under 15,000 daily active users to 500,000. By the time the product hit its two-year anniversary, more than 2.3 million users were using Slack every day. In late 2019, nearly six years from launch, that number exceeded 12 million, with more than 1 billion messages sent every week.

Many of Slack's early technology and design decisions were informed by the founders' experience building Flickr and Glitch. The usage of PHP and MySQL, for instance, was a logical one, given their experience building the photosharing website in 2004. In fact, much of Slack's basic server functionality has its roots in Flamework, a PHP web-application framework, borne out of the processes and house style developed at Flickr; you can find it on GitHub (*https://oreil.ly/IRayS*). Much of the real-time messaging infrastructure was derived directly from Tiny Speck's IRC-like internal tool.

In early 2016, Slack began to look at some alternatives to the Zend Engine II interpreter for PHP. There were two main contenders: upgrade to PHP 7 and use Zend Engine III, or try Facebook's HipHop Virtual Machine (HHVM). After some deliberation, leadership decided to roll out the HHVM runtime to its web servers. Once the rollout proved successful, the engineering team began to adopt the Hack programming language, a gradually typed dialect of PHP developed to run atop HHVM. At the time of publication, the portion of Slack's codebase that was once written in PHP is now written in Hack.

Both of the case studies in this section will focus on large refactoring efforts carried out on the portion of the codebase written in PHP and, later, Hack. To convey the nature of each problem as well as possible, the code samples in these sections will be in Hack. But don't worry! While the snippets help provide small, concrete examples of the problem we were tackling, they are not the focus of the story. Refactoring at scale is primarily about the process and the people involved rather than the code itself, and I hope that these case studies help illustrate exactly that. If you're still concerned about being able to parse the code samples, let me reassure you that at the time, Hack code still looked quite a bit like PHP. For those who aren't comfortable with either Hack or PHP, we'll walk through each snippet in detail so that you can get your bearings.

I'd like to draw attention to one final observation before we move on. At the time of publication, Slack has only been publicly available for six years. The code, the product, and the company are all relatively young. The code has had to scale rapidly to handle increasing customer usage as well as a growing number of engineers developing the product. Many of the large refactoring efforts that have begun throughout the company over the years have been in response to hypergrowth, both external due to high adoption and internal due to hiring.

CHAPTER 10

Case Study: Redundant Database Schemas

For the first of our two case study chapters, we explore a refactor I carried out with a few other members of my team during my first year at Slack. The project centered on consolidating two redundant database schemas. Both schemas were tightly coupled to our increasingly unwieldy codebase, and we had very few unit tests to rely on. In short, this project is a great example of a realistic, large-scale refactor at a relatively young, high-growth company with a modest number of engineers and an increasingly unwieldy codebase.

This project was successful primarily because we remained hyperfocused on our ultimate goal of consolidating the redundant database tables. We drafted a simple but effective execution plan (Chapter 4), thoughtfully weighing risk and speed of execution to deliver on our solution promptly. We opted for a lightweight approach to gathering metrics (Chapter 3), choosing a narrow focus on just a few key data points. We proactively communicated our changes widely, across the entirety of the engineering team, whenever we completed a new milestone (Chapter 7). We built tooling to ensure that our changes would persist (Chapter 9). Finally, we successfully demonstrated the value of the refactor by seamlessly shipping a new feature built atop the newly consolidated schema just weeks after its completion. This enabled us to get further buy-in to kick off further refactors (Chapter 5).

Although the refactor yielded the performance improvements we sought, we took a few missteps along the way. Due to significant pressure from our most important customers, we rushed to start making headway; we did not investigate why the schemas had converged, nor commit our plan to writing for other teams to consume easily (Chapter 4). We didn't seek broader, cross-functional support (Chapter 5), leaving the bulk of the work to our small team. Even then, we struggled to keep up the momentum, and the refactor dragged in its final few weeks (Chapter 8).

Before we dive into the refactor itself, however, it's imperative to understand what Slack does and the basics of how it works. If you aren't familiar with the product, I strongly recommend giving this section a thorough read. If you're a regular Slack user, feel free to skip ahead to "Slack Architecture 101" on page 174.

Slack 101

Slack is first and foremost a collaboration tool for companies of all sizes and industries. Typically, a business will set up a Slack workspace and create user accounts for each employee. As an employee, you can download the application (on your desktop machine, your mobile phone, or both) and immediately begin communicating with your teammates.

Slack organizes topics and conversations into *channels*. Let's say that you're working on a new feature that enables your users to upload files into your application faster. We'll call the project "Faster Uploads." You can create a new channel name, #feature-faster-uploads, where you can coordinate development with fellow engineers, your manager, and product manager. Anyone at the company curious to know how development is going on "Faster Uploads" can navigate to #feature-faster-uploads and read through the recent history or join the conversation and ask a question to the team directly.

You can see a simple example of what the Slack interface looked like during the first half of 2017, around the time of this first case study, in Figure 10-1.

Here, our example user is Matt Kump, an employee of Acme Sites. You can see the name of the workspace we're currently viewing at the top left, and Matt's name immediately below it.

The leftmost sidebar contains all of Matt's channels. We'll ignore the starred section for now and focus on the Channels section first. We can see from this list that Matt is involved in conversations about accounting costs (#accounting-costs), brainstorming (#brainstorming), business operations (#business-ops), and a handful of others. Each of these channels is public, meaning that anyone with an account at Acme Sites can discover the channel, view its contents, and join it.

You might have noticed that the #design-chat channel has a little lock where the others have the # symbol. This indicates that the channel is private. Only users who are members of the private channel can discover it and view its contents. To join a private channel, you must be invited by someone who is already a member.

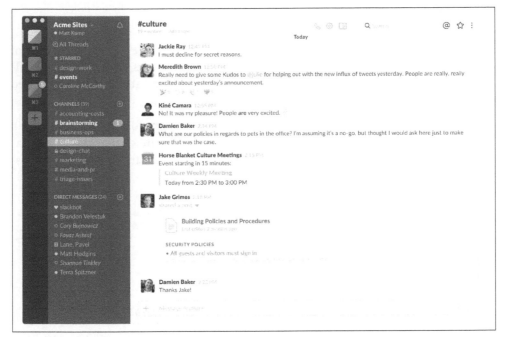

Figure 10-1. Slack interface circa January 2017

Farther down the sidebar is Matt's list of Direct Messages. We can see that he's in a number of direct, one-on-one conversations with fellow teammates like Brandon, Corey, and Fayaz. He is also in a group conversation with both Lane and Pavel; these work just like direct messages, but with a handful of teammates rather than just one.

 Understanding the distinction between public and private channels becomes important when we start discussing some of the key problems this case study refactor sought to solve.

You may have noticed that some of the channels in the sidebar appear bolded in bright white. This indicates that they contain new messages you haven't read yet. If Matt were to select #brainstorming, he would find some new content to read, and the channel in the sidebar would fade to match the others.

While there's much, much more to Slack, this covers the basics you'll need to understand before we dive into the historical context leading up to this case study.

Slack Architecture 101

Now let's explore a few basic components of Slack's architecture that are at the core of our study. It's important to note that some of these components have changed significantly beyond the refactoring effort outlined in this chapter, so the details provided here do not accurately reflect how Slack is architected today.

Let's take a look at a simple request to fetch message history for a given channel. I'll boot up my Slack instance and pop open one of my favorite channels, #core-infra-sourdough (shown in Figure 10-2), where a handful of infrastructure engineers discuss sourdough baking.

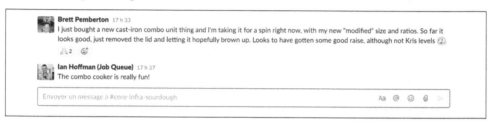

Figure 10-2. Reading the latest bread-baking advice in #core-infra-sourdough

If I monitored network traffic, I would have seen a `GET` request to the Slack API for `channels.history` with the channel ID for #core-infra-sourdough. The request would first hit a load balancer to reach an available web server. Next, the server would verify a few things about the request. This includes confirming that the provided token is valid and that I have access to the channel I want to read. If I had access, the server would fetch the most recent messages from the appropriate database, format them, and return them to my client. Voila! In just a few milliseconds, I could fetch the most recent content for the channel I selected.

How did the server know which database to reach out to in order to locate the correct messages? Within the product, everything belonged to a single workspace. All messages were contained within channels, and all channels were contained within a workspace. Having everything map to a single, logical unit gave us a convenient way of horizontally distributing our data.

Every workspace was assigned to a single database shard, where all of its relevant information was stored. If a user was a member of a workspace and wanted to get a list of all the public channels available, our servers would make an initial query to find out which shard contained the workspace's data and then query that shard for the channels.

If a large customer grew and began to occupy more space within a shard that it shared with other companies, we redistributed these other companies to different shards, giving the growing customer more wiggle room. If a customer was the sole occupant of their shard and they continued to grow, we upgraded the shard's hardware to accommodate the growth. All in all, our database structure looked as pictured in Figure 10-3.

Figure 10-3. Some workspaces distributed across shards

Next, we'll take a peek at how we stored a few key pieces of information in each workspace shard. Specifically, we'll look at *channels* and *channel membership*. At the start of 2017, Slack had a few tables responsible for storing information about channels. We had a table that stored information for public channels, called `teams_channels`. We had another table, `groups`, which stored information for private channels and group direct messages (messages among more than one user). Each of these tables contained basic information about the channel, things like the name of the channel, when it was created, and who created it. Figure 10-4 illustrates a few sample rows of two tables we used to store channel information.

teams_channels				
id	team_id	name	...	purpose
10001	20001	sourdough-baking		Discuss the highs and lows of sourdough baking
10002	20001	company-announcements		Important company communications

groups				
id	team_id	name	...	purpose
10007	20001	secret-acquisition		Updates relating to a potential acquisition
10008	20001	eng-promotions		Engineering promotion committee

Figure 10-4. Simplified table schema for `teams_channels` and `groups`

We stored information about members of those channels on `teams_channels_mem bers` and `groups_members`, respectively. For each member, we would store a row uniquely identified by the combination of workspace ID, channel ID, and user ID. We additionally stored some key pieces of information regarding that user's membership such as the date that they joined the channel and the time, as a Unix epoch timestamp, at which they last read content in that channel. Figure 10-5 demonstrates that these two tables were nearly identical.

teams_channels_members				
channel_id	team_id	user_id	...	last_read
10001	20001	30001		1553656778
10002	20001	30002		1553658978
10002	20001	30002		1553688978
10003	20001	30003		1553658978

group_members				
channel_id	team_id	user_id	...	last_read
10007	20001	30001		1553656778
10008	20001	30004		1553658978
10008	20001	30003		1553688978
10009	20001	30003		1553658978

Figure 10-5. Simplified table schema for teams_channels_members and groups_members

Finally, for direct messages, we had a single table called teams_ims (shown in Figure 10-6) to store information about both the channel itself and its membership.

teams_ims					
channel_id	team_id	user_id	target_user_id	...	last_read
10010	20001	30001	30003		1553656778
10011	20001	30002	30001		1553658978
10012	20001	30002	30003		1553688978
10010	20001	30003	30001		1553658978

Figure 10-6. Simplified table schema for teams_ims

In total, we had three distinct tables to store information about channels, and three distinct tables to store information about channel membership. Figure 10-7 illustrates the role of each table as it relates to the kind of channel it dealt with.

	public	private	DMs
channels	teams_channels	groups	teams_ims
memberships	teams_channels_members	groups_members	teams_ims

Figure 10-7. Chart designating the tables responsible for storing channel and respective membership information, depending on its kind (public, private, group DM, or DM)

Scalability Problems

Now that we have a better understanding of Slack's basic architecture and, more specifically, how channels and channel membership were represented, we can dive into the problems that arose as a result. We'll describe three of the most serious problems we encountered, as they were experienced by our largest customer at the time, which we'll refer to as Very Large Business, or VLB for short, for the remainder of the chapter.

VLB was eager for all of its 350,000 employees to use Slack. It had begun using the product slowly at first but began ramping up its usage aggressively during the first few months of 2017. By April, it had just over 50,000 users on the platform, nearly double that of our second-largest customer. VLB started hitting the limitations of nearly every piece of our product. At the time, I was part of the team responsible for Slack's performance with our biggest customers. For several weeks, our team shared a rotation whereby two of us needed to be at our desks in our San Franciso headquarters at 6:30 a.m. to be ready to respond to any immediate issues during VLB's peak log-in time on the East Coast. As our team scrambled quickly to patch problems left and right, we began to notice that each of them was exacerbated by the fact that we had redundant database tables for storing channel membership.

Booting Up the Slack Client

Every weekday morning, starting at 9 a.m. eastern time, VLB employees would start logging on to Slack. As more people began their workday, more load began to pile up on VLB's database shard. Our existing instrumentation showed us that the culprit was most likely one of the most crucial APIs we called on startup, `rtm.start`.

This API returned all the necessary information to populate a user's sidebar; it fetched all the public and private channels the user was a member of, fetched all the group and direct messages they had open, and determined whether any of those channels contained messages that they hadn't yet read. The client would then parse the result and populate the interface with a tidy list of bolded and unbolded conversations.

From the server perspective, this was an incredibly expensive process. To determine a user's memberships, we needed to query three tables: `teams_channels_members`, `groups_members`, and `teams_ims`. From each set of memberships, we extracted the `channel_id` and fetched the corresponding `teams_channels` or `groups` row to display the channel name. We also queried the `messages` table to fetch the timestamp of its most recent message, which we compared to the user's `last_read` timestamp to determine whether they had any unread messages. We executed the vast majority of these queries individually, incurring network roundtrip costs each time.

File Visibility

Sporadically throughout the day, we noticed spikes in expensive queries to the database. Our dashboards surfaced a few potential candidate callsites, including the function responsible for calculating file visibility at the core of most of our files-related APIs. Popping open the target function, we yet again came face to face with a set of complex queries.

When a user uploads a file to Slack, the servers write a new row to the `files` table denoting the file's name, its location on our remote file server, and a handful of other relevant pieces of information. Whenever a file is shared to a channel, we write a new entry to the `files_share` table, denoting the file ID and the ID of the channel to which it was shared. When a file is shared to a public channel, it becomes visible to any user on the workspace and is denoted as publicly discoverable by setting the `is_public` column to true on its `files` row. Thus, in the simplest case, the file is public, we know it is quickly, and we can reveal it to the user.

When a file isn't public, however, the logic becomes a little bit more complicated. We have to cross-reference all channels that the user is a member of with all the channels where the file was shared. As is the case for `rtm.start`, to determine a user's complete set of channel memberships, we had to query three distinct tables. We then combined those results with those from the `files_shares` table for the target file. If we found a match, we could show the file to the user; if not, we returned an error to the client.

Mentions

The query that caused the most consistent amount of load on VLB's shard for the full duration of the workday was the query responsible for determining whether a user (or the topics they subscribe to) were mentioned in a channel and hadn't yet read those messages. A *mention* can be any number of things within Slack. It can be a username or a username prefixed with the @ symbol. It can be a highlight word for which the user has enabled notifications within their user preferences. The client would then use that data to populate badges with the number of unread mentions to the right of the corresponding channel name in the sidebar. You can see one of the many complex mentions-related queries in its 40-line glory in Example 10-1.

This query, yet again, required fetching a user's memberships across the three membership tables. The tricky part was when we needed to exclude any memberships for which the associated channels were deleted or archived, requiring us to join the membership results with their corresponding channel row on either groups or teams_channels.

Example 10-1. Query to determine whether to notify a user of a mention; % symbolizes substitution syntax

```
SELECT
    tcm.channel_id as channel_id,
    'C' as type,
    tcm.last_read
from
    teams_channels tc
    INNER JOIN teams_channels_members tcm ON (
        tc.team_id = tcm.team_id
        AND tc.id = tcm.channel_id
    )
WHERE
    tc.team_id = %TEAM_ID
    AND tc.date_delete = 0
    AND tc.date_archived = 0
    AND tcm.user_id = %USER_ID
UNION ALL
SELECT
    gm.group_id as channel_id,
    'G' as type,
    gm.last_read
from
    groups g
    INNER JOIN groups_members gm ON (
        g.team_id = gm.team_id
        AND g.id = gm.group_id
    )
WHERE
    g.team_id = %TEAM_ID
    AND g.date_delete = 0
    AND g.date_archived = 0
    AND gm.user_id = %USER_ID
UNION ALL
SELECT
    channel_id as channel_id,
    'D' as type,
    last_read
FROM
```

```
    teams_ims
WHERE
    team_id = %TEAM_ID
    AND user_id = %USER_ID
```

Consolidating the Tables

Now that we have sufficient background on the problem we aimed to solve, we can begin to discuss the refactor. I wish I could say that consolidating `teams_chan nels_members` and `groups_members` into a single table was a well-planned and smartly executed project, but that would not be true. In fact, the more chaotic portions of the refactor are what inspired and informed a great deal of the ideas in this book. We kicked things off with a sense of urgency, didn't keep great tabs on progress as we went along, and in the end, although we knew we had decreased the load across most of our database tier, we could only point to a single metric to demonstrate roughly by how much. What ultimately made the project a success was the smart, dedicated set of individuals who helped us cross the finish line. Although our largest customers stood to benefit the most from the refactor, all of our customers ultimately benefited from the project.

We started the project somewhat immediately and without a written plan. Our top priority was to get the consolidation of the tables just to the point where we could migrate the one query that was hammering our database shards the most: the mentions query.

Although we knew that a great many queries would equally benefit from the consolidated table, their migration was strictly secondary. In Chapter 1, I strongly suggested that you not embark on a large-scale refactor unless you are confident that you can finish it. In this case, we certainly intended to finish the table consolidation; we just didn't know whether other, more pressing performance issues might creep up and need to be prioritized over the refactor. We were willing to take the risk, given the urgency of the problem at hand, fully aware of the consequences if we failed to finish the migration.

First, we created a new table, `channels_members`. We combined the schemas of the membership tables, completed with the same indices, and introduced a new column to denote whether a row originated from `teams_channels_members` or `groups_mem bers`, both to ease the migration and ensure that we could respect any business-logic dependencies around the initial tables. Figure 10-8 shows our goal state as compared to Figure 10-7, our starting state.

	public	private	DMs
channels	teams_channels	groups	teams_ims
memberships	channels_members		

Figure 10-8. Our goal state

Gathering the Scattered Queries

Rewriting our queries to target a single new table would not be easy. Slack's codebase was written in a very imperative style, with everything from short functions to long functions, distributed across hundreds of loosely namespaced files. Its original authors had stuck to what they knew well and steered clear of object-oriented patterns due to performance concerns with PHP. They preferred writing individual queries inline rather than relying on an object-relational mapping library and risk bloating the codebase early.

One-off queries to either `teams_channels_members` or `groups_members` were strewn across 126 files. Many of the queries hadn't been touched since well before the product launched. To top it off, we knew much of the code that contained these queries didn't have great unit test coverage. To give you a sense of what these might have looked like, I dug up some old code, which you can see in Example 10-2.

Example 10-2. An inlined SQL query to `teams_channels_members`

```
function chat_channels_members_get_display_counts(
    $team,
    $user,
    $channel
){
    // Some business logic

    $sql = "SELECT
        COUNT(\*) as display_counts,
        SUM(CASE
                WHEN (is_restricted != 0 OR is_ultra_restricted != 0)
                    THEN 1
                ELSE 0
            END) as guest_counts
    FROM
        teams_channels_members AS tcm
        INNER JOIN users AS u ON u.id = tcm.user_id
    WHERE
        tcm.team_id = % team_id
        AND tcm.channel_id = % channel_id
        AND u.deleted = 0";
```

```
$ret = db_fetch_team($team, $sql, array(
        'team_id' => $team['id'],
        'channel_id' => $channel['id']));

// A bit more business logic

return $counts;
}
```

Business logic code surrounding these queries would index directly into the resulting columns, cementing a tight coupling between our database schemas and the code. Whenever we introduced new columns, we had to update corresponding code to take it into consideration. Say we had a column on the `files` table called `is_public` to denote whether the file was public. If we later introduced additional logic that required us to check an additional property to determine whether the file was public, any code that relied on a simple check of `if ($file['is_public'])` would need to be updated to accommodate for that change properly.

To consolidate `teams_channels_members` and `groups_members` into `channels_mem bers`, we needed to identify all the queries to either table scattered across the codebase. A quick `grep` of the codebase and we were able to extract a list of all the locations where we queried `groups_members` or `teams_channels_members`. We plugged the list of files and line numbers directly into a shared Google Sheets file, shown in Figure 10-9.

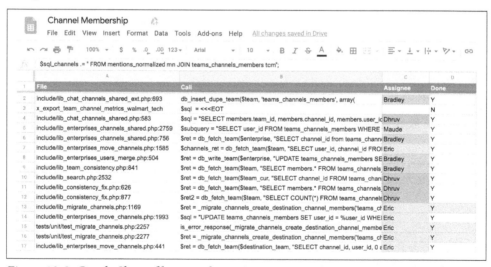

Figure 10-9. Google Sheets file to track queries to `teams_channels_members` *and* `groups_members`

We decided to create a single file where we could house all the queries related to channel membership. Our effort to revive our struggling membership queries conveniently arose around the same time engineers had begun having conversations about centralizing our queries. We were a growing team, trying to execute quickly, and needing to remember to update queries in haphazard corners of the codebase every time we altered a table was getting tedious. A few proposals had been shopped around, with engineers in favor of storing all queries to a given table in a single file. While some wanted an approach that would allow them to generate queries, given a set of parameters, leading us to build a more complex data access layer, others wanted to continue to be able to read the queries inline. We decided that with this project, we'd prototype minimal query generation as a means of limiting the number of individual functions in our new file. We decided to call this new pattern *unidata*, or ud for short, thus naming our target file ud_channel_membership.php.

Developing a Migration Strategy

Now that we had a table and a set of queries to migrate, we could get started. We needed to identify each of the queries from our initial grep, which inserted rows, updated values, or deleted rows. For each query, we created a corresponding function in our unidata library containing a copy. Each function would take a parameter to indicate whether to execute the query on teams_channels_members or groups_mem bers, alongside some logic to execute the same query conditionally against our new table, channels_members. The general idea is shown in Example 10-3.

Example 10-3.

```
function ud_channel_membership_delete(
    $team,
    $channel_id,
    $user_id,
    $channel_type
){

    if ($channel_type == 'groups'){
        $sql = 'DELETE FROM groups_members WHERE team_id=%team_id AND
                group_id=%channel_id AND user_id=%user_id';
    }else{
        $sql = 'DELETE FROM teams_channels_members WHERE team_id=%team_id AND
                channel_id=%channel_id AND user_id=%user_id';
    }

    $bind = array(
        'team_id'    => $team['id'],
        'channel_id' => $channel_id,
        'user_id'    => $user_id,
    );
```

```
    $ret = db_write_team($team, $sql, $bind);

    if (feature_enabled('channel_members_table')){
        $sql = 'DELETE FROM channels_members WHERE team_id=%team_id AND
                channel_id=%channel_id AND user_id=%user_id';
        $double_write_ret = db_write_team($team, $sql, $bind);

        if (not_ok($double_write_ret)){
            log_error("UD_DOUBLE_WRITE_ERR: Failed to delete row for
                channels_members for {$team['id']}-{$channel_id}-{$user_id}");
        }
    }

    return $ret;
}
```

Once we had successfully moved over all write operations, we wrote a backfill script to copy all existing data from both membership tables onto our new table. Note that we migrated write operations *before* starting a backfill to ensure that the data in the new table would be accurate. We then backfilled all membership data for our own workspace, followed promptly by VLB during off-hours to prevent any unnecessary load during their workday. We tripled-checked that no errant writes to either table remained outside of our new library, but given that the engineering organization was moving quickly, there was a nonzero chance we had missed one or two queries. We had not yet put any mechanisms in place to prevent an engineer on a different team from adding a new query without alerting us, so to ensure that the backfilled data remained consistent with the live data, we warned our engineering team about our process (see Figure 10-10) and wrote a script we could manually kick off to identify any inconsistencies and optionally patch them if desired.

 In some of the screenshots included in this chapter, you might see some references to TS. TS is short for Tiny Speck, the previous name of the company before Slack, the product, was launched publicly in 2014. If you see a reference to something being "enabled to TS," this just means that we're enabling the change to our own workspace.

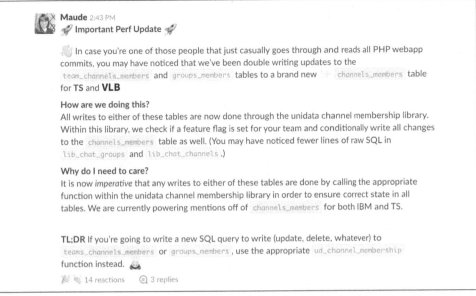

Maude 2:43 PM
🚀 Important Perf Update 🚀

🙋 In case you're one of those people that just casually goes through and reads all PHP webapp commits, you may have noticed that we've been double writing updates to the `team_channels_members` and `groups_members` tables to a brand new `channels_members` table for **TS** and **VLB**

How are we doing this?
All writes to either of these tables are now done through the unidata channel membership library. Within this library, we check if a feature flag is set for your team and conditionally write all changes to the `channels_members` table as well. (You may have noticed fewer lines of raw SQL in `lib_chat_groups` and `lib_chat_channels`.)

Why do I need to care?
It is now *imperative* that any writes to either of these tables are done by calling the appropriate function within the unidata channel membership library in order to ensure correct state in all tables. We are currently powering mentions off of `channels_members` for both IBM and TS.

TL;DR If you're going to write a new SQL query to write (update, delete, whatever) to `teams_channels_members` or `groups_members`, use the appropriate `ud_channel_membership` function instead. 🙏

✨ 🎉 14 reactions 💬 3 replies

Figure 10-10. Announcement that we've started double-writing to the new table

After enabling double-writing for VLB, we watched its database health carefully; `teams_channels_members` and `groups_members` rows were updated very frequently. Whenever a user read a new message, the client issued a request to the servers to update the user's `last_read` timestamp on their membership row. Now, with the addition of `channels_members`, we were issuing double the number of writes. We spent a day monitoring traffic to gain confidence that the workspace had enough bandwidth to handle the additional load.

Now that our tables were in sync and we were double-writing updates, we could execute on our most important milestone: migrating the mentions query. Whenever we were ready to give something a try in production, we first rolled it out to our own team. This was (and still is) the typical strategy for testing our work in production, whether it's a new feature, a new piece of infrastructure, or, in our case, a performance enhancement. We typically would have rolled out to free workspaces next, slowly working our way up the payment tiers, leaving our largest, most performance-sensitive customers last; but with this particular endeavor, we wanted to ease the load on those top-tier customers first. So we flipped our strategy on its head.

We enabled optimized mentions to our team. Because we didn't have much automated testing and our unit testing framework was unable to test the query properly, we relied on folks internally to spot any regressions before we enabled the query to any other customers. We carefully monitored channels where employees typically reported bugs. We later enabled this behavior for VLB.

Quantifying Our Progress

We knew that our databases were overloaded. We measured their health by looking at what percentage of their CPU was idle. Typically, this would hover at about 25 percent but would regularly dip to 10 percent and below. This was troubling because the more time it spent at less than 25 percent idle, the less likely it would be able to handle a sudden increase in load. VLB was putting our product through its paces, and we never knew which part of the product would lead to an unexpected uptick in database usage next.

When we began the consolidation effort, we already had multiple other projects running in parallel to help address the load. Among the range of ongoing workstreams, the added load due to double-writing, recurrent fluctuations, and product engineering continuing to build out new features, we couldn't rely on our database usage data to confirm that the refactor was effective. Besides, our monitoring data disappeared after about a week, so unless we had chosen a quiet day to capture some screenshots and record a series of data points, the data wouldn't have been available to us upon completion to serve as a good baseline.

Instead, we chose to rely primarily on query timings data. We instrumented each query with timing metrics, allowing us to confirm whether the new query was in fact more performant. EXPLAIN plans can be quite insightful, but nothing beats having actual metrics to track the time spent executing a query from the server's perspective. In an abundance of caution, instead of enabling the new treatment to all VLB users immediately, we randomly assigned incoming requests to either query. We first verified that the feature flag was enabled for the workspace and then randomly distributed the traffic 50-50. This enabled us to be a little bit more careful with our introduction of the change and confirmed that the new query was in fact more performant with a customer as large as VLB.

We waited a few hours before taking a look at our data. We needed to make sure that the new query was consistently faster, meaning it needed to be faster both when the database was under average load and when it was at peak usage. Thankfully, the data looked promising across the board with a 20 percent speed-up! You can see the original data we pulled in Figure 10-11. The first query joined across both `teams_chan nels_members` and `groups_members` and on average completed in about 4.4 seconds. The second query read from `channels_members` alone and on average completed in about 3.5 seconds. We managed to shed nearly a second by using the consolidated membership table. (Both queries were too long to show in full, so only the first few lines are visible in the timings chart.)

5 row(s), 7 column(s)						
sql	total	p50	p95	p99	maximum	avg_time
SELECT mn.*,tcm.last_read,tcm.last_read_abs,mnpp.state as is_pushed FROM mentions_normalized mn JOIN teams_channels_members tcm ON (mn.team_id=%team_id AND mn.channel_type=%channel_type_c AND mn.user_id!=%mentioned_user_id AND tcm.user_id=%mentioned_user_id AND mn.team_id=tcm.team_id AND mn.channel_id=tcm.channel_id AND mn.timestamp>tcm.date_joined*999999 AND mn.timestamp>tcm.last_read_abs AND mn.timestamp >= %_field_binding_0) LEFT JOIN subteams_users su ON (mn.team_id=su.team_id AND mn.item_id	4043474	2	11	37	3092	4.404268458261
SELECT mn.*,cm.last_read,cm.last_read_abs,mnpp.state as is_pushed FROM mentions_normalized mn JOIN channels_members cm ON (mn.team_id=%team_id AND mn.user_id!=%mentioned_user_id AND cm.user_id=%mentioned_user_id AND mn.team_id=cm.team_id AND mn.channel_id=cm.channel_id AND mn.timestamp>cm.date_joined*999999 AND mn.timestamp>cm.last_read_abs AND mn.timestamp >= %_field_binding_2) LEFT JOIN subteams_users su ON (mn.team_id=su.team_id AND mn.item_id=su.subteam_id AND su.user_id=%mentioned_user_id A	3967120	1	9	31	3657	3.511519943939
SELECT mn.*,tcm.last_read,tcm.last_read_abs,mnpp.state						

Figure 10-11. Timings data on one of the mentions queries for VLB

With the confirmation that our refactor did the trick for our most important use case, we could justify moving forward with the remainder of the consolidation. We referred back to our Google Sheet tracker and began divvying up the remainder of the read queries to engineers on our team.

Attempting to Keep the Team Motivated

Unfortunately, it was difficult to get the help we needed to finish the migration. Given so many fires to put out, everyone on our team was parallelized across distinct remediation efforts. It was tough to get anyone else to take a few hours out of their day to carefully extract a handful of queries. To top it off, most of the code surrounding the remaining queries was untested, making what should have been a simple, straightforward change quite dangerous. Spending an afternoon migrating queries was simply not enticing.

I considered reaching out to other teams in the Enterprise engineering team for their help and tapping a handful of other performance-minded developers across the company but, ultimately, decided to keep trudging through on my own, with the occasional help from my immediate teammates. Because the work was risky and not particularly intellectually stimulating, I thought it might be too much of an uphill battle to convince a wider circle of engineers to contribute. In hindsight, I think I could have found a way to make the effort more compelling, distributed the work more evenly, and likely shaved off a few weeks.

When progress slowed to a crawl just a few weeks later, I attempted to bribe the team with cookies, which you can see in Figure 10-12. While there is a number of more traditional options for getting engineers motivated to help out (see Chapter 8), sometimes food is the best incentive of all.

Figure 10-12. An attempt at bribery

Communicating Our Progress

Although our team was widely distributed across a number of projects, we still needed each other's support. We relied on one another for code reviews, talking through tough bugs, and the occasional gut check. To make sure we could be effective in those roles while remaining highly focused on our own endeavor, we would regularly debug performance problems in public channels (oftentimes our own team channel) and hold in-person weekly meetings to discuss progress and blockers. For me, that meant a regular avenue to call out what percentage of queries were still littered across the codebase and talk through any bugs or inconsistencies I'd spotted in the data.

Whenever we reached a meaningful milestone, like enabling double-writes to our own workspace, or enabling the new mentions query to VLB, we'd announce the change in both our team channel and in a few engineering-wide channels for added visibility. The more engineers that were aware of the changes we were making, the better! It meant that an engineer on another team was less likely to introduce a new query against either table we were actively deprecating without referring to our new library. It also meant that as we triaged incoming customer bugs, any engineer could isolate and solve a related problem much more effectively.

Stumbling upon the Inevitable Bug

No large refactoring effort would be complete without one or two pesky bugs, and this one was no exception. About a month into moving read queries into our new library, we began to notice a small but significant number of membership rows on the new table that were slightly out of date. After a day or so of poking around, we realized that sometimes we were successfully issuing a write to either `teams_chan nels_members` or `groups_members`, but failing to double-write to `channels_members`. Because our write functions returned whether the first write to the old table was a success and ignored whether the second write went through, callers of the function would assume everything was fine and continue executing.

We made the necessary change to return a failure if either write encountered a problem, but weren't sure whether there might have been another, more nefarious bug at play. To verify that we had fixed the one (and only) bug, we decided to repopulate `channels_members` for our own workspace from a clean slate. We initiated another backfill, pruning the table of all its contents and then populating it with copies of data from `teams_channels_members` and `groups_members`.

This should have been fine, except that I forgot at the time that our team was exclusively reading membership information from the new table. Just a few seconds after the script began, all my channels disappeared. Everyone across the entire company was booted out of all their channels. It took me a few minutes to flip the feature flag so that our team once again fetched its memberships from the original tables. Thankfully, most folks at the company had gone home by then and weren't closely monitoring their client, but I definitely gave some fellow employees a pretty serious scare.

Tidying Up

Once no more entries were left in our tracker, we slowly began enabling all other teams beyond our own (and VLB) to read from the new table. We let the changes sit for two weeks before deciding it was safe to stop double-writing data to the old tables. We wanted to be certain that our database tier responded well to the new table, that its data was consistently correct, and that no new bugs related to the refactor were logged. Had double-writing not been expensive from both a load and monetary perspective, we might have allowed the changes to bake a bit longer, but we were eager to remove the overhead.

Finally, we stopped double-writing, first for our own team, then for VLB, and finally for the remainder of our customers. As with every important step of our refactor, we communicated it broadly, as shown in Figure 10-13. We then quickly tidied up our new library by removing all references to `teams_channels_members` and `groups_mem bers`. We wrote some new linter rules, preventing engineers from writing new queries against either deprecated table and enforcing all new queries against the `chan nels_members` table to be properly located in our new centralized library. We wanted to prevent confusion among engineers about how far along we were with the refactor. Not everyone reads all announcements in cross-functional channels, especially if they are out on vacation or leave, so it's important to make sure you don't rely on those announcements alone for engineers across your organization to know what to do when they come across code that has been changed as part of your refactor.

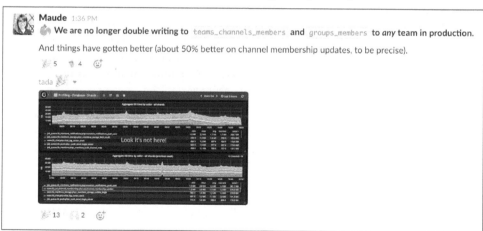

Figure 10-13. Announcing we were no longer double-writing for our own workspace

Here's a close-up of the graph in Figure 10-13's Slack message:

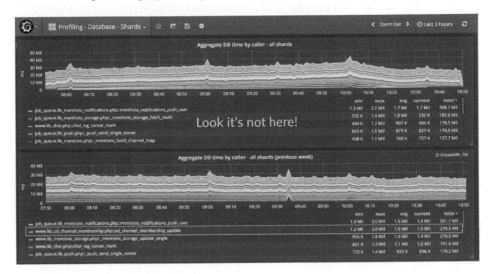

Of course, we didn't forget the most important final step: celebrating! As was tradition for much of the engineering team in San Francisco, we ordered a cake (Figure 10-14) adorned with the name of our new table to commemorate the completion of the project.

Figure 10-14. Funfetti cake to celebrate our refactor!

The project's complete trajectory is shown in Figure 10-15, highlighting the number of queries executed against each table on a daily basis from May to September 2017.

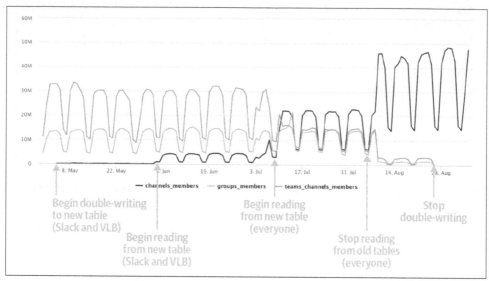

Figure 10-15. Query volume for `teams_channels_members`, `groups_members`, *and* `channels_members` *throughout the refactor*

Lessons Learned

There are a number of lessons to be learned from this case study, both from what went well and what could have gone better. We'll start with where the project struggled, describing the pitfalls of not having a written execution plan, forgoing understanding of how the code had degraded, skimping on the number of tests we wrote, and failing to motivate teammates. Then we'll discuss what went well, highlighting our sharp focus on dynamic milestones and a well-defined set of metrics.

Develop a Well-Defined, Well-Communicated Plan

Because the whole project began so fast, we didn't have much of a written plan. Our team was familiar with the process involved for migrating data from one table to another. We knew the mentions query was our top priority and that we would complete only as much of the migration as was necessary to do so; we would reevaluate later. The only time the process appeared in written form was when we posted updates in our team channel (rather than in a channel dedicated to the project); even then, these were only pertinent subsets of the overall plan.

The fact that we never deliberately wrote down each of the steps involved from start to finish meant that we were more likely to forget something critical along the way.

Perhaps most worrisome of all was the fact that we never shopped our plan around to other teams across the company to ensure that everyone had a chance to verify whether they might be affected by the change and voice their concerns if that was the case. We simply plowed through, on the assumption that performance was the most important thing we could be doing to improve our relationship with our largest customer (and, by extension, the most important thing we could be doing for the company). We also believed that we could implement the change in a way that would disrupt as few other engineering teams as possible.

This assumption proved to be wrong on multiple fronts. First, when a handful of inevitable bugs crept up and we hadn't adequately socialized the change, engineers responding to those bugs were unpleasantly surprised. Second, we overlooked a team altogether that would bear an acute impact from the change. About a month before we finished migrating the final few membership queries, a teammate reminded me that we should probably warn the data engineering team about the changes we were making. By moving membership onto a new table, and nearing the stage at which we would disable writes to the old tables, we risked disrupting most of their pipelines, including pipelines responsible for calculating important usage metrics. We were fortunate that the data engineering team was quick to respond and update the necessary pipelines, and a serious crisis was averted.

These mishaps show just how important it is to develop and vet a thorough execution plan. We were lucky that we recovered from these oversights quickly, but why leave to chance what could have been addressed more deliberately during the early planning stages? As was highlighted in Chapters 4 and 7, having a concrete plan is crucial to uncovering gaps early and minimizing cross-functional communication gaps.

Understand the Code's History

I highly recommend developers begin their code archeology expedition before they begin to execute their refactoring effort, because the added context can give a different shape and direction to the project. Unfortunately, due to the urgency of our work, we skipped the deliberate process of understanding and empathizing with the existing code and went right to execution. It was only well after we had begun migrating queries that I started to wonder why we'd made a distinction between `teams_channels_members` and `groups_members` in the first place.

As the weeks passed and there were still dozens of queries to migrate, I grew frustrated with the redundant tables and the way our SQL queries were strewn about. The more frustrated I became, the longer the project seemed to take (and the more tempting it became to cut corners in an attempt to reach the finish line faster).

After we had completed the refactor, I contacted a few of our early engineers to get some insight into why these tables had been distinct. I learned that keeping private and public channel information on separate tables isolated them from one another and served as a security precaution. Product history played a role as well; public channels and private channels felt like vastly different concepts in the early days of Slack. As the two concepts gradually converged, so did the table schemas.

Gaining this perspective proved helpful for subsequent refactors, informing how we went about consolidating `teams_channels` and `groups` into their own unified table. It gave me a newfound appreciation for decisions made early in Slack's history, and a more positive attitude toward refactoring as an opportunity to improve something that had probably served us well for some time but no longer could, rather than as an opportunity to improve "bad" code. This experience is precisely why in Chapter 2 I recommend that engineers take the time to understand where the code they seek to improve came from, and how circumstances may have led it to degrade over time. If we have more empathy for the code, we stand to keep a more open mind and be more patient throughout the refactor.

Ensure Adequate Test Coverage

In Chapter 1, I asserted that it's important to have adequate test coverage before refactoring, to ensure that the application's behavior is properly maintained at every step. In this project, the vast majority of the code we were modifying had been written early in Slack's development and, due to the push to get the product to market quickly, much of it lacked adequate tests. The refactor to consolidate the channel membership tables was under significant time pressure as well; performance for our largest customer was a growing concern, so we did our best to make the necessary changes carefully, opting to write tests for only the most critical untested codepaths.

This decision led us to ship a handful of bugs throughout the refactor, each of which could have been prevented had we taken the time to write the requisite tests. We arguably spent more time recovering from the regressions we introduced than we would have writing the tests in the first place. Having adequate test coverage is essential for a smooth refactor, preventing your customers from experiencing bugs and your team from spending time solving them.

Keep Your Team Motivated

Rather than continuing to plow through alone, I should have found a better way to get other engineers involved more seriously at the outset and again when progress slowed a few weeks later. The last 10 percent of queries took about the same amount of time to migrate as the first 50 percent. Once we had successfully improved the mentions query for VLB, we began to lose the sense of urgency we had experienced at the start of the project. With every new bug or inconsistency in our data, we lost a little steam. By the time the project was nearly complete, everything about it felt like pushing a boulder up a mountain.

What we had not considered was soliciting help from engineers outside our own team. We could have been more strategic about asking for help from those on other product engineering teams, asking them to migrate the queries within their own features. We could have sold them on the effort by demonstrating the performance boost they stood to gain. Distributing the work could have allowed us to halve the amount of time it took to complete.

If momentum on your refactor starts to slow, seek ways to give it a boost early, before progress slows further. Slow refactors are more likely to lose priority, leaving behind a significant amount of code stuck between two states, which, as was pointed out in Chapter 1, poses its own set of problems. Chapter 8 covered a number of ways to keep your team motivated; do not hesitate to ask for more support if you need it!

Focus on Strategic Milestones

We had preliminary data in the form of query EXPLAIN plans to support our hypothesis that combining the two membership tables would improve query performance. We needed further confirmation of that hypothesis during the early stages of the refactor so that we could pivot if the consolidation proved insufficient. By focusing on making only the changes necessary to enable the migration of the mentions query for VLB, we secured the confirmation we needed within just a few weeks and successfully alleviated load from the VLB database shard, buying us more time to see the remainder of the refactor through.

Proving your refactor's effectiveness early ensures that your team does not waste any time continuing to execute a lengthy project that may not yield the desired results. By focusing on strategic milestones, those meant to benefit from the refactor can reap those benefits sooner; this can help your team, further bolstering support for the effort while it is still underway. For more details on how to identify strategic milestones, refer to Chapter 4.

Identify and Rely on Meaningful Metrics

We had a specific set of metrics that enabled us to show conclusively that our project was successful for both our intermediate milestones and, once we'd completed the rollout, to all customers. By collecting EXPLAIN plans for queries before and after the consolidation, we were able to document progress as we migrated each of the more complex membership queries. By instrumenting the mentions query with timings metrics, we could monitor its performance in real time and immediately see the positive impact.

Keeping a close eye on your metrics helps you prove that your refactor is tilting the needle in the right direction throughout its development. If at any point the metrics stop improving (or worse, start regressing), you can dig in immediately, addressing problems as soon as they arise, rather than at the project's conclusion. Refer to Chapter 3 for suggestions on how to measure your refactor.

Takeaways

Here are the most important takeaways from our refactor to consolidate Slack's channel membership tables.

- Develop a thorough written plan and share it broadly.
- Take the time to understand the code's history; it might help you see it in a new, more positive light.
- Ensure that there is adequate test coverage for the code you're seeking to improve. If there isn't, commit to writing the missing test cases.
- Keep your team motivated. If you're losing momentum, find creative ways to boost it back up.
- Focus on strategic milestones to prove the impact of your refactor early and often.
- Identify and rely on meaningful metrics to guide your efforts.

CHAPTER 11

Case Study: Migrating to a New Database

Cowritten with Maggie Zhou,
Staff Infrastructure Engineer, Slack Technologies, Inc.

For the second of our two case study chapters, we'll explore a refactor carried out by a group of engineers from the product engineering team and infrastructure teams at Slack. The project was built on the consolidation of our channel membership tables discussed in the previous chapter. If you haven't read through the first case study yet, I recommend you do so; there's important context you'll want to understand to get the most out of this chapter.

Unlike the previous case study, which was primarily motivated by performance, this one was chiefly driven by Slack's need to enable greater flexibility in the product. Having channel memberships tied to distinct workspace shards made it difficult for us to build more complex features stretching beyond single workspaces. We wanted to enable complex organizations with multiple workspaces to collaborate seamlessly within the same set of channels and facilitate communication between distinct Slack customers, allowing companies to coordinate with their vendors directly within the application. To unlock this ability, we needed to reshard channel membership data by user and channel rather than by workspace. This refactor illustrates the many challenges that come with large-scale database migrations, multi-quarter projects, and heavily cross-functional engineering efforts.

The refactor was successful because we had a strong understanding of the problem we needed to solve and how our evolving product strategy had led us to outgrow past architectural decisions (Chapter 2). We planned the project thoughtfully, choosing to juggle a few more variables than were strictly necessary, knowing it would render the refactor even more worthwhile (Chapter 4). We derived a careful rollout strategy, developing tooling that enabled us to carry it out as reliably as possible (Chapter 8). Finally, throughout the entire effort, we maintained a simple communication strategy.

Although the refactor ultimately gave us the ability to stretch our product in new and interesting ways, it took nearly double the time we had initially estimated to complete. We were too optimistic in our estimates (Chapter 4); it took over a year to finish what we had originally anticipated would take only six months. We underestimated the product implications of the refactor and only learned to leverage the expertise of product engineers after spending several months making little progress (Chapter 6).

As with the previous case study, we'll start off with some important context, including a brief overview of why the way we distributed our data was becoming a bottleneck, and the motivations behind our adoption of a new database technology, Vitess. Once we've established a solid foundation and the motivations for our refactor, we'll describe our solution and walk through each phase of the project.

Workspace-Sharded Data

To appreciate the problems we sought to solve with this refactor, we need to describe how our data was distributed across our databases in MySQL. Before we kicked off our refactor, the vast majority of our data was sharded by workspace, where a workspace is a single Slack customer. We touched on this in the previous case study under "Slack Architecture 101" on page 174; you can see an illustration of how different customers' data was distributed across different shards in Figure 10-3.

While this worked just fine for a number of years, this sharding scheme grew increasingly inconvenient for two reasons.

First, we struggled to support our biggest workspace shards from an operational perspective. The shards housing our largest, fastest-growing customers suffered from frequent, problematic hotspots. These customers, already occupying isolated shards, were quickly approaching the data size at which we would no longer be able to upgrade their hardware space. With no simple mechanisms by which we could horizontally split their data, we were stuck.

Second, we were making important changes in our product that were actively leading us to break down the barriers between workspaces we had long upheld, both in the way our code was written and in how our data was structured. We had built features enabling our biggest customers to bridge together multiple workspaces and launched the ability for two distinct Slack customers to communicate directly within a channel they shared.

The mismatch between our product vision and the way our systems were architected meant that our application grew ever more complex. This was a perfect example of code degradation due to shift in product requirements (as you might recall from Chapter 2!). To illustrate this problem more concretely, in the year leading up to this case study, we sometimes needed to query three distinct database shards to locate a channel and its memberships successfully. This was confusing for our developers, who needed to remember the correct set of steps to fetch and manipulate channel-related data.

To address our operational concerns with MySQL and our difficulty scaling, we started evaluating other storage options. After weighing multiple solutions, the team decided to adopt Vitess (*https://vitess.io*), a database clustering system built at You-Tube that enables horizontal scaling of MySQL. With the migration to Vitess, we would finally be able to shard our data by something other than workspace, giving us the opportunity to free up space on our busiest shards and distribute our data in a way that made it easier for our engineers to reason out!

Migrating channels_members to Vitess

Given these circumstances, we decided to migrate the channel membership table, channels_members, to Vitess. Because this was one of our most high-traffic tables, resharding it would free up considerable space and load from our busiest workspace shards. The migration would also substantially simplify business logic around fetching memberships for channels that existed across workspace boundaries.

The project was spearheaded out of the Vitess infrastructure team, with help from a handful of product engineers who had intimate knowledge of our application query patterns against the channels_members table. We knew it would be a winning combination. The infrastructure engineers would contribute deep knowledge of the database system so that we could avoid any pitfalls during the migration and efficiently debug database-related issues as they arose; because they had the most expertise with table migrations to date, they'd be best suited to lead the project, with Maggie at the helm. The product engineers, including me, would provide crucial insight as to the new schema and sharding scheme and help with rewriting application logic to query the migrated data correctly.

We kicked things off in earnest by creating a new channel, #feat-vitess-channels, where we could easily bounce ideas off one another and coordinate workstreams. We invited everyone to join and jumped right into our first task.

Sharding Scheme

Before we could begin migrating channel membership data to Vitess, we needed to decide how it would be distributed (i.e., which keys to use to reshard the table). Here, we had two options:

- by channel (`channel_id`), to locate all memberships associated with a channel easily by querying a single shard
- by user (`user_id`), to find all of a user's memberships by querying a single shard

Having recently completed the consolidation of our membership tables per our first case study, my impression was that the majority of queries dealt with fetching membership for a given channel rather than for a given user. Many of these queries were crucial to the application, powering important features like Search, and the ability to mention everyone in a channel (via `@channel` or `@here`).

At the time (and still today), we logged a sample of all database queries to our data warehouse to keep tabs on our MySQL usage across requests to our production systems. To confirm my intuition that most of the traffic to `channels_members` relied on `channel_id`, I ran a few queries against this data, looking at sampled membership queries executed over a month-long period, and brought it to the team. The results are shown in Figure 11-1.

#	filters by channel ID	count
1	true	846150562
2	false	770456108

Figure 11-1. Number of queries run against `channels_members` filtered by `channel_id`

One of the product engineers working with us, who had more experience with Vitess, pointed out that sharding by user might be a better bet. Pulling from the same set of query logs, he showed us the top 10 most frequent queries hitting the table filtered by `user_id`. The results are shown in Figure 11-2. If we wanted our application to perform well, we would need to account for this behavior.

#	sql	filters by channel ID	count
1	SELECT * FROM channels_members FORCE INDEX (PRIMARY) WHE...	true	1129091681
2	SELECT * FROM channels_members WHERE team_id=%team_id AND...	true	268354996
3	SELECT cm.channel_id AS channel_id, cm.last_read, c.is_shared, c.is_m...	true	218944219
4	SELECT 'team_id','channel_id','user_id','date_joined','date_deleted','l...	true	134941810
5	UPDATE channels_members SET 'last_read'=%last_read, 'last_read_ab...	true	128874281
6	UPDATE channels_members SET 'last_read' =%last_read, 'last_read_ab...	true	86645894
7	SELECT 1 as count FROM messages m JOIN channels_members c ON...	false	69190411
8	SELECT channel_id, is_general, c.channel_type, name, date_archived, la...	false	65318561
9	SELECT c.* FROM %field:table c JOIN channels_members cm ON cm.c...	false	62554095
10	SELECT team_id, channel_id,user_id FROM channels_members WHER...	false	57343805

Figure 11-2. Top 10 most frequent queries against `channels_members` and whether they filtered the data by `user_id`

We weighed both options, doing some back-of-the-napkin math to determine the database querying capacity required to support either option. We ultimately decided to compromise, denormalizing the membership into two tables, one sharded by user, the other sharded by channel, double-writing for both use cases. This way, point queries would be cheap for both.

Developing a New Schema

Next, we needed to take a hard look at our existing workspace-sharded table schema and determine whether we wanted to modify it for both our user- and channel-sharded use cases. Although we could have migrated our existing schema to both sharding schemes, this refactor gave us a unique opportunity to rethink some of the decisions we'd made with the original table design. We'll take a closer look at the schema we derived for each, starting with the user shard. Example 11-1 shows the schema on the workspace shards, before the migration.

Example 11-1. CREATE TABLE statement showing the existing `channels_members` table, sharded by workspace

```
CREATE TABLE `channels_members` (
  `user_id` bigint(20) unsigned NOT NULL,
  `channel_id` bigint(20) unsigned NOT NULL,
  `team_id` bigint(20) unsigned NOT NULL,
  `date_joined` int(10) unsigned NOT NULL,
  `date_deleted` int(10) unsigned NOT NULL,
  `last_read` bigint(20) unsigned NOT NULL,
  ...
  `channel_type` tinyint(3) unsigned NOT NULL,
  `channel_privacy_type` tinyint(4) unsigned NOT NULL,
  ...
  `user_team_id` bigint(20) unsigned NOT NULL,
  PRIMARY KEY (`user_id`,`channel_id`)
)
```

User-sharded membership table

For the user-sharded case, we decided to maintain the majority of the original schema, with one exception: we made a significant change to how we stored user IDs. To understand the motivations behind this decision, we'll give a brief overview of the two kinds of user IDs we stored and how they came about.

At the start of the chapter, we briefly mentioned that Slack sought to enable complex businesses, split into multiple workspaces according to department or business unit, to collaborate more easily. Without any centralization, not only did employees have difficulty communicating across departments, it was also difficult for the company to manage each individual workspace properly. To this end, we enabled our biggest customers to bring together their many workspaces under a single umbrella.

Unfortunately, in grouping workspaces, we needed a way to keep users in sync. Let's illustrate how this works with a simple example.

Acme Corp. is a large corporation. It has a number of departments, each with its own workspace, including one for its engineering team and customer experience department. As an employee of Acme Corp., you have a single, organization-level user account. If you happen to be an engineer, you are a member of the Engineering workspace to collaborate with your teammates, and the Customer Experience workspace to help the support team troubleshoot customer issues.

What appeared to be a single account at Acme Corp., however, was actually multiple accounts under the hood. At the organization level, a user had a *canonical user ID*. The same user had distinct *local user IDs* for each workspace they were a member of. This means that if you were a member of the Engineering and Customer Experience workspaces, you had three unique user IDs, or, to generalize, $n + 1$ IDs, where n was the number of workspaces of which you were a member.

As you might imagine, translating between these IDs quickly became exceedingly complicated and bug-prone. Within a year of launching this feature, a number of product engineers hatched a plan for replacing all *local user IDs* with *canonical user IDs*. Because most of the data stored in Slack's systems refer to a user ID of some kind (authoring a message, uploading a file, etc.), a high degree of complexity was involved with correctly (and invisibly) rewriting these IDs.

The workspace-sharded `channels_members` table stored *local user IDs* in the `user_id` column. Because a project was already underway to replace all local user IDs with canonical user IDs, we decided to collaborate with them and ensure that we stored canonical user IDs across all user ID columns.

Channel-sharded table schema

Beyond our concerns with user IDs, we had some unease about the write bandwidth to the secondary, channel-sharded membership table. We examined the queries we planned to send to these shards to try to identify ways we could decrease write traffic. During that process, we noticed that most of the columns on the original table were entirely unused by their consumers, including the ones that were updated most often, like a user's last read position in the channel. For example, if we queried for all the memberships associated with a given channel, the application logic would usually only use the `user_id` and `user_team_id` columns. By omitting these unnecessary columns in our new schema, we could dramatically decrease the write frequency, giving our channel shards a bit more breathing room. Example 11-2 shows the table schema for the channel-sharded membership table.

Example 11-2. CREATE TABLE statement for the second of our new `channels_members` tables, sharded by channel

```
CREATE TABLE `channels_members_bychan`
  `user_id` bigint(20) unsigned NOT NULL,
  `channel_id` bigint(20) unsigned NOT NULL,
  `user_team_id` bigint(20) unsigned NOT NULL,
  `channel_team_id` bigint(20) unsigned NOT NULL, ❶
  `date_joined` int(10) unsigned NOT NULL DEFAULT '0',
  PRIMARY KEY (`channel_id`,`user_id`)
)
```

❶ Renamed `team_id` to `channel_team_id`

Detangling JOINs

We next needed to update our application logic to accommodate the changes to our schemas and point to the Vitess cluster. Thankfully, most of these changes were straightforward and before we knew it, we'd updated the majority of our application logic accordingly.

Where the migration became more difficult was with complex queries involving JOINs with other tables in our MySQL cluster. Because we were moving the table to an entirely new cluster, we could no longer support these queries and had to split them up into smaller point queries, performing the JOIN directly in the application code.

We knew at the project's outset that we would likely need to split up a handful of JOIN queries. What we did not anticipate was that most of them powered core Slack features and had been carefully hand-tuned for performance over a number of years. By splitting up these queries, we risked anything from slowing down notifications, to introducing data leaks, to bringing down Slack entirely. We were pretty nervous, but we needed to push on.

We put the day-to-day migrations on pause and compiled a list of the queries we were most concerned about, of which there were 20. Poring through the set, we worried that we didn't have the product expertise required to adequately detangle each and every one. We estimated that without any additional help from product engineering, we'd need months to detangle each of the JOINs successfully. Fortunately, a number of product engineers responded to our call for help and together we developed a simple process that we could apply to split up each query safely.

To illustrate each step, we'll walk through how we split up the query shown in Example 11-3, which was responsible for deciding whether a user had permission to see a specific file.

Example 11-3. A sample JOIN we needed to detangle; % symbolizes substitution syntax

```
SELECT COUNT(*)
FROM files_shares s
LEFT JOIN channels_members g
  ON g.team_id = s.team_id
  AND g.channel_id = s.channel_id
  AND g.user_id = %USER_ID
  AND g.date_deleted = 0
WHERE
  s.team_id = %TEAM_ID
AND s.file_id = %FILE_ID
LIMIT 1
```

We first needed to identify the smallest subset of data we could fetch earliest; this would help us minimize the intersection of data we needed to work with as early as possible.

With the file visibility query, we knew from typical usage patterns that the number of places where a file was shared was usually much smaller than the number of channels that a user was in. (We could also verify this assumption by looking at a query's cardinality.) So, instead of first querying for a user's channel memberships and cross-referencing those with the channels where the file was shared, we fetched the locations where the file was shared first and then determined whether the user was in any of these channels. You can see an example of the query split up into its two components in Example 11-4.

Example 11-4. The `JOIN` *with* `files_shares` *split into two queries*

```
SELECT DISTINCT channel_id
FROM files_shares
WHERE team_id=%TEAM_ID AND file_id=%FILE_ID

...

SELECT COUNT(*)
FROM channels_members
WHERE
  team_id=%TEAM_ID
  AND user_id=%USER_ID
  AND channel_id IN (%list:CHANNEL_IDS)
LIMIT 1
```

We then verified that the test coverage was sufficient. If it wasn't, we would write a few additional test cases to verify the results of the original query. Once we were satisfied, we wrapped the new logic in an experiment to enable a gradual rollout and give us the ability to rollback quickly in an emergency. We ran our tests against both implementations, fixed any bugs that crept up, and repeated the process until we felt confident with our new logic. Finally, we instrumented both calls with some timings metrics to track the execution time of both the `JOIN` and its detangled version. Example 11-5 provides a rough outline for what the file visibility check looked like with both query implementations and corresponding instrumentation.

 For the riskier query splits (including file visibility), we worked with the quality assurance team to manually verify the change in both our development environments and production before rolling it out to more users. The majority of the JOINs we sought to detangle dealt with critical Slack functionality, so we wanted to be particularly careful that our changes perfectly replicated intended behavior.

Example 11-5. Function for determining whether a user can see a specific file

```
function file_can_see($team, $user, $file): bool {

  if (experiment_get_user('detangle_files_shares_query')) {
    $start = microtime_float();

    # First, we want to find all of the channels where
    # the file was shared. Because we can share a file to the
    # same channel multiple times, we may find multiple files_shares
    # rows with the same channel ID but different timestamps
    # at which it was shared.
    $channel_ids =
      ud_files_shares_get_distinct_channel_ids(
        $team,
        $file['id']
      );

    # Next, we want to find the intersection of the channels
    # the file was shared in ($channel_ids) and the channels the
    # user is in.
    $membership_counts =
      ud_channels_members_get_counts(
        $team,
        $user['id'],
        $channel_ids
      );

    $end = microtime_float() - $start;

    # If there is at least one membership row, then the user
    # can see the file. If not, the user cannot see the file.
    _files_can_see_unjoined_histogram()->observe($end);
    return ($membership_counts['count'] > 0);
  }

  $start = microtime_float();
  $sql .=  "SELECT 1 FROM files_shares s
      LEFT JOIN channels_members g
      ON g.team_id = s.team_id
        AND g.channel_id = s.channel_id
        AND g.user_id = %USER_ID
        AND g.date_deleted=0
      WHERE s.team_id = %TEAM_ID
        AND s.file_id = %FILE_ID
        AND (g.user_id > 0) LIMIT 1";

  $bind = [
    'file_id' => $file['id'],
    'user_id' => $user['id'],
    'team_id' => $team['id']
  ];
```

```
    $ret = db_fetch_team($team, $sql, $bind);
    $end = microtime_float() - $start;
    _files_can_see_join_histogram()->observe($end);

    return (bool)db_single($ret);
}
```

We enabled the new implementation to our own internal Slack instance before rolling it out to real customers. This was an important step to confirm that we were properly ingesting timings metrics and further ensure that we had not unintentionally introduced a bug.

Slack's workspace has all sorts of quirks, and our usage patterns don't always match those of our customers. While it often makes for a decent litmus test for catching bugs early, the workspace was not a suitable candidate to help us determine whether the added latencies of the detangled queries were acceptable. For a subset of the JOINs, performance of the detangled queries was particularly aggravated on our own workspace, and as we continued the rollout to free teams, followed by larger paying customers, the metrics stabilized.

We repeated the process for nearly every JOIN, gingerly slicing queries apart, instrumenting them, and gradually rolling them out to customers. The only exception was two pesky mentions queries, which we left untouched for several months. Unfortunately, these queries posed a number of unique challenges, including JOINs against tables that were undergoing their own Vitess migration. We decided to defer on their migration until all their subcomponents had properly fallen into place. Overall, five of us took about six weeks on and off, with our time split between the refactor and other commitments, to finish migrating the majority of the JOINs.

It's often the case that refactors don't go entirely according to plan; we encounter hurdles that require us to reshuffle priorities or, in some cases, stop partway through a given step in favor of coming back to it later. Although it feels deeply unsatisfying to hit pause and shift gears, it can sometimes make a huge difference in our ability to deliver the overall project in a timely manner.

For this effort, had we waited for the remainder of the migrations we were depending on to land, it would have set the refactor back by several months. By instead choosing to move forward with the vast majority of the channels_members queries we had successfully rewritten, we were able to continue making headway, uncovering issues as they crept up; when the time finally came to revisit the mentions queries again, we were in a much stabler place to do so.

A Difficult Rollout

When we began our migration of `channels_members`, approximately 15 percent of our total queries per second (QPS) was powered by Vitess. We'd already migrated and resharded critical workloads, such as notifications-related tables, and the `teams` table responsible for listing each Slack customer instance. We had built reliable techniques and tooling to facilitate nearly 20 migrations, complete with dashboards and a framework for efficiently comparing data sets across the old and new clusters.

The `channels_members` migration was unique, however, in that it alone accounted for nearly 20 percent of our total query load, nearly doubling the QPS we had learned to manage on Vitess to date. Because of the scale, we were nervous about running into unexpected issues during the migration. That said, we were highly motivated to move these more sizable workloads off of MySQL, because it was struggling under the load of our largest customers. We were stuck between a rock and a hard place.

Our best bet was to lean heavily on the migration tooling we'd built during previous Vitess migrations. We hoped it would be stable enough for this table as well.

The rollout process we had developed for enabling migrations consisted of four high-level modes:

1. *Backfill*

   During this stage, we double-wrote queries to both the new cluster (with the new sharding scheme) and to the old cluster. This mode further allowed us to backfill our new cluster with existing data from the old cluster.

2. *Dark*

   This mode sent read traffic to both clusters and compared the results, logging any discrepancies in the data retrieved from the new Vitess cluster. Consumers of the read traffic were provided with results retrieved from the old cluster.

3. *Light*

   This mode sent read traffic to both clusters, again comparing results and logging any discrepancies as they arose. However, instead of returning results from the old cluster, Vitess results were returned to the application.

4. *Sunset*

   During this stage, we continued to double-write to both clusters but send read requests strictly to the Vitess cluster. This mode allowed us to discontinue the expensive process of reading from two distinct data sources, all the while enabling any downstream consumers to continue to rely on data stored in the old clusters until they were updated to read from Vitess. (This included systems such as our data warehouse.) At this stage, if any problems were uncovered, the only option was to fix forward; there was no easy or safe way to go back to consuming data from the legacy data source.

Fast, simple configuration deployments enabled us to swap easily between modes as well as ramp up and down within a single mode. The system also provided us with rather granular controls, whereby we could swiftly opt tiers of customers and users into distinct modes. We took advantage of being able to tweak these settings to ramp up and back down rapidly when we encountered any issues.

Backfill Mode

Every migration began with *Backfill* mode. In this mode, there were two primary goals. The first goal was to set the stage for running a complete backfill of the data from the old cluster in preparation for the migration of read queries. For the majority of our previous migrations, this phase was quite simple; the write queries for the new cluster would be identical (or nearly so) to the corresponding write queries to the old cluster. Because we were actively changing the data model, we ended up having to rewrite many of our application's SQL queries to conform to our new schema (including propagating the `share_type` correctly and translating local user IDs to their canonical counterparts). Luckily, thanks to the prior consolidation discussed in Chapter 10, we were able to readily identify each query requiring a rewrite.

The second goal was to unveil any performance problems associated with write load to the new cluster. For most of these migrations, we considered the *Backfill* and *Dark* modes to have relatively little (if any) performance impact on the application in production. This was primarily because:

- We used Hacklang's `async` cooperative multitasking mode to send queries to both clusters concurrently. We set a short, one-second (1s) time-out on the query hitting the new cluster in Vitess, so that in the very worst case, the performance penalty for these queries would be 1s minus the time it took to execute the query from the old cluster.

- We were not yet returning the results to the application from the Vitess cluster! This would occur in *Light* mode.

Again, our assumptions proved wrong with this migration. The user-sharded Vitess database cluster to which we were moving `channels_members` was already populated with highly used production data (including saved messages and notifications). As we ramped up *Backfill* mode, we began saturating database resources on Vitess, leading to time-outs and errors for queries to the critical tables already residing on the cluster. Digging in, we discovered that we had a number of update and delete queries lacking our sharding key (`user_id`), thus scattering them across every shard in the cluster. We made a configuration change so that these could run more efficiently, and then tentatively kicked off a second gradual ramp-up of *Backfill* mode. We quickly reached 100 percent and began the next stage, *Dark* mode!

Dark Mode

We entered the *Dark* mode portion of the refactor in earnest, having carefully rewritten most of the `channels_members` queries (including many of the troublesome JOINs) to read from Vitess, and successfully completed the backfill process in just over three months. Because our migration system enabled us to opt subsets of queries into different phases (i.e., one query could be in *Dark* mode while another was in *Light* mode), in an effort to parallelize as much of the refactor as possible, we began to ramp up *Dark* mode before we'd rewritten all our queries to read from the Vitess cluster properly.

Dark mode, as with *Backfill* mode, had two primary goals. Once again, one of our objectives was to reveal any potential performance problems associated with the read traffic being sent to the new cluster.

Performance

As we began ramping up traffic to read from Vitess concurrently with our legacy system, we noticed that a handful of queries with high QPS returned an alarming number of rows. The combination of high QPS with the large number of rows returned made the overall rows returned per second the largest in our cluster. Figure 11-3 shows that at peak, we were returning about 9,000 rows per second from a single shard's `channels_members` table. In fact, these queries were so frequent and memory-intensive that they caused out-of-memory errors (OOMs) to flood the database host itself! During the days following our ramp-up, we saw 1/256 of our hosts running out of memory every day.

At first, we believed that our cloud provider was at fault; perhaps something was wrong with the way we had provisioned our largest database cluster. Eventually, we realized that it wasn't a configuration mishap or random bad luck, and we swiftly ramped down to start isolating the source of the OOMs.

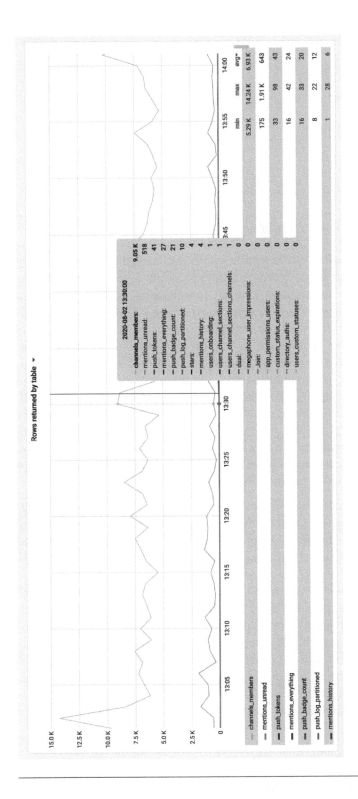

Figure 11-3. Rows returned from +channels_members+ on a single shard

Figure 11-4 shows our surprise with the OOMs during our weekly status update.

Maggie Zhou (she/her) 1 year ago
Status
100% DARK reads for all teams minus a few callsites*, and two remaining JOINs.

Big change this week
We ramped up more DARK reads and hit 5 OOMs on master tablets in 12 hours.

We're still working on uncovering the various causes of this problem and how to move forward so that high query load doesn't cause OOMs. In the meantime, we've actually re-ramped up *most* of the DARK reads.

Figure 11-4. Weekly project status reporting on OOMs

The refactor was a high-priority project both within the infrastructure and among engineering organizations at large. From a database reliability perspective, moving `channels_members` to Vitess was an important step in continuing to develop our muscle memory around operating the new system, so when the OOMs proved particularly elusive, we began working with the entire database team at Slack, debugging from all angles directly in the channel we had set up to coordinate the effort, #feat-vitess-channels. We attempted to resize the memory allocation for our MySQL processes, digging into memory fragmentation and allocation at both the MySQL and operating system levels. During this process, we upgraded minor versions of MySQL to have access to a new setting that allowed us to specify the nonuniform memory access (NUMA) interleave policy for the buffer pool! Meanwhile, we continued to split up more `JOIN`s, and began ramping up more *Dark* mode query load. Each time, we thought we might stop encountering OOMs, only to be disappointed as we kept encountering them as we ramped up more load.

At this point, the project had just surpassed the six-month mark, obliterating our initial estimate; the whole team very much felt as through we were consistently taking two steps forward and one step back. After weeks of trial and error, we discovered that other storage systems at Slack (including our monitoring cluster and Search cluster) had hit problems with a restrictively small value for `min_free_kbytes`, a low-level kernel setting responsible for controlling how aggressively the kernel decides to free memory. The larger the value, the more breathing room the kernel will give itself by shedding more data held in RAM. With the substantial number of queries returning a large number of rows at high QPS, we would sporadically hit spikes of requests that required a sudden allocation of a large amount of RAM, leading to OOMs, because the kernel couldn't free RAM quickly enough to return results. Bumping this `min_free_kbytes` to a higher value enabled our hosts to manage the memory pressure associated with these queries better and finally resolved our OOMs.

We spent eight whole months in the *Dark* mode phase; not only did we spend more time in this phase alone than we had initially anticipated spending on the project as a whole, it accounted for nearly two-thirds of the entire endeavor once we'd completed it. What happened?

Data discrepancies

Given our configuration changes, we were comfortable ramping up 100 percent of the traffic to the Vitess cluster without the risk of affecting site-wide performance. At this point, nearly all JOINs were detangled, with all point queries updated to read from the Vitess cluster as well. During this second step, our primary goal was to reveal any discrepancies in the data sets returned from the new queries. We could easily compare the two sets side by side because we concurrently ran our queries against both the new and old clusters and logged diffs as we encountered them (using results from the existing query against our legacy data source as the source of truth). We aggregated discrepancies in a number of ways so that we could get a broad sense of the scope of the problems we needed to address, in addition to logging primary keys whenever a pair returned different results.

We spent a few weeks in this phase, meticulously combing through the diffs. Because our user-sharded schema incorporated more information than the original, workspace-sharded `channels_members` table, we were juggling many more variables during the rewrite process than we might have otherwise. We sought to improve the developer experience for engineers working with shared channels and Enterprise Grid, requiring us to consider tricky product logic thoughtfully with each query we migrated. This meant that the potential for mistakes was much greater than had we done a one-to-one migration (as was the case with every table we had moved to Vitess to date).

Large portions of the differences in the data sets were due to single problems; fixing a single instance would often lead to a large reduction in the volume of diffs logged. For example, if on the legacy system we were selecting a different set of columns than on Vitess, every query would return mismatched results, logging a diff. As we reported on in Figure 11-5, finding and fixing the discrepancies to ignore mismatched columns decreased the number of diffs logged against the channel-sharded table from 10 percent of all queries to just 0.01 percent.

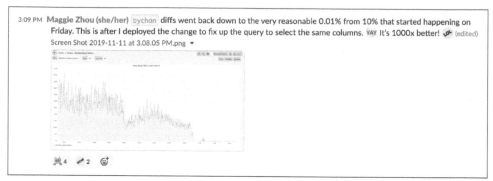

Figure 11-5. Reducing diffs on the channel-sharded `channels_members` table

Here's a close-up of the graph in Figure 11-5's Slack message:

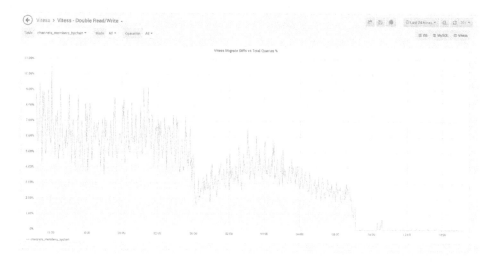

Alas, not all diffs were as easy to fix. Reading through the differences in data sets, we uncovered a few spots where our logic for shared channels was not quite right, and a few others where we had made mistakes in our backfill. It was tedious work and, due to the product implications, oftentimes required a profound understanding of the inner workings of our application. Although our manipulations were hidden between feature flags and experiments, the changes we were making had real ramifications for our production systems, and we had to proceed with real caution. Given these factors and the fact that the project was progressing at a slow crawl, we asked for more resources from product engineering.

Bringing new folks onboard brought new life to the project. Those of us who had been involved for many months were eager to get new perspectives on the many problems we'd been facing. We used pairing to ramp up new engineers quickly, joining forces to debug a small set of data discrepancies. It was the perfect context from which to demonstrate the Vitess migration tooling and the phased rollout process, and to talk through the new schemas. The work was tedious, but with a bigger arsenal of engineers at our disposal, we managed to boost our momentum drastically and banish the final few discrepancies. We did not get down to zero diffs, but settled for feeling good at 99.999 percent correctness. Since we knew that each `channels_mem bers` row could change quite rapidly as a user read messages in Slack, moving their `last_read` cursor state, we felt comfortable with some amount of discrepency that could be attributed to rapid read-after-write situations. Digging into the remaining .001 percent of differences, when we examined rows directly in the database after a diff occurred, we noticed that the rows would converge to the same state.

Wrapping up the *Dark* phase was significant. Knowing that 100 percent of `chan nels_members` traffic could run in a performant way on Vitess *and* return correct results was absolutely crucial to the overall success of the refactor. Although we weren't quite finished yet, being able to close the book on *Dark* mode was a relief to everyone. Finally, we were ready to ramp up to *Light* mode for a small subset of beta users within the company.

Light Mode

During *Light* mode, we wanted to test-drive the data retrieved from executing queries against the Vitess cluster, certifying that swapping over traffic to our new tables would not introduce any user-facing regressions. We were fairly confident that there would be relatively few bugs, in great part because of the work completed during the previous phases to address data discrepancies. However, because channel membership is at the core of Slack, if there were any bugs at all, they risked being quite serious. So we started our *Light* mode ramp-up carefully, starting off with a small group of volunteers at Slack, with the eventual goal to enable it to our entire customer base.

Most things worked fine, but we quickly ran into a problem when sometimes, after joining a channel, users would be unable to send messages. We immediately ramped down the experiment and dug into query logs, which we kept on all database hosts for up to two hours. These logs allowed us to debug easily, grepping for any modifications to the user's membership row in the given channel and the callers responsible for them.

We quickly identified the culprit: a background process, triggered after any Grid user joined a workspace-level channel they'd previously been a member of, which would locate and replace membership rows that had a canonical user ID with the user's local user ID. This was a problem because our new database schema in Vitess intentionally used canonical user IDs; after the process had rewritten the user ID, we could no longer locate the user's membership row, thereby preventing them from sending messages.

We were puzzled about why this process existed and curious to understand whether we needed to preserve this strange behavior or had uncovered a more nefarious problem. A journey into Slack conversations and git history from years prior revealed that the code was written to paper over a problem specific to an Enterprise Grid feature, where we sometimes wrote placeholder membership rows with canonical user IDs and updated them once users rejoined those channels.

This issue did not manifest itself in the discrepancies we inspected during the *Dark* mode phase, nor did it appear during several rounds of manual quality assurance (QA) and in the unit tests we wrote, because it only arose under precise, highly uncommon circumstances. Fortunately, we determined that we no longer needed this process and deleted it entirely. Problem solved!

From start to finish, we spent one month ramping up *Light* mode to all customers. Once we'd gained confidence in the overall correctness of the data in the Vitess cluster with our small set of volunteers, we continued the ramp-up. We began with our own Slack instance and then went on to teams on the free tier, followed by paying customers, and finally our largest Enterprise customers. During the ramp-up, we noticed that our customer with the greatest number of shared channels was seeing time-outs on the API called when viewing a channel (`conversations.view`). We quickly noticed that one of the Vitess `channels_members` queries executed during the API call was timing out. Unfortunately, because the query was relatively low volume, we hadn't been alerted to the problem during the *Dark* mode phase. We immediately rolled back *Light* mode for the customer, fixed the query, and ramped right back up.

Sunset Mode

A mere three days after successfully opting all customers into *Light* mode, we began the final stage, *Sunset* mode. During this phase, although we continued to double-write to both data sources, we only routed read traffic to the new Vitess clusters. By enabling *Sunset* mode to our users, we decreased the query load on our overloaded legacy systems by 22 percent, giving them much-needed breathing room. Figure 11-6 shows the dip in query volume we observed across our workspace shards.

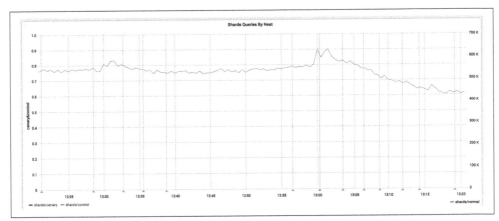

Figure 11-6. Removing read queries from the legacy workspace-sharded clusters

Tidying Up

After *Sunset* mode, a handful of important tasks remained. Namely, once our data warehouse dependencies had been properly migrated to consume channel membership data from Vitess, we needed to drop the old workspace-sharded `channels_mem bers` tables. We bade them farewell roughly a month later. We then spent the following weeks tidying the channel membership unidata library, carefully unwinding any feature flags and removing double-writing logic.

Dropping writes from the legacy shards was a huge, timely win. We removed 50 percent of writes and completely eliminated replication lag on the enterprise shard for our largest customer (VLB from Chapter 10), just as it was beginning to struggle under the pressure of the incessant write traffic. In the days leading up to dropping the table, the shard had been experiencing replication lag upward of 20 minutes. Figure 11-7 shows the steep drop in write traffic to VLB's enterprise shard.

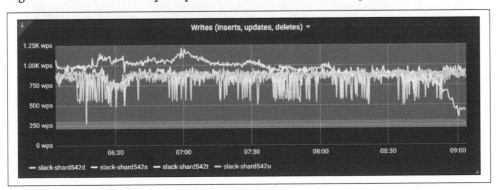

Figure 11-7. Removing writes from VLB's shard

Figure 11-8 shows a distinct lack of spikes in replication lag following the removal of the write load.

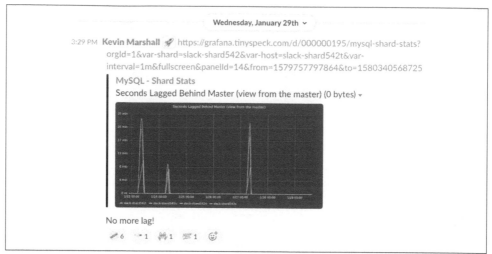

Figure 11-8. No more replication lag!

Here's a close-up of the graph in Figure 11-8's Slack message:

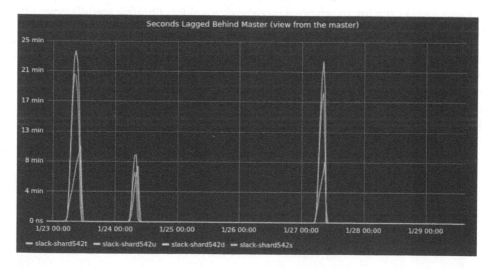

Unfortunately, just as we were finishing up, the coronavirus was beginning to spread, and our offices around the world shut down, with Slack's entire workforce transitioning to working from home. With the global shift to remote work, Slack saw a sharp increase in demand; we were acquiring new customers at a breakneck pace, and our existing customers were sending more messages than ever before. The entire infrastructure team, including those of us winding down the `channels_members`

migration, urgently shifted their focus to scaling our systems to unprecendented levels. Although we were relieved to bring the refactor to a close, we were never given the proper opportunity to revel in our achievement.

With this project at a close, other engineers at Slack started scheming about ways to take advantage of the newly resharded table. Quickly, prototypes of new features started emerging even when we were in SUNSET mode, and many following projects were staffed on multiple teams quickly to take advantage of the new data model and simplify other queries around both Grid and shared channels.

Lessons Learned

As with our previous case study, there are a number of important lessons to be learned from our migration of channels_members to Vitess. We'll start with ways the project might have gone better, describing how we might have set more realistic estimates and sourced the right teammates sooner. Then we'll discuss ways it succeeded, detailing our decision to increase project scope carefully at the outset and the merits of our simple communication strategy.

Set Realistic Estimates

By the time we started our migration of the channels_members table to Vitess, we had done a number of Vitess migrations already. We had built and refined tooling to improve the process, making it easier and safer with every iteration. We based our initial estimates on our experience with our most recent migrations, which had been decidedly quicker than the first few. We optimistically assumed that this migration would be no more difficult than the last.

We should have known, however, that channels_members would be a different beast for a number of reasons. First, the query load far exceeded any of our previous migrations. Second, we decided to shard the data across two keys, user and channel, rather than just one. Finally, we chose to use canonical user IDs and make meaningful changes to the schema to improve developer productivity, thereby further increasing the complexity of the project. Our estimates should have reflected these important decisions and their implications.

The team took a morale hit when we surpassed our original estimate, and engineering leadership turned a more watchful eye on the project. Fortunately, we were able to secure more resources and move forward with the refactor, but our estimate certainly did not set the expectations it should have at the start.

Setting unrealistic estimates can have much more serious consequences: the refactor might lose priority, and engineering leadership might lose faith in your ability to drive large software projects. Your career risks taking a hit. Had we taken the time to brainstorm each of the potential pitfalls and leaned on the strategies discussed in

Chapter 4, we might have set better expectations for both ourselves and our stakeholders at the start of the refactor.

Source the Teammates You Need

When we started the project, we assumed that the majority of the work would be best handled by infrastructure engineers. We could reach out to product engineers as necessary, asking questions or seeking code review on an ad hoc basis. Only once we ran into difficulties detangling the JOINs did we ask for more significant resourcing from product engineering. It was at that point that we realized that we could work faster by working alongside engineers who were intimately familiar with the queries we were migrating. Their involvement was crucial throughout the lengthy *Dark* mode phase, during which we debugged a number of data discrepancies that led to strange behaviors in the product. Had they been more present from the beginning, we might have migrated queries more quickly and more correctly (including the JOINs), cutting down on the time spent in later phases.

As discussed in Chapter 5, sometimes the teammates you have are not the ones best suited for the job. Because large-scale refactors have far-reaching impact, they often involve engineers from different teams and disciplines. The team you identify at the start of your project is very rarely set in stone. If you believe your team is no longer the right one, figure out who it is missing and seek out those individuals. If you think you need more resources than you had initially anticipated, ask for them.

Plan Scope Carefully

An important decision we made early in the refactor was to use canonical user IDs for all user ID–related columns in the Vitess `channels_members` schemas. We knew that Slack was aiming to adopt canonical user IDs throughout, but the first few phases of the project were unlikely to conclude before our table migration was complete.

By choosing to adopt canonical user IDs, we intentionally increased the scope of the refactor. We could have spent the time canonicalizing user IDs on our legacy workspace-sharded clusters first, only migrating to Vitess once the data had been properly updated. Likewise, we could have migrated the table without canonicalizing the IDs and initiated the process once it had safely landed in Vitess. We believed that by doing both at the same time, we would save both time and effort. (While we had no great way of measuring this, we do believe it turned out to be true!)

In Chapter 4, we learned that keeping a moderate scope is important to ensure that a refactor is completed within a reasonable amount of time and does not affect more surface area than is necessary. However, there are circumstances when adding some additional scope is worthwhile and will ultimately make the effort more successful. Be mindful of these opportunities during the project planning stage and make a deliberate decision to take advantage of them well before the project is in full swing. This way, when you communicate your plan more broadly, stakeholders will have an opportunity to voice an opinion about the additional scope, and everyone's expectations should be appropriately aligned.

Choose a Single Place for Project Communication

Throughout the refactor, we leaned heavily on our project channel, #feat-vitess-channels, to collaborate, coordinate, and provide important updates. Because it served as our central point of contact, everyone kept up to date with new messages. It was a great place to ask questions or post code for review; you were sure to get a response within a few minutes. On several occasions, teammates would debug issues in threads for others to chime in or catch up on later. During the *Light* mode portion of the refactor, users who had volunteered to be opted in to the new queries would come to #feat-vitess-channels to report bugs and other strange behavior they'd encountered. If it was related to moving channels_members to Vitess, you could find it in this channel.

Most importantly, #feat-vitess-channels was a place for us to keep each other motivated. As the refactor dragged on, with engineers cycling on and off and *Dark* mode continuing to throw us a number of curveballs, it became increasingly difficult to stay optimistic about our progress. Engineers from across the company would occasionally pop in with an encouraging "You got this!" or a series of emoji reactions to a weekly status update. Small, thoughtful acts of support can go a long way to boost team morale, and having a convenient place where colleagues could share their encouragement helped make it a common occurrence.

By keeping all communication pertaining to the project in a single place, it's easy for everyone involved with the refactor to stay on the same page. Teammates can join and leave the effort without extensive knowledge transfers. External stakeholders can check in on the latest progress without pinging you directly. Perhaps most importantly, it can be a place of support and encouragement. For ideas on how to establish good communication habits, refer to Chapter 7.

Design a Thoughtful Rollout Plan

The migration of the channel membership table to Vitess had a well-defined rollout strategy split into four concrete phases. At each stage, we had a strong vision of when we should opt different groups of users into our changes (i.e., users at the company first, followed by customers on the free tier, regular paid customers, and our largest customers last). On top of this procedure, we used highly reliable tooling built explicitly for the Vitess migration use case, which enabled us to quickly ramp up (and down) each of the different modes to distinct slices of users at our preferred pace.

Each of these factors helped us move forward quickly, but perhaps the most effective piece was our ability to roll back immediately if we began to notice a detrimental impact to our users. Having that power at our fingertips meant that we weren't afraid to move forward aggressively. It was particularly useful when we entered the *Light* mode phase as we used volunteers within the company to read data from the Vitess cluster.

Even the most thoughtfully planned, meticulously executed refactor will lead to a handful of bugs, and it is often impossible to identify them all before beginning a roll-out. If you can control who is opted in to your changes at important milestones, and can roll back swiftly, you'll be able to make progress much more nimbly, surfacing potentially terrible regressions well before they become a serious incident.

Takeaways

Here are the most important takeaways from our refactor to migrate `channels_mem bers` from our workspace-sharded clusters to user- and channel-sharded clusters in Vitess.

- Set realistic estimates. Optimism is great, but missed deadlines can have serious ramifications.

- Source the teammates you need; the ones available to you or currently on your team may not be the ones best suited for the job. Don't be afraid to ask for new (or more) resources if you need them.

- Plan project scope carefully. Any added scope should be accounted for during the planning phase to set expectations appropriately.

- Choose a single place for project communication and stick to it.

- Design a thoughtful rollout plan and invest in building the tooling you need to make ramp up (and down) as easy as possible.

Index

About the Author

Maude Lemaire is an engineer at Slack Technologies, Inc., where she works to scale the product to support some of the world's largest organizations. She spends most of her time chasing down people, making network calls in a loop, refactoring unwieldy chunks of code, consolidating redundant database schemas, and building tools for other developers. Maude cares deeply about the developer experience and has actively sought out simpler, more efficient ways to structure code in each of her roles, at different levels of the stack.

Maude obtained a BSc. in Honours Software Engineering from McGill University.

Colophon

The animals on the cover of *Refactoring at Scale* are walruses (*Odobenus rosmarus*), large marine mammals found in the Arctic and subarctic regions of the North Pole.

Walruses are well known for their long, sharp tusks that aid them in breaking ice, climbing out of the water, establishing dominance in a herd, and defending themselves from predators. Short fur sparsely covers the walrus's thick skin, which ranges in color from gray to a yellow-brown. A much thicker layer of blubber provides warmth and stored energy, allowing them to survive in harsh conditions.

These slow-moving carnivores prefer to live in areas of ice and shallow water to allow easy access to food and will migrate seasonally to find ice of optimal thickness. Short front flippers and larger hind flippers propel this one-ton (on average) creature through the water, while its whiskers, more so than its eyes, are used for navigation and food identification. Walruses mostly consume large amounts of mollusks and other shellfish, but have been known to occasionally eat larger animals such as seabirds and even seals.

Global climate change and human predation have caused the walrus's conservation status to be listed as Vulnerable. Many of the animals on O'Reilly covers are endangered; all of them are important to the world.

The cover illustration is by Karen Montgomery, based on a black and white engraving from *Natural History of Animals* by Vogt & Specht. The cover fonts are Gilroy Semibold and Guardian Sans. The text font is Adobe Minion Pro; the heading font is Adobe Myriad Condensed; and the code font is Dalton Maag's Ubuntu Mono.

O'REILLY®

There's much more
where this came from.

Experience books, videos, live online
training courses, and more from O'Reilly
and our 200+ partners—all in one place.

Learn more at oreilly.com/online-learning

Milton Keynes UK
Ingram Content Group UK Ltd.
UKHW050635140824
446857UK00016B/109